Necronomicon presents

Shocking Cinema of the Seventies

Edited by
Xavier Mendik

NOIR
Publishing
PO Box 28
Hereford
HR1 1YT
E-mail: noir@macunlimited.net

Necronomicon presents
Shocking Cinema of the Seventies
Edited by: Xavier Mendik
ISBN 0 9536564 4 6
© Xavier Mendik and all contributors 2002, all rights reserved
First Published 2002 by:
Noir Publishing
Copyright © Noir Publishing 2002
Necronomicon presents - a periodical publication
Photos from Scimitar Films and the Noir Publishing Collection
Cover Photo:
L"Anticristo/The Antichrist, Alberto de Martino
By courtesy of Capitolina Produzioni Cinematografiche

British Library Cataloguing in Publication Data:
A catalogue record for this book is available from the British Library

Editor's Acknowledgements

The editor wishes to thank all of the writers who contributed so much hard work to this volume. I would also like to offer my gratitude to Michael Winner for providing not only an excellent introduction and interview for this book, but also for giving so much of his support, time and encouragement to *Shocking Cinema of the Seventies*.

I would also like to express my gratitude to colleagues and friends at University College Northampton for their support with this and other related projects. In particular I would like to offer sincere thanks to both George Savona (Head of School of Cultural Studies) and Peter Brooker (Director of the Centre of Culture and Criticism), for doing so much to cultivate 'Mendik Megalomania' over the last four years. Special thanks are also due to the staff (past and present) from the department of Media and Popular Culture including Sonya Andermahr, Charlie Blake and Mike Sanders as well as to Paul Johnson from the Cult Film Archive for his proof-reading and constructive comments on this volume.

For all his support and guidance throughout the course of this project, I wish to offer particular thanks to Andy Black at Noir Publishing, who also honoured me with the wonderful opportunity to edit an edition of the *Necronomicon* series.

For their assistance with the sourcing of rare images I would like to thank Harvey Fenton of Fab Press, as well as Steven Jay Schneider. The images used to illustrate the chapter 'Come On-A My House: The Inescapable Legacy of Wes Craven's *The Last House on the Left* are courtesy of Harvey Fenton and the author David A. Szulkin. They are derived from Mr Szulkin's book *Wes Craven's Last House on the Left: The Making of a Cult Classic* (second edition) and are copyrighted to this volume. The stills that accompany the article 'Urban Legend: the 1970s Films of Michael Winner' are from the Director's own collection, and I would like to thank him for giving us access to these images. The rest of the stills in this volume are courtesy are from the Noir Collection and are reproduced here in the spirit of publicity.

Some of the production and promotion costs for this edition of *Shocking Cinema of the Seventies* were met via a bid from the School of Cultural Studies Research Cluster at University College Northampton. Both the editor and the publisher wish to offer their thanks to those involved with the fund for their invaluable assistance.

This volume is dedicated with love to Nicola and Zena, for helping me through fits and starts.

CONTENTS

Contents

Introducing
the Shocking Cinema of the Seventies
Michael Winner

In the 1970s I moved fully into the American scene. I could have had no better introduction than the start of my friendship with Burt Lancaster on *Lawman* in 1970. When I first met Burt He asked me why Jered Maddox, the fanatical law-abiding Sheriff, ended up shooting in the back one of the men he had come to arrest. The man had thrown down his gun and was running away. Burt said to me "Why does he shoot him in the back?" I said, "Because he's a bastard, Burt." And because the man had drawn on him and after that the rules of engagement were entered into and everything was okay." This is similar to the later *Dirty Harry* movies where an over-zealous, rule breaking Lawman became a figure to be supported. It was a theme later taken into my movie *Death Wish*. For years nobody would make *Death Wish* because film companies said, "You can't have a film where a citizen shoots other citizens and is still a hero." What they didn't realise was the paranoia in America, the desire to wipe out all types of evil, had become so great that the old rules were over.

On a personal level, it was immensely exciting to make a Western at all! And to make it in Mexico with an all-American cast of such brilliant and famous actors from old-timer Robert Ryan to new-comer Robert Duvall.

America was never at ease with Richard Nixon who became president in 1969. A feeling of dispossession and unease, encouraged by the Vietnam War, overtook the nation.

Reviewing the *Stone Killer* in 1973, Roy Frumkes in the *US National Board of Review* said, "Social muddle emerges as an honest portrait of America's divergent nature. Winner's two previous films *The Mechanic* and *Scorpio* were heavy with themes of social, political and criminal paranoia. The present climate in this country is laden with mistrust and Winner seems, in retrospect, to have been intellectually very close to it." This mistrust started with the 70s and spread from Nixon to life in general. After a brief sojourn in Cambridgeshire with Marlon Brando making *The Nightcomers* – an experience to be treasured!–I did another Western with an all-American cast: *Chato's Land*.

I remember speaking at a lecture at the Arnolfini in Bristol about this picture being to do with the current American scene, Vietnam and President Nixon and thinking "Oh typical!" when the local reviewer described my remarks as pretentious bullshit. The American press saw it very clearly. Frances Herridge in the *New York Post* said "If you find any likeness to our war in Vietnam, the film-makers would probably not object."

Norma Maclean Stoop in *New York After Dark* wrote "Jack Palance is very good as the indecisive posse leader who sees everything in terms of past glory, for which I am afraid, read: Johnson or Nixon."

The 70s produced allegorical movie-tales that reflected American society. They also saw a considerable increase in levels of blood and violence. This had commenced with *The Wild Bunch* in 1969 and was taken up by *A Clockwork Orange* in 1971. These pictures would not have passed the censor a decade later. 1972 saw me work in Hollywood for the first time because Charles Bronson asked me to direct *The Mechanic*. I came into a world of hippies and alternative lifestyles, where people fought to get away from the realities of the bend political situation-viz the departure of Spiro Agnew -and the Vietnam War.

The Mechanic remains a classic film noir the world over. But it is probably relegated to something less, by the British, who can diminish anything! The rave reviews that all these films got in America, including my 60s films *The System, I'll Never Forget What's 'Is Name* and *The Jokers* gave me great confidence. It put me on the Hollywood A List.

It was also a period, where I got to direct in Hollywood and New York, which had always been a dream. I was immensely impressed with how hardworking, cohesive and self-motivated film units were there. The British had a few good crews, but even those had to be egged to stop them discussing the tea-break and taking votes on whether the caterer should be changed. In America the dedication was superb. On *The Mechanic* the end of the hardboard track had to be painted to match into the ground, a fairly common practice in movies. In England, a "standby painter" would always be on the set. He'd lay out rows and rows of paint and brushes and would sit waiting to be called.

Seeing this board needed painting, I called out "Standby Painter!" One of the property men said "We don't have a standby painter here, Mr Winner. If you want to paint something, do it yourself!" and he threw me a can of spray paint from the Prop truck. The unit expected me to be appalled at this. But I was delighted! I took the spray paint and started to spray the end of the hardboard. In fact, the prop man took over and thereafter in England I refused to have a standby painter. British Unions at the time were very strong. My production manager said "Well, who shall we put on the unit list as the standby painter?" I replied, "At the top of the list put Producer, Director and Standby Painter Michael Winner."

In 1972, I found myself in the centre of the American neurosis. I was staying at the Watergate hotel on the night it was robbed, making *Scorpio* a film set in the Central Intelligence Agency. We were the first and only company ever to film in the Central Intelligence Agency. When I asked Howard Osborne the Head of Internal Security why he thought we had been allowed in by CIA Director Richard Helms he said "I think Helms wanted to show the place was not as sinister as people thought." Our script showed the CIA doing fairly dreadful things. United Artists were so terrified of a political comeback they insisted I showed the CIA the script in advance. It is to the great credit of an often-maligned organisation that the CIA let us go ahead. *Scorpio* brought in the other element of the 70s which was that the Cold War was still very much alive. America was afraid of Communist domination outside its territory as well as the overthrow of society by a whole collection of groups within its territory. These ranged from student protestors to the Black Panthers to gangs of muggers and other villains.

When we shot part of *Death Wish* in Harlem we had to lay on a vegetarian meal for the Black Panthers and negotiate territorial rights with them. I looked forward to our dinner at two in the morning, which is when we were eating. Sadly their table with the vegetarian meal remained unoccupied. Perhaps the Panthers got a better offer!

In 1973 hostilities in Vietnam ceased with the signing of a cease-fire and by 1975 the last US personnel had left. Also by then the very homely and mild Gerald Ford took over the Presidency to be followed by the low key rustic Jimmy Carter. I think that what we know as the 70s in America, a period of great trauma with the proposed impeachment and resignation of Nixon, the Vietnam War, student riots balanced by flower power, in reality expired shortly after the middle of the decade, just as the so-called Swinging 60s in England didn't really start until 1964.

The motion picture world continued to echo the political nervousness but by 1976 *All the Presidents' Men* was a nostalgic look back to a time that had sailed by. Just as by the end of the 70s *Apocalypse Now* was a surrealistic dream of past times.

Cinema became less political as the 70s rolled on. I myself went into firstly a comedy about old Hollywood with *Won Ton the Dog Who Saved Hollywood* – I dare to call this a rather underrated film! This was a year when Hollywood was convinced everybody was interested in movies about Hollywood. A great many were made. None of them found much of an audience! So I went onto do a horror film, *The Sentinel*, which became a portrait of New York threatened now, not by the muggers as in *Death Wish*, but by the underworld of hell.

Death Wish remains the archetypal 70s movie. One which is lectured about in American universities, and one which in America is considered to have changed the whole direction of cinema. It was on many US critics Ten Best of the Year lists. It permitted a gun-toting hero not to be confined to a soldier or a policeman, but anyone who was doing away with evil people. It was immensely copied and still is today. It broke a number of taboos. Except in Westerns with John Wayne and others a citizen has never been applauded for illegal acts. Also the word "Death" was considered just that–Death in the cinema. Nobody would allow a film to be made with the word "Death" in the title. Studio executives thought it would be a downer. Films with that word had always been a failure.

Dino de Laurentiis sent me new advertising and insisted I change the title to *The Sidewalk Vigilante*. I was editing the film myself in London, as always. That is cutting by hand all the celluloid and joining it myself with scotch tape. I ordered the title *The Sidewalk Vigilante* to replace the Death *Wish* title we already had. I was sitting in my cinema at home feeling a well of rejection from my editing assistants when this title came on the screen. I rang Dino and said, "I'm going to deliver you a film called *Death Wish*. Short of you getting an injunction to prevent me, that's what will happen."

Dino obviously felt my fervour on the matter was correct. But even ten days before release he rang begging me to reconsider, it was his authority to do what he wanted anyway! He said "Michael I can't sleep, I keep thinking about the title *Death Wish* and I can't sleep." I said, "Take a pill, Dino."

In fact, *Death Wish* both as a title and as an aura sums up America in the 70s. It had come out of the hope of the Kennedy era. Camelot had changed to a Hieronymus Bosch painting. The thought that a President could act as Nixon did undermined America's entire belief in its own democracy.

Yet, the fact that he was caught and paid the price seemed to me a strong plus for the American system. I thought the 70s were a wonderful time! The political upheavals, the flared trousers, the beads all men wore, even Abba! But it faded to a new normality by the end of the decade. It was no surprise that in 1979 the Academy Award Best movie was *Kramer verses Kramer*, a nice film about nice people in a soap opera drama. And the following year, as the 80s commenced, it was *Ordinary People*. America had re-found its confidence. American cinema wanted to settle down. For a while at least.

Michael Winner

Part One: Hollywood on the Edge
Xavier Mendik

More than any other recent period, American film of the 1970s has become a favoured object of scrutiny for film scholars and movie fans alike. Central to this examination has been the fact that both the content and structure of seventies Hollywood can be seen to mirror the wider social and political tensions which gripped America during this period. In the light of Vietnam, the Watergate scandal, political and civil unrest, the construction of the Hollywood narrative altered to reveal a much more pessimistic and downbeat tone. Indeed, it is noticeable that dominant cycles of the era (such as the thriller, western and horror genres) seem dogged by moral ambiguity. This uncertainty saw 'illegal' violence coded as legitimate response, the forces of white authority depicted as marauding savages and the 'monstrous' as a mere mirror image to 'normal' society. Equally, the seventies also saw the emergence of new U.S. film types tailor-made for the chaos engulfing the era. These included the 'paranoid-thriller', which clearly reflected wider doubts surrounding the legitimacy of official government structures, as well as the disaster movie which revealed various layers of American society as vulnerable to attack from both manmade and natural disasters.

The opening section of *Shocking Cinema of the Seventies* provides a snapshot of the changes and turmoil that beset American cinema and society during the 1970s, by considering examples from key genres of the era. What unites the following articles is an examination of the tension between the genuine dispossessed and underground 'voices' that these narratives seek to express, and Hollywood's attempt to limit and contain any social criticism of the issues under review. It is this notion of the Hollywood text as a battleground between utopian and regressive tensions which is documented in Benjamin Halligan's article 'The New Mesmerica: *Zabriskie Point*, *The Last Movie* and *Two-Lane Blacktop*.' Here, Halligan warns against totalising seventies Hollywood as a radical break with past political and cinematic traditions. By using a case study of films such as *Zabriskie Point*, *The Last Movie* and *Two-Lane Black Top*, the author reveals how the social discontent and cinematic experimentation of the late 1960s was gradually reincorporated in the celluloid mainstream. In the case of all three movies under review, counter-cultural ideals met mainstream budget funding, resulting in not liberation or repression, but rather a disorientating sense of alienation that affected both film form and characterisation. In the case of Monte Hellman's *Two-Lane Black Top*, the established iconography of the road movie is manipulated in a film that reduces character motivation, the importance of the American open-road and even the image track itself to a minimum. While Halligan's analysis of this and other movies of the era provides an interesting account of the tensions present in the Hollywood of the period, the importance of his analysis extends to consider the type of entertainment which replaced it. By using the term 'Reaganite Entertainment', the author describes a type of popular fiction which lasted beyond the 1970s and defined much of what we think of as eighties Hollywood. Halligan's label describes 1970s works such as *Close Encounters of the Third Kind* and *Star Wars*, which jettisoned any engagement with the problems in contemporary reality in favour of a nostalgic style reliant on established Hollywood traditions. As well as introducing a feel good factor back into a nation scarred by Vietnam and Watergate corruption, Reaganite entertainment also reinforced the power of the Hollywood studios by promoting big budget, special effect laden productions.

Alongside Halligan's work, it is also the tension between the socially progressive and the morally conservative that is central to Mark Sample's article 'There Goes the Neighbourhood: The Seventies, The Middle Class, and *The Omega Man*.' Here, the author makes an innovative reading of the previously marginal science fiction film *The Omega Man*. Although the movie can be seen as part of a post-apocalyptic trilogy which starred Charlton Heston, it remains the least discussed in terms of its possible links to the wider tensions of the 1970s. What Sample argues is that contemporary reviewers failed to read the film's theme of a white, middle-class, middle-aged man as the only survivor of a bacteriological plague within the domestic hysteria of the era. Thus, rather than seeing *The Omega Man* as a future-tense drama, the author sees the plight of the protagonist Robert Neville (Heston), as reflecting the fears surrounding the film's audience at that time. Thus, *The Omega Man's* focus on contagion mirrors contemporary middle class concerns around the growing (and aggressive) urban underclass, black militancy and the youth counter-culture of the period. As Sample indicates, Neville remains a man unable to relinquish his habits of bourgeois civility no matter how much the confines of his domestic space are threatened by infected marauders. (Their actions mimicking the phobia around the emerging phenomenon of mugging which was traumatising urban areas during this period). In response to the contradictory situation of a good populous turned bad by a very American 'infection', the film creates a paradoxical hero in the figure of Robert Neville, who responds to this malaise with a mixture of apathy and violence. As Sample indicates, the film's opening scene establishes Neville as an ambivalent figure: part freedom fighter/part vigilante whose endless pleasures of cruising the freeway are only disrupted by his repeated attempts to pick off the infected opponents who threaten to cut into his leisure time.

Beyond his role in science fiction films of the seventies, Charlton Heston also emerges as one focus in Stephen Keane's article 'The Stars Don't Always Survive: Disaster Movies as Savage Cinema.' Here, Keane considers the placement of such established Hollywood stars in the disaster film cycle popular during the decade. By focusing on a return to the established star system of golden Hollywood, this article once again explores the tension between social discontent and moral conservatism as expressed by seventies film cycles. Keane does concede that the concept of 'cinematic chaos' central to the cycle can be traced back to biblical epics as well as fifties science fiction. However, the genre emerged as a popular focus in the seventies through titles such as *Airport*, *Earthquake*, *The Towering Inferno* and *The Poseidon Adventure*. Although cliched plots and characterisations are frequent explanations that have prevented the critical re-evaluation of the disaster film, it is primarily their over-reliance on star structures that condemned them as ideologically laden. From this traditional perspective it seems that while the disaster film reveals all layers of American society as vulnerable, it also renders them as capable of closure and resolution courtesy of the courage and leadership of the Hollywood A-list. In the case of Heston, several commentators have noted how his roles in works such as *Airport* and *Earthquake* reproduced the divine qualities of his earlier casting as Moses in *The Ten Commandments*. However, as Keane notes, rather than use their stars as ideological vehicles, these works tend to abuse them and the qualities they are seen to represent. In one of the many amusing asides that marks this chapter, he notes that although Heston is responsible for guiding an uncontrollable aircraft to safety in *Airport*, he is also washed away in a torrent of water and muck at the end of *Earthquake*. It is not merely the case that the stars *actually* suffered during the making of these films (as Keane indicates with his references to the trials of Gene Hackman during the making of *The Poseidon Adventure*). Rather, it is the fact that they subvert a star hierarchy that would otherwise equate top billing with invincibility.

While the disaster movie revealed the ease with which the American landscape could be disrupted, the vigilante film proved even more disturbing by pointing to unprecedented levels of violence existing within the Stateside psyche. The most controversial example of the 1970s vigilante film remains *Death Wish*, which is discussed in Xavier Mendik's article 'Urban Legend: The 1970s Films of Michael Winner.' Here, Mendik contextualises the film's reputation and reception alongside a wider consideration of its director, Michael Winner. Although Winner's films of the era offer a disturbing vision of 1970s America, they have frequently been neglected as right-wing and reactionary readings of contemporary events. For instance, *Death Wish* has been read as part of the conservative 'Hollywood counter revolution' identified by theorists such as Michael Ryan and Douglas Kellner. For these writers, the film attempts to isolate and privilege white, middle-class rage as a legitimate reaction against the violent and irrational drives of an urban underclass. In so doing, the film can be seen as part of a wider ideological campaign to diminish the liberal advances of the late 1960s counter-culture, with its radical emphasis on the advancement of ethnic, social and sexual minority interests. While acknowledging the historical importance of these theoretical accounts of 1970s Hollywood cinema, Mendik seeks a more positive reappraisal of *Death Wish* which stresses the radical impetus of not only the film, but Winner's other work from the era. Specifically, the author argues that rather than isolate and validate the actions of its hero Paul Kersey, the film develops a series of unsettling parallels between the character and the muggers that make up his prey. For Mendik, *Death Wish* and Winner's other films of the 1970s depict a cynical view of capital relations and its link to 'civilisation' which produces a widespread and uncontrollable urge towards violence across all sectors of American society.

While the actions of vigilantes such as Paul Kersey functioned to erode distinctions between illegitimate violence and socially viable revenge, the paranoid thriller emerged as the ultimate in contemporary American auto-critique. It is this cycle, which Paul Cobley discusses in his chapter 'Reading the Politics of Conspiracy in 1970s America.' Here, a case study of two films is provided: *The Parallax View* and *The*

Conversation. For Cobley, these works demonstrate the key features of the paranoid thriller. Specifically, such texts focus on some form of political/social corruption that profoundly alters the appearance of everyday reality, as well as suggesting illegality as operating at a number of levels of officialdom. Although contemporary critics attempted to underplay the emergence of this cycle and its links to scandals such as Watergate, the connection is underscored by the repeated themes of marginal protagonists who witness assassinations that are then concealed within sinister bureaucracies. In the case of Warren Beatty's character from the *Parallax View*, his status as a press reporter instantly links him with Bernstein and Woodward, the real life investigators of Nixon's crimes. The film, which features Frady as an unwitting witness to the shooting of a Senator, even carries the flavour of conspiracy debates that surrounded the earlier assassinations of political figures such as John F. Kennedy and Martin Luther King. As Cobley notes, the film's focus on the Parallax committee that is supposed to investigating the Senator's death even bears resemblance to the Warren Commission set up to investigate Kennedy's killing. Although *The Conversation* was more positively reviewed than *The Parallax View*, critics once again diminished its link to contemporary American fears about political corruption. However, for Cobley, the film's theme of a professional surveillance expert who accidentally overhears a murder instantly connects the narrative with the type of 'spying' equipment used by Nixon and his aides during the controversial election campaign. As with the other examples of this cycle, *The Conversation* thus creates a paranoid environment where the knowledge of institutional malpractice severs the so called 'paranoid' individual from any sense of wider, shared social structures.

The New Mesmerica: *Zabriskie Point, The Last Movie* and *Two-Lane Blacktop.*

Benjamin Halligan

Hollywood in the Seventies: A Decade of Celluloid Lawlessness

One measure of the unsuspected success of *Bonnie and Clyde* (1967) and *Easy Rider* (1969) was the ten year period of filmic lawlessness they left in their wake. The major studios all scrambled to sign up the New Hollywood *auteurs*, whose films, no matter how nonsensical, iconoclastic and 'way out' they seemed to the executives, would milk the problematic late 1960s youth market. Thus the studios had attempted to shift the market boundaries to assimilate a counter-culture which was now no longer confined to a cultural ghetto, or the exploitation circuit. It took until the latter half of the 1970s before a consolidation of the defining themes of post-*Easy Rider* cinema occurred, with the reinvention of the mainstream through the restoration of a sense of 'relevance', of 'maturity' and, principally, of the studio control that had been lost so fatally in the mid-1960s.' In this way, the experience of Vietnam was reinvented with Academy-approved films and 'issue films' like *The Deer Hunter* (1978) and *Apocalypse Now* (1979), of Watergate and the resultant conspiracy theory paranoia with *All The Presidents Men* (1976), *Capricorn One* (1978) and *The China Syndrome* (1979) and of the counter-culture and protest movements with *Big Wednesday* (1978) and *Reds* (1981). But these films, which were underwritten by troubled liberal sentiment, were soon to be overshadowed by the next wave: the brutal emergence onto the market of the Reaganite cinema of the 1980s, as defined by Spielberg with *Close Encounters of the Third Kind* (1977) and *E.T.* (1982) and George Lucas with *Star Wars* (1977).

This construction of a cinema of escapism, and on a scale not seen since the Golden Age of Hollywood, and with the strength of purpose of the make-believe of these films, may be read as a strong reaction against–a revenge even, on–the 'anarchy' of post-*Easy Rider* Hollywood. The clean quality of their imagery can be contextualised in a similar way: the grainy location-derived look of New Hollywood was replaced by the gloss and sharpness of Spielberg's family scenes. The small town Christmas lights-esque aesthetic of his fleets of well-wishing UFOs and the fast food restaurant whiteness and shopping mall lighting of Lucas' Death Star, all assembled with a renewed use of invisible cutting, big-budgets, star performances, emphatic soundtracks and studio sets showcasing technical wizardry over narrative development and trajectory.

During the same period mythology was also being restored to the North American cinema. The damage that had been done to the mythologies propagated by

Zabriskie Point

film-makers such as Cecil B. DeMille, King Vidor, John Ford, Frank Capra and D W Griffith by films such as *The Rain People* (1969), *Five Easy Pieces* (1970), *Carnal Knowledge* (1971), *The Last Picture Show* (1971), *Tracks* (1976) and deconstructive satires such as *Myra Breckinridge* (1970) and *Beyond the Valley of the Dolls* (1970) was rapidly repaired. The new frontiers were either aggrandised (the cycle of space operas or reintroduction of super hero yarns) or trivialised (teenage angst, *Fast Times at Ridgemont High*, 1982, and the cycle of 'Brat pack' films). Film distribution changed too: once opening weekends became the majority of box office return it was only necessary for films to be familiar, not 'good.' When Manny Farber stopped writing about film at this time, it seemed a symptom more than a sign.

Towards a Cinema of 'Disneyfication'

This re-establishing of the pre-eminence of a Hollywood mainstream of the Right was notable for the way in which the experiential aspect of the New Hollywood cinema was assimilated, Disneyfied, and reproduced as an experiential cinema of escapism. This can be seen in the scope and end scenes of *Close Encounters of the Third Kind*, where the experiential aesthetic is now at the service of the creation of a sense of collective awe and collective purpose. This replaces the role of experientialism in *Easy Rider*–seen in the cemetery drug trip, the campfire conversation and the endless, rolling landscapes. Here experientialism serviced the creation of a heightened reality of

Zabriskie Point

hallucination and mesmerism, of 'oneness' with the vast surroundings, pointing to a feeling of brotherly peace and the creation of a new America.

Not only did this re-establishment end New Hollywood, but it sealed-off the period of experimentation, (roughly 1967-1977). It was an era defined by a filmic language determined by confrontation, by elliptical narrative form and by a grainy, make-shift quality to the image. It was an era that had been enthralled by the European New Waves, particularly the Godard films of the 1960s. One consequence of the mimicking of the 1960s European New Waves was the way in which New Hollywood films managed to closely reflect the times and places in which they were made (in the most immediate, for example, by the movement away from studio filming to filming on location).

Easy Rider prefaced this period of experimentation, exactly set out the parameters, broke out of the studio and, most importantly, detailed the formation of the counter-culture. The film begins in the sensibility of 1966–a sequence of a deracinated Phil Spector, as Connection (then at his paranoid and coked-up height), selling cocaine to Captain America (Peter Fonda). This opening sequence alludes to the narcotic foundations of the counter-culture, established in 1966 through figures such as Ken Kesey. In a similar manner, The Commune sequence alludes to the 1967 Summer of Love sensibility, while the bad acid trip in the cemetery and Billy's (Dennis

Hopper) death at the hands of rednecks at the close of the film alludes to the loss of the utopian dreams of revolution and the changes that marked the end of the counter-cultural movements after 1968: Nixon's re-election, the Hells Angels at Altmont, the escalation of the conflict in Vietnam, the shooting of rioting students by the National Guard in Kent State, Ohio, the death of Hendrix, the violent clashes between police and students at the 1968 Chicago Democratic Conference–in short, the shift from the liberal society of the 1960s to the authoritarian society of the 1970s.

New Hollywood Against the Grain

The majority of retrospective approaches to and critical studies of this period have only been able to salvage those films which adhere to a structure with a semblance of that which now constitutes 'quality' American cinema. That is narratives which are issue-driven, liberal, tending to film places and people that can be seen to push against the norms of the Hollywood aesthetic, but with a controlled aesthetic all the same and a sense of the evocation of their period. Thus, Hal Ashby can be understood in terms of his blue collar dramas and the finding of 'poetry' in every day life. For instance, his working class roughnecks in *The Last Detail* (1973) empathising more with the prisoner they escort across the wintry countryside and bleak cityscapes than the military system they are employed to uphold. Thus, Scorsese can be understood in terms of the 'art' that he brings to the aesthetics of a film such as *Taxi Driver* (1976)–endless dwelling on the light of New York by night, its neonness, the liquid light on the wet windscreen of the taxi, the blue interior light of midnight diners, the light of 16mm projection in a porn cinema. This is offset by painful blasts of overexposed day light, as disconcerting to the audience as they are to the film's wired protagonist. Thus, *Midnight Cowboy* (1969) reworks the buddy movie via Steinbeck-like myths of escape and a better life, albeit in-between New Wave blasts of a kinetic New York: hookers, gay encounters in cinemas, glitzy poverty, a happening/party and streetwise petty criminals. Thus, *The Last Picture Show* reworks the 1950s-derived images of home and family that have been the exalted foundation of both Republican and Democrat policies during the 1980s and 1990s.

Films that do not fit comfortably into retrospective readings of this period are those which embody the elements unique to the period 1967-1977. As a result, they cannot so readily be assimilated into contemporary re-imaginings of the political discourse of this period. These films include *The Last Movie* (1971), *Night of the Living Dead* (1968), *Gas-s-s-s* (1970), *Sweet Sweetback's Badasssss Song* (1971), *The Honeymoon Killers* (1969), *Dirty Harry* (1971), *Magnum Force* (1973), *The Man Who Fell To Earth* (1976), *The Passenger* (1975), *The Parallax View* (1974), *Eraserhead* (1977), *Zabriskie Point* (1970), *Medium Cool* (1969) and *Two-Lane Blacktop* (1971). *The Holy Mountain* (1975) aimed at a Western audience, might also be included. These films are mainly apocalyptic and offer little prospect of a future in the portraits of America they present. They both fight against the audience yet rely on that audience. In the case of Antonioni, Jodorowsky, Hopper, Hellman and Corman, they work to create a 'hippie' cinema yet reject the hippie ethos. They embody Jean-Jacques Lebel's maxim–"Art = $hit"–adopted by The Living Theatre at this time, yet are 'art.' It is this untenable nature that both courted rejection from the initial audiences and dissuaded re-assessment by later critical writers and film historians since they could not be effectively retrospectively 'sealed into' the period of experimentation.

The three films that best embody this problematic sensibility are, significantly, films the studios thought would directly repeat the success of *Easy Rider*: MGM's *Zabriskie Point* (a psychedelic free-love odyssey, to be directed by an Antonioni fresh from filming Swinging London for *Blow-Up*, 1966), Universal Pictures' *The Last Movie* (to be directed by Dennis Hopper and marketed as *Easy Rider*'s sequel) and *Two-Lane Blacktop* (also Universal, to be another road movie with hippies). The commercial failure of these films, and the bafflement and anger with which the former two films were met, suggested that their post-1968 take on the counter-culture movements made for uncomfortable viewing with their initial 'counter culture' audiences. Hopper, Hellman and Antonioni all deny a sense of importance or significance to the counter-culture. Their films are fundamentally nihilistic rather than utopian. They robbed the counter-culture of its self-awarded significance.

1. Art Cinema Meets Death Valley: *Zabriskie Point*

For *Zabriskie Point*, director Michelangelo Antonioni seemed to plunder the surface of reality for his experiential aesthetic (the hippies and their dress sense, the

The Last Movie

love-in, the psychedelic happening, the campus debates and violence, the generation clash), without allowing it to inform the structure and narrative of the film itself. The two central images in Antonioni's film work in a dialectic that contextualises the revolt of the young in a seemingly demeaning way: the hypnotic montage of Antonioni's seventeen camera-set up of an exploding luxurious desert retreat (extreme slow-motion shots of consumer goods, the detritus of American civilisation) with the shots of Death Valley (explosive formations of rock, frozen–the slow-motion of millennia rather than minutes). Both images have a coda. The exploding house has been frequently read as an image of the desire for the destruction of consumer culture.[2] But Antonioni's filmic language at this point is ambiguous and subjective–the house explodes only in Daria's (Daria Halprin) mind's eye. Daria leaves the vision of the exploding house and drives away. Antonioni frames the orange burn of a setting sun in a red sky, onto which he imposes the end title. The exploding house which may be related to the explosive energy on Daria's part is thus contrasted with the controlled and natural explosive energy of the sun. The two images juxtaposed suggest that the energy of the youth is a natural energy, that what is taken by the authorities (also present in the film) as violent dissent, anarchic revolt and a shirking of civil responsibilities is, in fact, evolutionary and also present in the very landscape of America.

The coda to the Death Valley sequence works in a similar way and with a similar ambiguity. Perhaps overcome by the existential moment (the feeling of insignificance in the face of the vastness of the natural scenery in front of them) Daria and Mark (Mark Frechette) make love. They are seemingly 'joined' (but again this seems to be subjective and illusory on the part of the protagonists) by numerous other couples (and triples), all also making love, in the valley. It is an affirmation of life (love-making) in the face of the dead landscapes of Death Valley (the ancient rock formations). They do not make love because they are free from the constraints of society, as would have been assumed and expected at the time of the film's release but, rather, they make love in the light of a taste of their own mortality and insignificance in the face of the 'deathscape' of Death Valley. The unreal orgy does not illustrate a free-love America but, rather, indicates the couple embracing a sensual world rather than accept their political responsibilities (that is, the un-illusory world) and their mortality. The couple grasp at the one expressive tool they possess: the ability to make love. It is a primitive rather than cerebral act. Jerry Garcia's accompaniment (the track *Love Scene*, which consists of a solo guitar improvisation) mirrors this concentration on the primal lineament of their actions. The love-in is not freedom, but a form of escape and denial.

2. The Lost Myths of *The Last Movie*

The Last Movie has an equally ambivalent attitude towards the reality that it plunders. The film plays off 'found' reality (sex, improvisations, parties, a semi-documentary about Sam Fuller shooting a Western in Peru) with various fictional narratives (a love story, a Western, a prospectors' adventure story, Jean Rouch-like ethnographic footage). The fictional narratives are drawn from the 'memory' of

American film. The narrative broadly alludes to the independent productions of the 1950s (in the figure of Fuller), John Huston of the 1940s (in its partial reworking of *The Treasure of the Sierra Madre*, 1948) and the Biblical epic of the 1930s (crowds of extras assembled for the camera–filming as a religious ceremony). Alongside these references, also cited is mythology of the Golden Age of Hollywood (the "movies" arriving in Peru with the crew, glamorising the ordinary and transforming reality), and the very origins of cinema itself in the 'primitive rituals' of filming that are re-enacted. This occurs through a mesmeric aesthetic and experiential narrative structure (albeit a structure seemingly by default). The act of filming itself becomes a religious ritual to the Peruvians once the film crew have pulled out and Hopper, as the stuntman Kansas, winds-up as the sacrificial victim once the act of filming has been inverted. (The Peruvians use a fake camera, made of bamboo, to 'film' real violence–hence Kansas, initially seen faking stunts for Fuller, is now engaged in actual violence for the fake camera).

Dennis Hopper deconstructs film myths, particularly that of the cowboy film and the West, by exploding them: he continually alludes to the film-making process (by casting himself, a Western shot in Peru, Brechtian inter-titles, non-matching cuts, the lack of an aesthetic style, the paraphernalia of cinema itself) and this overwhelms the fragments of fictional narrative. Thus, reality continually intervenes in his film, unbalances all aspects of the suspension of belief in the fictional film, and leaves chaos in its wake. The film can both embrace and collapse the myth of the old West and civilisation, and of Hollywood, which come to be directly correlated: revisionism, myth-making, illusion, lies. Thus, *The Last Movie* succeeds as it collapses in on itself, culminating in a re-enactment of the myth of Western civilisation: the crucifixion.

3. Reflexivity on the Open Road: *Two-Lane Blacktop*

Two-Lane Blacktop reaches another such dead end, beyond which it cannot advance via the same cinematic means. Namely, it assails myths and utilises a mesmeric aesthetic and structure. It is similarly nihilistic–deconstructing and stripping away the genres that it vaguely nods towards (the road movie, the buddy movie, the Western, the European art movie)–until nothing but the mechanism of cinema itself is left. The effect is like watching its most immediate predecessor, Ray's *They Live By Night* (1949), with all the drama stripped away–leaving only the locations, the movement and the road. It is the road that is the principal character in the film, as its title suggests. The film is the open road and everything else is unimportant. The soundtrack is near jazzless, rockless, soulless–scored instead with the constant flat roar of car motors. The fragments of music that are used (being mainly diegetic, from car stereos and diner jukeboxes) are notable for a kind of unauthenticity: white-boy country (Kris Kristofferson's *Me and Bobby McGee*), white-boy rock (The Doors' *Moonlight Drive* and *Satisfaction* by The Rolling Stones) and Hit Parade-friendly rock 'n roll (Chuck Berry's *No Particular Place To Go*).

The film's visual aesthetic is equally disinterested at times: the camera often pans from a rostrum rather than tracks, so the viewer is even denied the subjective experience of relating to the anti-heroes through sharing a sense of the momentum of moving with the cars. As with the director Monte Hellman, the viewer remains only an observer. Against the featurelessness of the New Mexico landscapes and the barely perceivable narrative, all the extraneous narrative conventions of the road movie genre seem to fall away: the race peters out, no-one ever arrives anywhere and the few representatives of authority that are depicted quickly disappear.

Hellman sets *Two-Lane Blacktop* in the contemporary America of 1971. Its two central protagonists are two listless young men known only as 'The Driver' and 'The Mechanic.' The pair engage in hotrod races for money as they make their way across the country (the purpose of their journey is never made clear). Along the way they meet the waif-like 'The Girl', with whom they both form fleeting relationships. The majority of the film concerns the duo's cross country race against a character referred to as 'The G.T.O.' This contest is struck up after a mild confrontation with the character at a gas station. Despite his constant talk to the contrary, the narrative reveals The G.T.O. to be as directionless as the two central male leads he is opposition with. However, in one of the alienating plot moves which defines *Two-Lane Blacktop*, the race quickly becomes unimportant to all three and by the close of the film has been forgotten altogether. During this time, The G.T.O. moves from an antagonistic to a paternalistic position with both The Driver and The Mechanic. (These bonding sessions occur in a series of stilted conversations at gas stations, diners and in each others cars). During this time, The G.T.O. also attempts (unsuccessfully) to form a relationship with The Girl. The film ends inconclusively, during a diversionary race on a disused airport landing strip.

As the above synopsis indicates, *Two-Lane Blacktop* offers a minimalist take on the *Easy Rider* mythology. It strips the film down to its essentials, finding in the 'central' race of the film not so much a narrative device, but a ritual centred on the road. All narrative comes from the road: The G.T.O (Warren Oates) sees the road as an endless narrative; it presents the opportunities for chance meetings. Indeed, it comes as no surprise that one such chance meeting, with Oklahoma Hitchhiker (Harry Dean Stanton) turns out to be an attempted homosexual encounter on the part of the Hitchhiker. With these bit-players The G.T.O enters into and elaborates on a variety of stories: he tests jet 'planes, he is a Korean war veteran, he is a Vegas gambler going to New York to spend his winnings, he is scouting for film locations, he is on his way to decorate his mother's house, and finally (to two soldiers), that he is The Driver, claiming he won The G.T.O in a race in which he drove a Chevy he himself had constructed. He even repeats the phrases that seem to embody his attitude to life more than once, on one occasion to a sleeping hitch-hiker. But the narrative of the road represents more than just a diversion for The G.T.O. It is also the opportunity to enact only the appearance of the gleaning of life lessons. Towards the end of the film, when he claims he is The Driver, he notes of winning the fictional race:

> "I'll tell you one thing. There's nothing like building up an old automobile from scratch and wiping out one of these Detroit machines. That'll give you a set of emotions that'll stay with you. Know what I mean? Those satisfactions are

permanent."

For *The Driver* (played by the pre-fame singer/songwriter James Taylor) and *The Mechanic* (Beach Boy drummer Dennis Wilson) the road becomes more vital: it is the *raison d'être*. *The Mechanic* invests the Chevy with more significance than the other (human) characters, at one point noting: "She don't seem to be breathing right. While on the road they brood: Morrisonesque, Mansonesque."[3]

The Driver's car, a Primer grey '55 Chevy with a 454 cubic inch high-performance engine, seems nothing more than a highly tuned mechanism on wheels. Every part seems to yield to access, to be primed and greased. The engine is constantly examined, consulted, tampered-with, fine-tuned and almost fetishised. The engine seems to make-up for the hollowness in the men. The G.T.O's car, a yellow 1970 Pontiac G.T.O, is from the opposite end of the spectrum: it is complete, a statement, a body. It is designed for comfort, for music (to be selected from an eclectic in-car collection), for stretching out on the black leather seats, unlike the Chevy's entirely functional interior.

The G.T.O, *The Driver* and *The Mechanic* match their cars accordingly. The Driver and The Mechanic act like awkward musicians with a between-numbers self-consciousness. They seem expelled from the beach and are now rootless drifters, surfing only on the hot blacktop. With Wilson the obsessiveness of the Beach Boys music is still present: the constant tweaking of the car engine replaces the perfectionist recording techniques of their songs. But now he is solely defined by his driving – the constant hum of his engine replaces the harmonies of his music. They are creatures of the road, as is The Girl (Laurie Bird), who comes across as an exile from the *Easy Rider* commune, a sullen, fragile hippie, indifferent to the world around her. She is first seen entering the Chevy while The Mechanic and The Driver eat in a diner. They return to the car and drive off with complete nonchalance. Her dialogue is equally detached. At one point she replies:

"East? That's cool, I've never been east."

Conversely, The Driver and The Mechanic are near wordless. They eat and drive. When they do talk, they talk of driving. The dialogue is sparse, riffing off Pinter-like repetition and Beckett-like absurdity. Hellman cast Taylor after seeing his image on a Sunset Boulevard billboard, and he frames and directs him in terms of manipulating his image, stripping it of any sense of authentic personality. Their anonymity works as affirmation of their sole status and role again and again: *The* Driver, *The* Mechanic. Hellman denies the protagonists a history. Any expositional authority that the viewer may assume of dialogue which might reveal a history is negated by its low-level mix: the engines drown it out.

The Fast Lane and the Filmic: Visual 'Alienation' in *Two-Lane Blacktop*

While the film is marked by a minimalist use of dialogue, the final image of

Two-Lane Blacktop represents the last act of the pairing-down of sound and the genre. Here, even the fictional nature of the film is stripped away. The Driver, shot from behind (a repeated visual motif in the film), accelerates along a featureless road. The sound has been removed. The film slows, freeze-frames and, seemingly, catches in the projector. A distant whirring on the soundtrack – which could be either the sound of the car motor or the sound of the film projector, bridges the images of the driving and the burning celluloid. The frame burns, smokes, holes of white light blast through it, and Hellman, after a beat, fades to black.

This final shot represents the very opposite of the opening image: darkness, engines and voices on a multi-layered soundtrack, a depth-of-field frame crowded with anonymous people shot with restless and mobile camera work. The smoke recalls the final image of *Easy Rider*: the burning motorcycle of the dead Billy. The brightness and the silence of the soundtrack recalls the final scenes of *2001: A Space Odyssey* (1968). Yet this moment is most frequently associated with a similar instance half-way through Bergman's *Persona* (1966).

As in *Persona*, the film's final image represents the same kind of violent rupture in the narrative and works as a reflexive gesture of the mechanisms of film projection. But, for Hellman, it is also the final nothingness – even the image has been stripped away from the film, the only thing that is left is white light. It negates the thin strands of narrative still left and offers a final ambiguity, simply erasing the characters. In context it represents a climatic negation in terms of the narrative. It occurs during a race within a race – The Driver has embarked on a quick race to make some "bread" during the cross-county race with The G.T.O. This ending means nothing – only that there is no lesson, no moral, no conclusion.

As in the films of the European *auteurs* to whom Hellman looks, those given to narrative austerity, existential gestures and stylish expressions of alienation (Erice, Antonioni, early Resnais, Melville, Duras, Bresson), *Two-Lane Blacktop* is a film in which both nothing and everything happens.[4] The film is a succession of sequences, utilized by Hellman as opportunities to leave out the narrative beats, to retain a flat dramatic trajectory. This is particularly unusual for American cinema, even New Hollywood cinema, which has traditionally worked towards a refinement of narrative. American cinema lacks the documentary roots of European cinema, and the belated start, principally with Griffith, looked straight towards Dickensian constructions and realism, as argued by Eisenstein.[5]

The result is that, as a rule of thumb, the narrative is at the heart of the American film, and works its way out into the *mise-en-scène*. The *mise-en-scène* becomes a device for exposing narrative. Hence American films are usually described in terms of narrative whereas European films are usually described in terms of the aesthetic and the *mise-en-scène*. Hellman's relationship to this classical difference is revealing, since he came from a quarter of American film-making that was dominated by the unrefined narrative. His early films were horror and exploitation flicks for late 1950s / early 1960s poverty-row production companies such as American International

Pictures–those feeding straight to the drive-in market.

Although mostly dismissed, such films can now be read in a unique fashion: a kind of documentation of 'nothingness.' Once the hokey stories have been put to one side, it is life that is left. The light, the faces, the inflections of voice, the dancing, the clothes and hair styles, the space – insights into the most momentous period of "nothing happening": suburban American of the 1950s and early/mid 1960s. The cheapness and sparseness of the *mise-en-scène*, unlike in the polished and well-financed *The Birds* (1963), a comparable exploitation, allows life to leak into the frame. This life-centered approach with its unconscious traces of *cinéma vérité* also characterises *Two-Lane Blacktop*. From the way a hippie thanks The G.T.O for a lift with "'Preciate it"; to the telephoto shots of The Girl picking her way through the spectators of a car race and asking people in the street for money. (This sequence even employs shades of documentary since it utilised unsuspecting real people and was shot with a hidden camera).

Like Antonioni in the 1960s, the Hellman of *Two-Lane Blacktop* seems to edge towards a new kind of cinema, one made of fragments of drama, traces of narratives, isolated moments of human interaction, underlined by a refusal to refine the narrative. In this respect, Hellman places himself outside the European/American divide in the balance between narrative and *mise-en-scène*. This is another reason why his work has been problematic in terms of the assimilation of New Hollywood into the cinematic and critical mainstream. This approach determines the mesmeric aspect of *Two-Lane Blacktop*. The compulsion to watch that the film achieves seems to come from a desire to find the narrative on the part of the viewer. The invitation is to read small details in a way that lends narrative to the film–and the details are drawn as much from Hellman's observations of life as from the narrative construction of the car race. Consequently, his camera probes while remaining at a distance, shuffling images together in a way that draws equal drama from both the slight narrative as it evolves and the images drawn from the locales of the film and the partly-amateur cast.

The elaborate stop at a run-down petrol station, which culminates in the challenge of the race is one such example. It is like a scene from the end of the world. The agreement is made: the race will be for Pink Slips–that is, for the ownership of the cars, that is, for the very essence, the very existence of the characters. This stand-off between The Driver and The G.T.O occurs in a bland petrol station, to which a few mobile homes seem to have attached themselves. A pump assistant, a mechanic, a cashier and a couple of old timers pass unnoticed through the scene. The G.T.O, who arrives first, swigs restlessly from a coke bottle while The Driver leans with studied casualness on a petrol pump. The G.T.O is shot in profile. Such framing and his 'comfortable' clothing (bottle green v-deck sweater, loud neckerchief, black driving gloves) mimics that celebrity-endorsement genre of advertising prevalent in the early 1970s: 'Warren Oates recommends...' For The G.T.O, the garage is a rest-stop, for The Driver and The Mechanic, it is another opportunity for car maintenance – and for Hellman to shoot them as they lounge around, in the manner of Factory extras in a Warhol movie, essaying the coolness of inexpressivity. For the first few of minutes,

Hellman cuts back and forth between the characters as they do nothing – or work on appearing to do nothing – like a stand-off in a Leone Western, until The G.T.O breaks the spell. First, a formulated opinion, delivered without a breath or pause: "I don't like being crowded by a couple of punk road hogs fair across two states." He then affirms this statement with: "I don't."

They engage in a mild exchange, all the time the language suggesting a combat of comparative virility, and inextricably intertwined with the prowess of their respective cars. After a couple of instances of unprompted 'buzzing' of the Chevy by the G.T.O before this sequence, the confrontation is both inevitable and, for Hellman at least, down playable. Yet once The Driver has cut-short the half-hearted slanging match and has initiated the challenge for the cross-county race to "Washington DC" (Oates' utterance of which makes it sound like a legendary lost brothel), The G.T.O seems uneasy with the consequences of his own bullishness and subsequent inability to back down. At the same time, a sense of rapport and warmth is immediately established: The Mechanic and The G.T.O peer at a map as The Driver watches both, eating potato chips. The Mechanic and The Driver seem especially unperturbed.

After the featurelessness of the previous scenes, and the over-exposed, whited-out landscapes glimpsed through the windscreens of the cars, the station is surprisingly 'loud' – signs proliferate, all just words: Fresh Coffee; Regular; Drink Coca-Cola; Ladies; Dr Pepper; Oil; UTE Station; Whipped Chocolate. The camera is restless, prowling about the forecourt, moving back and forth as The G.T.O gets into, and then out of, his car, keeping in medium shot. The bright midday light heightens the aesthetic – the colours do not so much glow, but shine. The Techniscope process works to sharpen the grain of the colours.

Meanwhile, other strands of the film's narrative are touched upon: The Girl gets into The G.T.O's car, as immediately trusting of him as she is of the other two men, and examines his music tapes. The plump hitchhiking cowboy/businessman (Bill Keller) in a tight, creased suit wonders off, barely noticeable, having had enough of The G.T.O's small talk and instant camaraderie. Moments before, The Girl walks in on him while using the garage toilet. He freezes like an animal caught in car headlights, looking perplexed and startled beneath his cowboy hat and behind his thick glasses, completely unable to react to the situation.

Another such diversion is the brief conversation between The Girl and The Driver, framed sitting on a wooden fence. Reverse angle shots would lend too much emphasis to the throw-away dialogue and so the camera remains fixed. He talks, softly and inexplicably, about "freaky bugs"–something seemingly half-remembered from a nature documentary that had made an impression on him when he younger. This invites a type of superficial and slogan-like reading of the film's posturing–as do the lyrics "freedom's just another word for nothing left to lose" that drift across the scene from The G.T.O's stereo. Hellman here seems to be pre-empting the expected framework that critics and viewers might apply to a viewing of the film: doomed hippies looking for elusive freedom yet a sense of continuity, the metaphor of bugs laying eggs before dying. The obviousness with which gestures towards such readings are made by Hellman works to reject such reading–another of the many rejections that characterise the film. Hellman's 'meaning' is elsewhere, and knowingly edges towards the ineffable–it is the way that The Driver is partly turned in from the camera during this conversation, his mop of black hair, blowing in the wind, replaces his face. The way Taylor's hair blows remains constant in the film–and offers more expressivity than his face, a mask of dark brooding. The movement of the hair indicates the slowing-down of the film in its last few seconds. It offers the anecdote to Wilson's stereotypical white teeth, tan and thick rusty-blond hair.

Conclusions and Fragments: The Influence of the Forgotten New Hollywood

The remembered New Hollywood was marked by a refinement of the art of derivation. Here, the artistic freedoms of the European New Waves and the gestures towards alienation were all 'cleaned-up', repackaged and resold. The price for bucking this trend in the few films from the time that offered a genuinely progressive vision, are seen in *Zabriskie Point*, *The Last Movie* and *Two-Lane Blacktop*. These works seem to accept and acknowledge their own redundancy through a dramatisation of reflexivity and rejection, with the result that they have remained misunderstood and forgotten for decades. In that these films also dealt with the post-1968 remnants of the counter-culture, this notion of redundancy was invariably connected to the redundancy of the whole counter-culture at this point. It was, perhaps, inevitable that they should be rejected by those of the counter-culture who had found themselves in the 1970s bereft of the dreams of 1968.

The author would like to thank David Cairns, Vaughan Green and Matthew Wilder for their assistance in the preparation of this article.

Notes

1. Peter Biskind, *Easy Riders, Raging Bulls: How the Sex 'n' Drugs 'n' Rock 'n' Roll Generation Saved Hollywood* (London: Bloomsbury, 1998),p.122. Biskind cites *Paint Your Wagon*, *Hello, Dolly!*, *Sweet Charity* and *True Grit* as emblematic of this mid-/ late 1960s situation in which the studios seemed hopelessly out of touch with their audiences. This attitude paved the way for the success of *Easy Rider* and New Hollywood.
2. Indeed, Antonioni shot an original, unused, ending for the film: a 'plane sky-writes "Fuck You America."
3. Wilson would have had first-hand help with the latter aura – Charles Manson and Family moved into his house in 1968. Wilson encouraged Manson's song writing and recorded his *Cease to Exist* for the 1969 20/20 album as *Never Learn Not to Love*. A fearful Wilson soon abandoned his home to the Family. The Tate-LaBianca murders occurred shortly after.
4. See Beverly Walker, 'Two-Lane Blacktop', *Sight and Sound*, Volume 40, Issue 1 (Winter 70/71), 34-37 (p.35). Here, Hellman cites Minnelli's *The Clock*, Lelouch's *Un Homme et Une Femme*, Nichols' *The Graduate*, Wilder's *The Apartment* and Truffaut's *Tirez sur le Pianiste* as influences.
5. S. M. Eisenstein, 'Dickens, Griffith, and the Film Today', in *Film Form: Essay in Film Theory*, ed. By Jay Leyda (London: Dennis Dobson, 1963), pp. 195-257.

There Goes the Neighbourhood: The Seventies, the Middle Class, and *The Omega Man*

Mark Sample

Charlton Heston's Seventies Persona

Beginning in the late sixties and continuing into the early seventies Charlton Heston appeared in a series of three dystopian science fiction movies, dismissed by critics at the time and remembered by audiences more for their camp value than for their deep social meaning. The first and last of these films, *Planet of the Apes* (1968) and *Soylent Green* (1973), are regularly quoted in contemporary popular culture, often referenced, for example, by the American television shows *Saturday Night Live* and *The Simpsons*. The middle film, however, has languished among the obscure dregs of the seventies, and attempts to remake it (most recently, the rumours go, with Ridley Scott directing) have repeatedly failed. This is unfortunate because the film, *The Omega Man* (1971, dir. Boris Sagal), is perhaps the most socially significant of the trio. Loosely based on Richard Matheson's 1954 novel *I Am Legend*, the official narrative of *The Omega Man* could not be clearer: humankind has been driven to the brink of extinction by an infectious bacillus which transforms men, women, and children into zombies, and only Robert Neville-played by Heston-can save it.

In the final scene a dying Neville lies in a pool of blood, arms outstretched, palms up, in a pose self-consciously reminiscent of Christ on the Cross. Neville's blood, like Christ's, is the blood that heals, the blood that renews, the blood that gives life. For Neville's blood is the only blood on earth immune to the deadly contagion. This apocalyptic scenario masks the real tensions operating in *The Omega Man*. It is a film about urban anxieties, not disease. It is a film about ambivalence towards the Other, not plague-ravaged zombies. It is a film about America in the seventies, not a fictional world filmed in Panavision.

Carnivalesque Futures

The future envisioned by *The Omega Man* is a bleak one indeed. Neville, an army scientist who injects himself with an experimental vaccine, is literally the last man in Los Angeles. Most of the city's inhabitants have died in a germ warfare attack, and two years later there are still corpses rotting in the hazy LA sun. A small band of diseased, zombie-like survivors occupy the City of Angels as well, but they are quickly established by the narrative as hardly human. The relationship between Neville and these zombies, and how that relationship is constructed to render the plague survivors as a grotesque 'Other' is central to understanding *The Omega Man*'s significance. It is useful to frame this relationship in terms of the bourgeoisie (the middle class, as represented by Neville) and the carnivalesque (the world in which official hierarchies are inverted and all is defiled and degraded). Two critical approaches guide my reading of *The Omega Man*: Mikhail Bakhtin's enormously influential celebration of the carnivalesque, *Rabelais and His World*; and Peter Stallybrass and Allon White's 1986 reworking of Bakhtin, *The Politics and Poetics of Transgression*. Stallybrass and White argue that carnivals are not, as Bakhtin supposes, inherently subversive. There is "no a priori revolutionary vector to carnival and transgression," they write.' According to them, the carnival or spectacle is not a liberating expression of the lower classes so much as it is a means through which the middle class reasserts its own position in society. This is achieved by fragmenting, marginalizing, sublimating, and repressing forces which represent a threat to the status quo. It is only when political antagonism intensifies that the carnival is transformed into a site of symbolic struggle. Especially during times of social stress and rapid change the middle class attempts to comfort itself by projecting its anxieties onto lower social classes, representing them in a manner which reaffirms the status of the middle class.

The carnivalesque, then, is often a site of displaced anxiety, and *The Omega Man*, as a film preoccupied with the changing world of the seventies, resonates with this anxiety. Among the many ways the middle class protects itself against the

The Omega Man

The Omega Man

carnivalesque is through two different imaginings of the human body, which Bakhtin refers to as the "classical" and the "grotesque."[2] The classical body is self-contained, its orifices sealed or hidden entirely, a finished product alone and raised on a pedestal. It is the body of the Renaissance, something like Michelangelo's *David*. The grotesque, on the other hand, is always part of a throng, its mouth gaping, its arms and feet obtrusive, dirty and vile, a body "in the act of becoming."[3] Much of the visual force of *The Omega Man* derives from this opposition between the classical and the grotesque body. There is Robert Neville, portrayed with the trademark Hestonian bearing, self-assured and self-righteous, a singular heroic figure, standing tall and mighty. Then there is the Other, those cadaverous humans ravaged by the plague, the so-called "tertiary cases." Cloaked in black, hunched over, open sores on their pallid skin, wearing mirrored sunglasses to protect their photosensitive eyes, the zombies are creatures of the night, the embodiment of the grotesque. Always depicted as part of a mob, the zombies call themselves the "Family," as if they were some sort of cult. Indeed, for the most part they have lost their individuality and act with a herd mentality, chanting and performing whatever ritual their leader Matthias commands. But the zombies are more animal than human; when Neville powers on the floodlights outside his stronghold, the Family members in his courtyard scatter like a pack of rats.

Though there are two versions of the human body in *The Omega Man*, physical differences alone cannot fully account for the dichotomy between classical and grotesque bodies. The film reveals that the spatial arrangements of these bodies are significant as well. Stallybrass and White note how the carnival and all it represented: the filth, the mobs, the laughter, the libidinal flows-became geographically marginalised; what once took place at the centre of town was first confined to certain neighbourhoods, then pushed out of town entirely, moving more and more to the periphery. At the same time, one of the developing features of the middle class was self-exclusion from festival activities.[4] No more would the bourgeoisie enjoy the carnival as part of the carnival; they became onlookers rather than participants.

This distance between the bourgeoisie and the carnivalesque is best understood in *The Omega Man* in terms of Neville's LA penthouse. An enclave among the contaminated ruins of the city, Neville's home represents the space of the middle class, a refuge of protected domesticity. Here Neville is safe, living among his lights and appliances powered by a diesel generator, surrounded by artwork on his walls, sculptures on his mantel, a chessboard on his desk, wine in his glass-in short, all the trappings of a bourgeois life. Like today's gated communities, his home is a sanctuary where the tenets of civilisation can be upheld. It is a sanctuary Neville refuses to leave. When he is invited to join a small group of humans who are still uninfected with disease and fighting for survival in the mountains, Neville explains the importance of his LA home: "Well, that's where I live. That's where I used to live. That's where I'm going to live. And not Matthias or his Family or any other son of a bitch is going to make me leave." Like a long-time city dweller who refuses to budge from a posh neighbourhood once crime rates rise and the 'riffraff' move in, Neville is determined to maintain his place in society.

Outside Neville's fortress await the Family and its insidious, mocking laughter. Led by Matthias, who before the plague was a television news anchor, the zombies parade through the streets in nightly festivals, kindling bonfires, burning all that the scientist Neville holds dear: books, artwork, globes, tools. As Neville watches from his balcony, a classical figure poised above the crowd, he observes, "At it again, I see. What'll it be tonight? The Museum of Science? Some Library? Poor miserable bastards." From their peripheral position as outsiders the zombies are looting the elements of high culture. And nothing is safe, not even Neville's fortress. When the Family threatens to break into Neville's apartment, catapulting flaming torches through his windows or scaling across his accordion-wired balcony, Neville shouts, "Why the hell can't you leave me alone?" His powerlessness to stop this invasion of his space by the carnivalesque, we shall see, reflects one of the middle class's greatest anxieties.

The threat Neville faces is not one of mere inversion or status reversal, in which the zombies simply turn his world upside-down. The threat is something far more complex, a hybridisation in which the classical self is contaminated by the grotesque Other, resulting in a new, unstable category. It is a blurring of boundaries, and the danger it heralds is, according to Stallybrass and White, "the possibility of shifting *the very terms of the system itself*, by erasing and interrogating the relationships which constitute it."[5] Though Neville may not consider his situation in these terms, he intuits that his identity and the social system which produced it are at

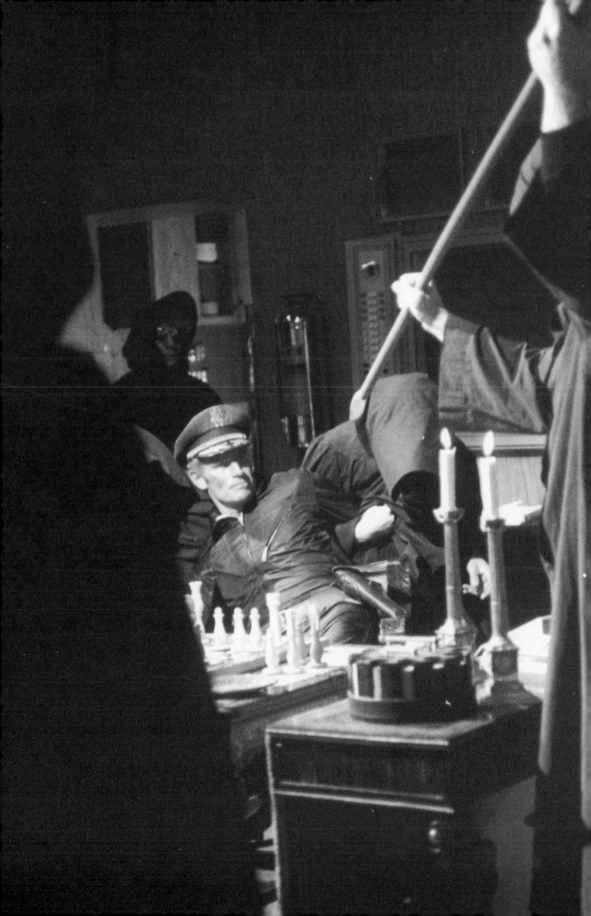

stake. Alarmed by this possibility, Neville begins to speak of the Family as a kind of "vermin," a rhetorical strategy which calls to mind Hitler's Final Solution. Like Freud's Rat Man, like Hitler himself, Neville is both fascinated and horrified by what he perceives as vermin, especially with the zombies' ability to hide and to contaminate all that they touch. Neville even captures one of the zombies in an attempt to study it. As a series of flashbacks match his voice-over, Neville explains his scientific endeavour to Dutch, one of the surviving humans in the mountains: "Once I caught one of Matthias's people last year. I tried everything in the shelves on him." The flashback sequence ends with the zombie grappling against Neville in his lab; a lethal injection from Neville ends the struggle, and the zombie sags to the floor. Since the vermin cannot be tamed, it must be exterminated.

The Terror of Surveillance

Which is precisely Neville's project in *The Omega Man*. Neville spends his days sweeping through the city on a one-man search-and-destroy mission. Though it is not apparent at the time, this is exactly what the opening scene is all about. The establishing shot frames a lone car driving on the freeways of Los Angeles before zooming out to a panoramic bird's-eye view of the city, which simultaneously projects a fantasy of freedom unheard of on LA's highways and the implied impossibility of that dream. Cut to a close-up of the car: a convertible, its top down, driven by a white male, sunglasses on, his hair blowing in the wind. The image of virility is supplemented with a sudden motion-the man slams the brakes, skidding the car to a stop, bursts from his seat, and fires a machine gun at shadows moving through the windows of a distant building. Neville's methodology becomes clearer as the plot progresses. He has divided the city into sectors and systematically moves through these, looking for evidence of the Family. He takes notes every ten blocks or so, observing a grocery store that had been broken into here, and signs of "foraging", there.

Neville is obsessed with finding the Family's lair, what he calls the "nest," and his need to locate and map out the Family is rooted in his recognition that the Family's invisibility is dangerous: the zombies can attack anytime, anywhere. Stallybrass and White stress the importance of surveillance as a means for the bourgeoisie to control the lower classes. "Throughout the nineteenth century," they write, "the 'invisibility' of the poor was a source of fear."[6] The solution was to police the dangerous elements of the lower classes through surveillance; this is the panopticon discussed by Bentham and later elaborated on by Foucault. In a prison setting, the panopticon operates via a guard stationed in a central tower. The guard observes the inmates in their cells below, circularly arranged around the tower, while he himself cannot be seen by the prisoners. It is a control mechanism that automatically conditions the prisoners, for they know that there is a possibility that any deviant behaviour will be detected and that serious consequences-punishment-would follow. Aware of their 'permanent visibility,' or at least the threat of permanent visibility, the prisoners self-monitor their actions and act as the warden wants them to.[7] According to Stallybrass and White, the middle class has often adopted this principle of the panopticon to control the poor and other undesirables. For example, nineteenth century English aristocrats countered the threat

The Omega Man

of the poor's 'invisibility' by building roads into and through slums, thinking that their benign gaze would be enough to inculcate the poor with the morals and ideals of the upper class.[8]

But there is a paradox here: by looking at the lower classes-at the Other-the middle class risks becoming contaminated itself. Hence the rise of informal and formal laws regulating contact with the filthy, the diseased, the grotesque. *The Omega Man* can be read as a textbook of these regulations. Consider Neville's advice to Lisa, one of the humans who had escaped the plague by hiding in the mountains and who is now living in the city, hoping to persuade the seemingly invulnerable Neville to help the human survivors. Before Lisa ventures into the streets, Neville warns her, "Stay on the ground floors, near the doors, in the light. If you see anything, shoot." Of course, such admonitions go unheeded, and Lisa becomes a zombie herself by the movie's end. Lisa failed to see without being seen.

Neville, on the other hand, possesses several means of surveilling without putting himself at risk. He rigs a modern-day panopticon in his apartment: a video wall wired to an elaborate closed-circuit camera system, displaying various images from outside his apartment. From inside Neville can safely monitor his surroundings, a middle class hero forestalling the collapse of social space through incessant surveillance. Just as important as the panopticon-and closely related to it, architecturally speaking-is the balcony, where, as Stallybrass and White note, "one could gaze, but not be touched."[9] A means of separating oneself from the festivals of the street, the balcony plays an important role in *The Omega Man*. It is from the balcony that Neville can look down upon the zombies as they laugh around a bonfire yet remain separate from them. It is from the balcony that he can pick off the Family, one by one, sharpshooting his high-powered Browning automatic rifle, complete with infrared scope, down into the crowd.

Outside Neville's apartment mayhem reigns. Inside, reason rules. This divide between madness and reason provides another means of distinguishing the bourgeois from the grotesque. Influenced by the work of Foucault, Stallybrass and White speak of "the contained outsiders-who-make-the-insiders-insiders."[10] In other words, the Other is a construction of what-we-are-not which helps us define what-we-are. Attaching a scientific discourse to insanity and then institutionalising the insane is a means to maintain classical bourgeois reasoning by clearly staking out what is insane and what is not. The presence of an asylum buttresses the logical world of those who live outside its barred doors. But in its portrayal of a "world upside-down," *The Omega Man* even inverts the asylum. Neville is the one who is contained, and only on the inside is he safe. Outside he is surrounded by zombies, who are diagnosed by Dutch as having "psychotic delusions" and "occasional stages of torpor."

Though immune to the disease Neville struggles to maintain his sanity, since it is one sure way to differentiate himself from the Other. But, and this is where ruptures in the narrative appear, it is not at all clear he is succeeding. He fires at shadows. On Sunday evenings he dresses up for dinner with himself, wearing a velvet jacket and ruffled satin shirt. He plays chess against "Caesar"-a bust of a Caesar Augustus. In the deserted streets he hears the ringing of countless pay phones, and in response he desperately screams, "There is no phone ringing, damn it! There is no phone!" In this lonely world of one Neville talks to himself endlessly; in a car dealership he sells himself a car, while in his apartment building's elevator, he pretends to be the doorman. When Neville first encounters Lisa he even questions his own vision: "Is this how it starts? The trip to the laughing academy? No, you silly bastard. It starts with you asking yourself idiot questions." The "it" here is madness-the "psychotic delusions" shared by the Family. And "laughing," like the inane hooting of the Family, is a symptom. Thus two qualities held up by bourgeois society as binary oppositions, reason and madness, are shifting, sliding into one another, just as domestic and carnivalesque spaces are collapsing into one another. It is from these slippages and the resulting hybridisation that the tensions in both *The Omega Man* and real life arise.

There Goes the Neighbourhood: American Middle Class Anxieties in the Seventies

It now seems appropriate to link the tensions raised in the film to the concept of myth proposed by the French anthropologist Claude Lévi-Strauss. For Strauss, myth, even a myth set far in the past (or far into the future, for that matter) deals with the time in which the myth was created, rather than the time the myth tells about.[11] Thus

The Omega Man is really about America in 1971, when the film was produced, not America in 1977, when the post-apocalyptic narrative takes place. Lévi-Strauss also proposes that "the purpose of myth is to provide a logical model capable of overcoming a contradiction."[12] The myth, in other words, is an attempt to resolve crises in society. This notion of a myth motivates a brief historical survey of the years leading up to 1971.

America had just emerged from one of the most turbulent decades since the Civil War: racial conflicts, riots, assassinations, an unpopular war, the yippie and hippie movements. The new decade did not bring a halt to any of these tensions; in fact, what is commonly thought of as 'the sixties' in the popular consciousness did not really end until well into the seventies. Recall that several of the era's defining events occurred at the threshold of the seventies. The Stonewall riot in the summer of 1969 galvanised the gay rights movement, while the Altamont and Woodstock music festivals in the same year illustrated the power and threat of music and of the younger generation.

Challenges to the established order continued into the early seventies: Charles Manson and several of his followers-another 'family'-were found guilty of seven murders in late 1970; anti-war demonstrations shut down universities across America; four students were shot dead at Kent State in Ohio and the ratification of the 26th Amendment, lowering the voting age to 18, was imminent. In this era there was racial violence, with armed Black Panthers cut down in police raids; there was arson, there was looting. Prison riots. Mandated bussing. Increasing inflation. Strikes. In short, it appeared to many middle class Americans that the world they had constructed since the end of World War Two was falling apart.

Throughout *The Omega Man* Neville is confronted with menaces that can be read as threats not only to himself, but to the non-diegetic middle class American audience viewing the film back in 1971. Neville is merely a metonymic stand-in for the rest of bourgeois America. As Neville watches the burning of books, powerless to stop the pillaging of high culture, his contempt registers with mainstream America, and his anguish is similar to what some academics and conservatives (not necessarily mutually exclusive groups) feel over attempts to do away with or enlarge the traditional literary canon. Political movements such as feminism likewise threatened mainstream America with the 'loss' of its values, just as the Family threatened Neville. And of course, just as the grotesque can pollute ideas and values, it can also contaminate things and possessions. In the climactic action sequence of *The Omega Man* several members of the Family force their way into Neville's apartment. The camera suddenly switches from a series of long, steady shots into a rocky, cinéma-vérité style, which emphasises the weariness of Neville; he can only sit and watch as the Family trashes the place with bats, splintering bookcases, breaking medical equipment, smashing dishes, hacking apart paintings and tapestries. Literally then, the Other breaks in and loots bourgeois America. Appropriately enough, the camera lingers upon the last item to be smashed, the quintessential prop of the middle class lifestyle: the television set.

So what does it all mean? How can the world inside *The Omega Man* be reconciled with the world outside it? By the time of *The Omega Man's* release, Lyndon Johnson's "Great Society" and its accompanying federal welfare programs, aimed at narrowing the gap between rich and poor, was only several years old. Congressional passage of several Civil and Voting Rights Acts in the mid-sixties was intended to ensure that all American citizens, regardless of race or class, received the same rights. In April of 1971 the Supreme Court unanimously upheld bussing in *Swann v. Charlotte-Mecklenburg Board of Education* as a means to achieve integration and maintain a racial balance in public schools. I wish to suggest that although the popular news media celebrated these achievements, an undercurrent of ambivalence ran through middle class America. Many Americans wanted those less fortunate to move up the social ladder. Many Americans agreed that integration was better than segregation. Many Americans hoped the war on poverty would succeed. Who could argue against such visions, so true to the ideals of the American Dream? Yet middle class America was also deeply concerned about this newly proposed social mobility.

The Omega Man is a manifestation of this ambivalence-and this is where the film's true power lies. Consider that at first the Family seems to represent a militant political group like the Black Panthers. Matthias singles out Neville for not bearing "the marks" of the Family, and members refer to each other as "brothers." Moreover, Matthias's right-hand man, an aggressive African-American male who advocates the use of violence, calls Neville's fortress a "honky paradise." In short, the Family appears to correspond directly to middle class America's fears of African-Americans. But to insist upon such a closed reading of *The Omega Man* is to ignore other facets of the film's narrative. For instance, Neville becomes romantically involved with Lisa, a young African-American woman. The film even preaches against racial epithets; when Dutch mentions that the orphans he takes care of get "spooked" easily, Lisa corrects him, "Watch your mouth!" So the film presents two contradictory discourses about race relations; Neville, and America, move back and forth uncertainly between them.

Related to the idea of mixing races and mixing classes is the fear of contamination, which I have already discussed in terms of the gaze and the touch. Superficially, this fear is about something so small that it cannot be seen: the germs that spread the plague. In fact, if *The Omega Man* had been made a decade later one might read the film as an AIDS allegory. But we must exempt that reading, instead looking for an explanation of the plague's symbolism which takes into account the experiences of the early seventies. Could the film be about the Cold War or détente? A flashback newscast reveals that the contagion was unleashed in a Cold War border dispute. With film clips of dying Americans running in the background, the news anchor-Matthias-announces: "Whether a state of war between China and Russia still exists is not important any longer. Our fellow countrymen are dying. The very foundations of civilisation are beginning to crumble under the dread assault of that horror long feared: germ warfare."

Racial 'Mixing' and the Fear of Youth

But was China near the brink of war with Russia in 1971? That is debatable. But this much is certain: germ warfare was the last thing on the American public's mind. Instead, Americans were thinking about issues like bussing and integration. Neville himself locates where the middle class's priorities lie when he explains that his blood is "genuine 160-proof old Anglo-Saxon." Neville is not worried about a virus infecting him; he is worried about the movement of the Other into his social position, embodied by his blood. Neville is troubled by a type of miscegenation, not strictly of race, but of the carnivalesque. That mingling of the high and low elements of society is the "dread assault" on the "foundations of civilisation." What Neville fails to realise is that the siege has long been underway. After all, his blood is not pure 200-proof Anglo-Saxon-only 160-proof, or 80 percent. This slip on Neville's part is revealing, for it suggests that within ourselves lies the origins of our downfall. Neville, though blind to the fact, is already a hybrid. The assault comes not from without, but from within, in the part of ourselves we pass on to our children.

Indeed, perhaps the fear that is most veiled in *The Omega Man* is the fear of youth, a youth that celebrates hybridisation. Appropriately enough, traces of this anxiety surface while Neville attends the cinema. Taking a break from his extermination project, Neville wanders into a theatre, fires up a generator, and threads the projector. The movie: *Woodstock* (1970, dir. Michael Wadleigh). It is a film that documents perhaps the most socially significant festival of young people in the nation's history, protesting, singing, eating, drinking, smoking, challenging every convention their parents had handed down to them. It is truly a world upside-down. Neville has apparently seen the movie a hundred times, for he lip-synchs the entire show, speaking along word-for-word with the songs and interviews. It appears as if Neville has no problem with the ideas represented in *Woodstock*; he even seems sympathetic with one hippie's wish for a world where you are not "afraid to walk out on the street."

However, this is not the real Woodstock he is watching. It is only a two-dimensional film version in which the threats, the spectacles, the carnivalesque have been flattened and reduced, if not expunged completely. Neville appears to take comfort in this Woodstock, but Matthias reminds Neville what the real Woodstock signifies: a new world in which Neville "has no place." Matthias declares that Neville "has the stink of oil and electrical circuitry about him. He is obsolete." This condemnation of Neville might just as easily apply to the middle-aged, middle class American audience that Neville, in the guise of Charlton Heston, represents. Pointing directly to Neville, Matthias continues: "You are discarded. You are the refuse of the past." When Charlton Heston, one of the greatest leading men of the fifties, tall, strapping, and intelligent, still in his prime in 1971, is called "obsolete," it marks the end of an era. No more Moses, no more Ben-Hur, no more El Cid. Heston's obsolescence is later reaffirmed by Ritchie, Lisa's kid brother. Ritchie tells Neville that "you just don't belong" in this new world ruled by the carnivalesque. The younger generation has spoken, and Neville/Heston serves no more purpose. Neville can only quietly respond, "Nice of you to let me hang around."

If *The Omega Man* is indeed a myth designed to reconcile contradictions, then it is doomed to fail. The oppositions *The Omega Man* attempts to overcome are legion: the classical body versus the grotesque, the gaze versus the touch, reason versus madness, the movement of social classes versus the protection of class interests, the irrepressible tide of youth that wipes away the past. None of these are overcome in *The Omega Man*. The final scene betrays the closing credit's bright music and veneer happy ending, in which Dutch saves a vial of Neville's life-giving blood. This is intended to be happy? Neville's lover has become infected and is now a zombie. Neville himself lies dead, killed by Matthias, who has taken over Neville's home and now stands on the balcony, where Neville, the last of the middle class, once reigned. What went wrong? Very simply, Neville failed to navigate between the ever-shifting extremes that made up his world. Stallybrass and White conclude their work by noting that "the carnivalesque was marked out as an intensely powerful semiotic realm precisely because bourgeois culture constructed its self-identity by rejecting it."[13] But this rejection can never be complete; the repressed always returns. At best, a kind of diaspora occurs, in which the real-world anxieties represented in *The Omega Man* can only be faced if very well disguised. Disguised, perhaps, as science fiction and displaced onto a dystopian vision of a plague-ravaged society. What cannot be disguised, however, is Neville's downfall. He is a hero, yes, but a dead one. And what good is a dead hero to the middle class when the hero himself is-or was-the last of the middle class?

Notes

1. Peter Stallybrass and Allon White, *The Politics and Poetics of Transgression* (New York: Cornell University Press, 1986), p.16.
2. Mikhail Bakhtin, *Rabelais and His World*, trans. Hélène Iswolksy (Bloomington: Indiana University Press, 1984), pp.18-30.
3. Ibid., p.317.
4. Stallybrass and White, pp.176-79.
5. Ibid., p.58.
6. Ibid., p.134.
7. Michael Foucault, *Discipline and Punish: The Birth of the Prison*, trans. Alan Sheridan (New York: Pantheon, 1977), pp.200-204.
8. Stallybrass and White, p. 139.
9. Ibid., p.136.
10. Ibid., pp.22-23.
11. Claude Lévi-Strauss, *Structural Anthropology*, trans. Claire Jacobson and Brooke Grundfest Schoepf (New York: Basic Books, 1963), p.209.
12. Ibid., p.229.
13. Stallybrass and White, p.202.

The Stars Don't Always Survive: Disaster Movies as Shocking Cinema

Stephen Keane

Disaster: The 'Lost' Genre of the 1970s

In contrast to classic genres like the Western or film noir and popular genres of the present such as horror and science fiction, disaster movies have remained relatively neglected in film studies both past and present. Taking 'disaster' at face value it could be said that catastrophe has been such a longstanding and pervasive aspect of cinema that the task of writing about films with disaster in them is far too demanding. From early Biblical epics and 1950s sci-fi B movies through to recent action /disaster/science-fiction hybrids, disaster has always been a spectacular draw.' The opposite problem with the term, 'disaster movies', is that it refers to films entirely predicated around disaster, without the benefit, it would seem, of swords, sandals and laser beams. This is to say that disaster could be said to be their only point of interest. For a while back in the 1970s, however, watching ordinary folk and the filthy rich getting bombed, burned, drowned and generally crushed to death proved extremely popular-but only for a while.

The simple dismissal of disaster movies of the 1970s is that they were formulaic and spectatorial, with ingenious moments of destruction invariably wasted on cardboard characters. These movies came and quickly went because the narrative possibilities were limited and the law of diminishing returns was such that after numerous planes in peril, an overturned ship, a burning skyscraper and Los Angeles laid to waste by an earthquake there was nowhere else to go. If the microcosmic characters often failed to maintain interest in the middle of all this spectacular destruction this is not to forget that the other key draw of disaster movies of the 1970s was their use and, I'd like to argue, *abuse* of stars. The basic, conservative reading of disaster movies of the time is that far from being savage they were highly moral affairs. What better way to carry audiences along, therefore, than have them identify with certain upstanding stars leading the weak but willing through to survival? What better way to offer an alternative reading by pointing out that the stars themselves often perish?

As a way into offering this alternative reading I am, of course, indebted to certain principles laid down in Nick Roddick's 'Only the stars survive: Disaster movies in the seventies.'² Although Roddick only uses the star/survival equation as a hook, it does prove central to his argument concerning the 'sacrosanct' nature of disaster movies; that somehow, despite all the destruction around them, the stars always seem to

survive. Although *Airport* (1970) can be said to have sparked off the disaster movie cycle of the 1970s, Roddick correctly asserts that it was *The Poseidon Adventure* (1972) which:

> confidently established its basic narrative model: a random collection of people centred around a small group of what Variety calls 'topflight thesps' (stars), caught up in a spectacular disaster and, despite a reduction in numbers –minimal for topflight thesps, massive for everyone else–overcoming apparently impossible odds in order to survive.[3]

As an impetus for approaching the pumped-up spectacle and sheer carnage of this extremely popular phase of the cycle circa 1972-74, Roddick uses producer Irwin Allen's characteristic Hollywood pitch in order to establish the basic industrial formula: "We have a perfect set-up of a group of people who have never met before and who are thrown together in terrible circumstances. In the first six minutes, 1,400 people are killed and only the stars survive."[4]

As far as context is concerned, Roddick does warn against making simple cause and effects judgements. Disaster movies of the 1970s may well have met "some basic need in the mass audience"[5] but that general, basic need can only be attributed to basic, general crises of the time:

The Poseidon Adventure

a sort of post-Watergate depression, a national inferiority complex after the Vietnam debacle, or even a 'bread and circuses' attitude caused by 'the erosion of democracy and the Western materialist way of living'–all of which are both a little too convenient and wholly impossible to substantiate.[6]

The compromise is that instead of seeing Charlton Heston as a direct alternative to Richard Nixon or making too many links with the slaughter in Vietnam, for example, disaster movies of the time were fundamentally concerned with more pervasive workaday concerns surrounding "the spectre of corporatism."[7] This is where ideological readings begin to follow a certain, conservative line but also inadvertently open up the possibility of more radical readings. Borrowing certain tricks from Biblical epics, certainly the elemental forces that wreak havoc in these films are as much a reminder of the eternal as the contextual. But terrorists and corporate bosses alike are also partly responsible for the disasters in these films, either directly or indirectly putting innocent people at risk with their concerns over money and bureaucracy. With regard to the perceived irresponsibility of those in power, Roddick states:

> Such men who in the normal, liberal, capitalist, democratic run of things have risen to positions of power through commercial enterprise or by due (or even undue) process of election are, it is implied, not fit to run society... This fear, fuelled by Watergate and exploited by the 'super-cop' cycle, is evidently a very real one. And disaster movies respond to it in a typically demagogic fashion: by portraying the transfer of power from the old, the incompetent and the corrupt to the new race of super-heroes, brave, morally upright and technologically brilliant. Behind them, the people can be united into a corporate identity, free from the divisions and the individual selfishness which characterised them before the disaster.[8]

Must The Stars Survive?: Winners and Losers in the Disaster Stakes

It naturally follows that, whether looked at in terms of those partly responsible for the disaster or the flock of innocents following the new, self-appointed group leader, disaster movies punish 'the wicked', 'the weak' and 'the criminal.'[9] From out of the rubble and into the bright light of a new day, it is principally the stars who act as a focus for the issue of the survival of the fittest. They may well play the decent professional middle ground of pilots, engineers, architects and firemen but they also have the advantage of being better than the average person in terms of both their superstar qualities and the authoritative characters they portray.

As Roddick explains the basic use of stars in disaster movies, the narrative compression of 'a random gathering of people' is further facilitated by pre-existing star personas. The films themselves call for ensemble casting and particular actors bring instant recognition:

> Disaster movies are peopled by archetypes who react to the given situation in function of their sex, class or profession and not in function of any individual

The Poseidon Adventure

identity. What is more, the archetypes are extended by the known personality of the star playing the part: in accordance with the usual formula, what we respond to on the screen is not someone called Stuart Graff (*Earthquake*) or Alan Murdock (*Airport 1975*), but someone far more substantial called Charlton Heston.[10]

Adapting the singular Charlton Heston factor somewhat, Maurice Yacowar points out that Graff is also married to the 'romantic legend' that is Ava Gardner. Thus, the double expectation is that "husband Charlton Heston will gravitate towards her in the crunch, particularly when his mistress is lightly accented as an alien (French Canadian Genevieve Bujold)."[11]

Principally, Roddick and Yacowar's readings are based upon conservative assumptions, namely that stars known for playing heroic types will go on to do the same in disaster movies, thus further ensuring that the stars survive and actors known for playing corrupt characters will duly die. Charlton Heston plays Charlton Heston and the implications are that we can expect him to rescue the plummeting plane in *Airport 1975* as confidently as he rode his crippled chariot in *Ben-Hur* (1959), for example. In this case he does and that is extremely reassuring. The opposite attraction of disaster movies, however, is that the stars don't always survive. They may die heroically and the films themselves might well play on the usual expectations exactly in order to create the opposite effect, but the twist is that not even images set in stone can live up to disaster. So while it might have been entirely appropriate to have the rock-like, chisel-jawed Charlton Heston face up to *Earthquake* (1974) it was an unexpected pleasure to see the man who parted the Red Sea in *The Ten Commandments* (1956) get washed down the drain along with his marriage at the end of the film.

The Poseidon Adventure

Particularly in light of the new alternative filmmaking that had begun to transform Hollywood in the late 1960s (*Bonnie and Clyde, The Graduate, Easy Rider, Midnight Cowboy* etc.), the first of the disaster movie cycle of the 1970s, *Airport*, probably deserved to be labelled "The best film of 1944."[12] In their scathing ideological critique, Michael Ryan and Douglas Kellner see the film as a hymn to American ingenuity. Principally *Airport* presents us with an enclosed corporate calamity in which the General Manager (Burt Lancaster), the dashing pilot (Dean Martin) and the engineer (Arthur Kennedy) cut through bureaucratic orders in order to clean up the mess caused by a belligerent working-class bomber.[13] Stylistically the film is an anachronistic slice of Old Hollywood with the underlying feeling that at any moment soon Burt Lancaster will simply melt the snow from the runway with his gleaming teeth or that Dean Martin will croon the bomber into submission.

Certainly, as a disaster movie, *Airport's* fatality rate of just one (the mad bomber) is likely to disappoint. Apart from the higher death toll as expressed by Irwin Allen, stylistically *The Poseidon Adventure* is a shock to the senses. For good and bad Lawrence Shaffer sees it as the epitome of the Good Dumb Film, 'kinaesthetic', raw, bone crunching: "Classics of the genre include *The Wild Bunch*... *The French Connection*, and *Bullitt*... With all these, consciousness may not be raised but it is energised, through being allowed participation in such things."[14] Let down slightly by its 'dumb' content, nevertheless *The Poseidon Adventure* is one of the most spectacularly mechanical and, above all, experiential films of the early 1970s: "although the film is somewhat of a toss-up between Disney and Dante it does finally land on the Dante (heads) side."[15]

In contrast to Burt Lancaster or Dean Martin, who beamed and occasionally gnashed their way through the 1950s and 60s, *The Poseidon Adventure* is led by Gene Hackman, fresh from the success of his anti-hero cop, Popeye Doyle, in *The French Connection* (1971). Here Hackman bites and snarls his way through the upturned scenery. Hardly a rock like Charlton Heston, he is nevertheless earthy and dependable:

> He is the one surrogate we could have wished for to lead us out of the quicksand of this most graphic of all *elemental* nightmare films... Which is not to say that Hackman is like some adolescent fantasy figure like Wayne or Flynn, only somewhat more resilient, resourceful, and courageous than ourselves... Where Flynn and Wayne have an a priori braggadocio unrelated to plot specifics, Hackman's virtues are identical with his problem solving. Hackman never seems sure of the outcome, as Flynn and Wayne do, because,

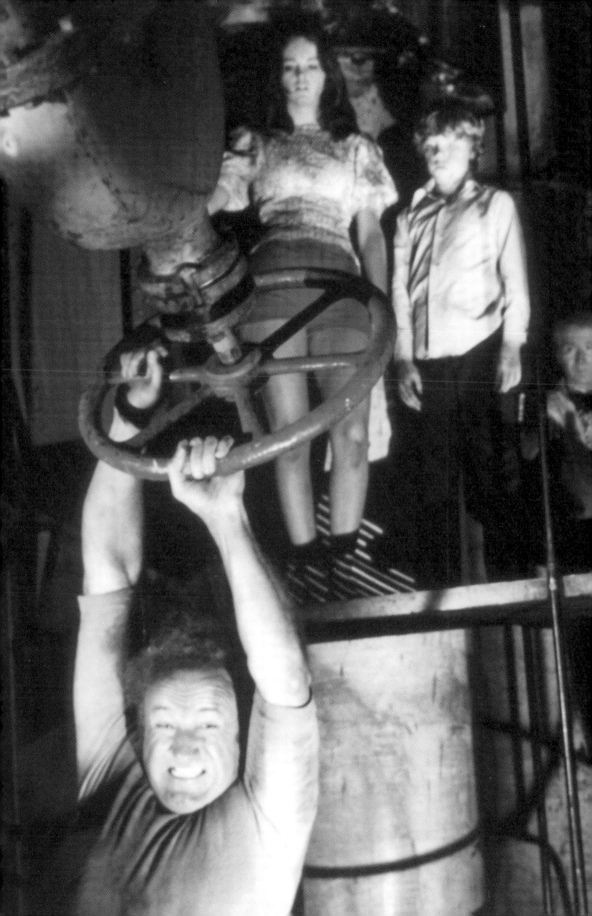

for one thing, he never thinks of the outcome, only the steps along the way.[16]

This goes some way to explaining Hackman's appeal in the film but in playing a particularly belligerent anti-hero priest there are other factors to consider. As his opening sermon makes clear, Hackman's Reverend Scott preaches to the strong, those willing to take control of their own destiny, and throughout the film he is caught between self-righteous arrogance when things go right and railing against God when things go wrong. The key moment in this respect is when he leads the main group away from the flooded ballroom. Climbing up a lopsided Christmas tree, the next big wave hits and those held back by the stubborn purser and fatalistic chaplain are drowned. In the central disaster of the film the image of a benevolent God is completely overturned by an act of God and the passive belief in salvation completely taken to task. But what of Scott's own, alternative ideology? The film isn't afraid to question blind faith in the orthodox or the unorthodox. Throughout Scott is presented as angry, belligerent and even messianic. Particularly in his final sacrifice the film deploys its mythic, moral symbolism with all the subtlety of a wrench, but what better way to rid a turbulent priest than have him fall into nothing less than the burning fire of an upside-down, boiler room hell?

I would argue that the more bitter and twisted the disaster scenarios throughout the 1970s, the more solutions are tested to their limits in these films - even to breaking point. It could be argued that Scott has to die because he rails against God or it could be argued that he is, in fact, proven right in refusing to accept the herd instinct and gather his flock his own way. Depending on which view you take, his death can be read as thoroughly deserved or a defiant act of supreme self-sacrifice. On a more structural level, what I find most interesting about *The Poseidon Adventure* is that the 'only the stars survive' formula is also pushed to its very limits. In a sense, the ideal disaster movie would be one that satisfies innate industrial demands and subsequent ideological readings by having its stars play the morally upright characters and its character actors the greedy and cowardly ones. In one fell swoop, the heroic stars survive and the rest get what they deserve. But it doesn't work that way. By way of testing the relative demands of the industrial and ideological, therefore, it's worth considering the hierarchical cast list of *The Poseidon Adventure*.

The poster for the film splits the eleven main characters into seven stars and four co-stars. Whether we look at the seven stars in terms of their very own hierarchy or consider them all as a veritable ensemble, the list proceeds as follows: Gene Hackman, Ernest Borgnine, Red Buttons, Carol Lynley, Roddy McDowall, Stella Stevens, Shelley Winters. From a very clinical and statistical perspective, by the end of the film four of these stars are dead-or, only 43 per cent of the stars survive. Following on from this crumbling hierarchy, the four co-stars are Jack Albertson, Pamela Sue Martin, Arthur O'Connell and Eric Shea, only one of whom actually dies-or, 75 per cent of the co-stars survive.

Even if we were to cut the ensemble of stars down to the first two, the main problem is still the fact that the main star, Gene Hackman, doesn't survive. One might

The Towering Inferno

have at least expected the bullish ex-cop, Rogo (Ernest Borgnine), to die instead, but if this seems too clinical a judgement consider Michael Ryan and Douglas Kellner's cheeky one-line summary of the group's main progress: "They undergo numerous tests, and the weak (two women, most notably) fall by the wayside."[17] If Scott and Rogo can be considered the strongest characters and the rest weak, why is it that most of the weak also survive Scott? Similarly more men die than women and as many women survive as don't, so why this casual link between the weak and the women? The fact is that the more such blanket ideological readings follow the same pattern of the survival of the fittest, the exceptions in the films become much more important than the assumed generic rules. We could well follow Ryan and Kellner's significant, throwaway comment and say that Linda (Stella Stevens) and Belle (Shelley Winters) die just because they're women but this wouldn't explain why the other two women survive. In which case we'd have to look at the reasons why these particular women die and the other two don't. Bottom line, it could be said that Linda has to die for her past sins as a prostitute and the common enough parody version of Belle is that she dies because she's too fat; conversely, Nonnie (Carol Lynley) and Susan (Pamela Sue Martin) survive because they're young, pretty and do what they're told. I would say that Linda's death is more of a plot device than anything (the personal loss that finally leads Rogo into taking charge), but what the weak-flesh reading of Belle's death ignores is that she dies in an act of bravery, diving into a perilous waterway and saving Scott's life. Accidental deaths can be read as either deserving or unfortunate where not mechanical plot devices or the excuse for a spectacular mid-narrative nosedive.

Similarly heroic deaths can be read as martyring the point home, breaking the rules, confusing the issues or wanting to go out with a bang.

The Towering Inferno

Industrial readings of the 1970s disaster cycle are such that the disasters and characters in the films themselves can be said to have resulted out of the combined draw of spectacle and stars (the ideal being that the stars were as spectacular a draw as the spectacular disasters). With regard to spectacle *The Towering Inferno* (1974) is quite possibly the most impressive of all disaster movies, not only in terms of the 1970s but also in comparison with more recent and often computer-generated standards as evidenced in fiery films like *Backdraft* (1991) and *Volcano* (1997). Model and matte shots stand up well (with enough fire and smoke to disguise the miniatures and enhance the perceived scale) and the set pieces are particularly well staged, with both stunt men and stars right in the heart of the perilous action. Individual stunts are particularly well staged in this respect but the main contrast is that, whereas today stars might face up to a blue screen, this and the other main disaster movies of the time really put their stars under pressure. As if all that water wasn't enough to almost drown the cast of *The Poseidon Adventure* (and dislodge Gene Hackman's wig), there are particular close-ups of Paul Newman and poor old Fred Astaire when the water tanks explode at the end of the film that make watching *The Towering Inferno* a real peril and a curious pleasure. Ideological readings are such that we go to see disaster movies to watch the rich and greedy get their comeuppance. The allied draw of disaster movies of the 1970s is watching famous film stars really working for their money.

The Towering Inferno is also the most star-studded of disaster movies, the point being that star power really does live up to the power of its spectacle. Paul Newman and Steve McQueen are the obvious top-line stars in this respect but as Maurice Yacowar points out in relation to the rest of the cast: "an inherited sentiment plays around Jennifer Jones and Fred Astaire, Robert Vaughn repeats his corrupt politician from *Bullitt*, and Richard Chamberlain reprises his corrupt All-American from *Petulia*, itself an ironic inversion of his Kildare."[18] Yacowar's list is interesting in that it does establish *The Towering Inferno*'s clever mix of old and new Hollywood stars. The 'inherited sentiment' of Fred Astaire and Jennifer Jones is certainly played around with and both the creepy Vaughn and slimy Chamberlain do get their comeuppance. Not all of the bad guys in the film do die but part of the wonderful predictability is that we can't wait for these two characters, at least, to get what they deserve. But how will Fred Astaire and Jennifer Jones fare? The best disaster movies remain true to the indiscriminate nature of disaster and for all its reassurances *The Towering Inferno* isn't afraid to shatter some of our illusions and play havoc with sentimental expectations along the way.

In contrast to the grainy *Poseidon Adventure* and shaky *Earthquake*, *The Towering Inferno* is shot with clear and striking visuals. As Richard Dyer explains:

[*The Poseidon Adventure*] is closer in time to those moments in the

commercial cinema when underground experiments with 'dislocation of perception' surfaced, e.g. *Easy Rider*, *2001*, Roger Corman, *Midnight Cowboy*, etc. With its fascinating overturned interiors and its journey upwards into ever more labyrinthine depths, it played around with our perceptions of the normal world, and it cast the whole thing in a mock heroic mode, including a ranting priest, brave Jewish momma, and an escape up a Christmas tree. *Earthquake* encased its title event in a series of banal dramas, but it did try, naively, to simulate, with juddering camera and trembling seats, the experience of being in a 'quake. There is nothing like this in *The Towering Inferno*.[19]

However, this is not to dismiss *The Towering Inferno* as clinical in its form or predictable in its subsequent narrative, rather to explain that it stood out from an increasingly cluttered genre. The film's clarity makes its disaster and action scenes all the more shocking and a further reason for its popularity was its equally distinct use of stars. As Dyer begins, using Fred Astaire and Jennifer Jones to portray a twilight romance is, indeed, particularly affecting. Similarly in the modern casting Faye Dunaway adds "a sensuality and a strength"[20] to her role which distinguishes her character from the usual disaster movie bias of cloying wives and screaming girlfriends. But key to the whole film is, indeed, the 'master-stroke' casting of Newman and McQueen, if only for their piercing blue eyes:

> Those eyes are a feature of Newman and McQueen's images, but meaningfully exchanged looks between men are an important element in the narrative of *The Towering Inferno*. Several of the incidents... end with two men looking hard and trustingly at each other–they've come through something perilous together and survived through mutual dependence. Looking square and silent at each other is a model of transparency and trust between males (it is a mode deriving from Westerns, and particularly dwelt on in Spaghetti Westerns).[21]

Two points that Dyer doesn't expressly follow are, first, these stars' wider images and, second, further connotations in their blue eyes. As the reference to Westerns makes clear, stars also bring with them reassuring signs from other genres (Charlton Heston being a good case in point). Newman and McQueen have starred in contemporary inflections on the Western but as respective roles in *Cool Hand Luke* (1967) and as "the Cooler King" in *The Great Escape* (1963) also indicate, these two are the kings of cool united in a film full of heat. Dyer does refer to the 'cool and dark' look of *The Towering Inferno*'s modern interiors, gradually overwhelmed by the 'yellows and reds' of the fire,[22] but even more significant is the cool, liquid property of blue. Fred Astaire has blue eyes but they're old and watery. Newman and McQueen have icy, piercing, steely stares and only they can face up to the flaming disaster ahead.

This blue-eyed focus doesn't always work (Richard Chamberlain and Robert Wagner also have blue eyes) but it's such an attractive way in: "So when at the end of the film Newman and McQueen also look at each other, with those blue eyes, and say they are going to co-operate on new buildings... it is the culmination of a pattern that affirms both that something can be done and that men, in their strong silent way, can do it."[23] There is, however, an equally effective divergence when it comes to the other stars and co-stars in *The Towering Inferno*. It could be said that Astaire's past image is much stronger than his character in determining his fate in this film. The previously light-footed Astaire plays a light-fingered con man. With such a dubious character, lying his way into the opening night so that he can fleece rich widows, you'd expect the disaster to make him pay. Particularly bearing in mind that he begins by picking on the perfectly nice Jennifer Jones, why is it that Astaire survives and this poor old widow, having helped rescue her grandchildren and the family cat, falls to her death?

While we're in the business of playing the Disaster Movie game and assessing the relative worth of the characters, why should the gracious Jennifer Jones die and William Holden's main boss figure live? Holden is just as responsible for the disaster as his weasly son-in-law, Chamberlain, most of all in cutting construction costs but also through holding off on cancelling the opening night when Newman comes to him with a burnt-out wire at the beginning of the film. Strengthening the question even further, why should the innocent Jennifer Jones die and the man who is at least partly responsible for her death live? Perhaps Jones is being punished for her 'Lust in the Dust' image as established in *Duel in the Sun* (1946), but here she plays the complete opposite, a nun-like widow. Holden always had hedged his bets by playing anti-hero

The Towering Inferno

figures but at this stage in his career he was on to playing downright corrupt characters, his role in *The Towering Inferno* being almost a practice run for his cynical television executive in *Network* (1976).

The compromise option is one that levels all readings of the moral melting pot of disaster movies–redemption. The point about Astaire is that he falls in love with Jones, admits his sins to her and has to pay when his newfound love dies. That is, he becomes a better person because of her and because of her death. And for his part Holden survives exactly so that he can go on to build a better, safer world. Newman might well survive to design safer buildings, with McQueen always there for health and safety advice, but Holden is the sort of man who will go on to provide the money. As he says to his grieving daughter: "All I can do now is pray to God that I can stop this from ever happening again." Disaster movies don't always play fair but even in death there are (hard) life lessons to be learned. It's all in the stars. Only the repentant survive.

Transitions and Retrospect

What is often forgotten in treatments of the New Hollywood is that disaster movies represent a key, *transitional* genre. So, on one level disaster movies did put the New Hollywood into corporate mood after the left-field success of films like *Bonnie and Clyde* (1967) and *Easy Rider* (1969). But compared with *Star Wars* (1977) and a whole stream of blockbusters through to recent disaster/sci-fi hybrids like *Independence Day* (1996), I would say that the savage nature of 1970s disaster movies becomes much more manifest. As Michael Ryan and Douglas Kellner also admit, there's something in the move from 'anxiety' to 'affirmation', disaster to escapism, that makes disaster movies of the early to mid-1970s much less clean-cut than what was to follow in mainstream cinema.[24]

What I find particularly interesting in such retrospect is the way in which disaster movies of the time are said to have appealed to family audiences. Roddick's distinction between spectacle and violence is very pertinent in this respect. As he says of the disasters themselves: "although they are spectacular in terms of special effects and superlative in terms of stunt work, there is little explicit suffering or violence in them."[25] Particularly in contrast to the new cinematic gore of films like *The Texas Chainsaw Massacre* (1974) and *Death Weekend* (1976)–to use Roddick's examples–certainly disaster movies represented relatively wholesome family entertainment. Roddick's argument is that 'violent deaths' are actually kept to a minimum and are restricted to one main 'striking example' per film: "the man who falls to his death in the lighting installations in the inverted saloon of the Poseidon; Robert Wagner and Susan Flannery burned to death in the apartment in *The Towering Inferno*; one or two passengers and crew crushed by shifting cargo and fittings as the plane hits the water in *Airport '77*."[26] While this might hold true with regard to the *Airport* films, in vastly inflating the spectacle and pumping up the body count I would say that *The Poseidon Adventure*, *The Towering Inferno* and *Earthquake* provide us with some of the most graphic death scenes in movie history. If these can still be regarded as spectacular, rather than bloody deaths this is also because they are often instantaneous rather than lingering–a sudden crushed body here and there as opposed to people openly bleeding to death. As if such indiscriminate sudden impacts weren't ambiguously violent but bloodless enough to give *The Poseidon Adventure* an 'A' or 'PG' rating here in Britain, the particular 'AA' or '15' certificate trick of *The Towering Inferno* was to present its burning bodies as part of the spectacle. When Richard Wagner and Susan Flannery do die, they die wonderfully photographed, choreographed, slow motion deaths. Both violent and spectacular, radical and reactionary, these disaster movies, in particular, stand out as perfect examples of mainstream shocking cinema of the seventies.

This article represents a streamlining and development of some of the issues raised in my book, *Disaster Movies: The Cinema of Catastrophe* (Wallflower Press, 2000). See, in particular, Chapter 2, 'Fighting the Elements' [on *The Poseidon Adventure* and *The Towering Inferno*].

Notes

1. For pointed histories of the disaster genre see Susan Sontag, 'The Imagination of Disaster' (1965), in *Against Interpretation, and Other Essays* (London: Andre Deutsch, 1987), pp.209-25; Fred Kaplan, 'Riches from Ruins', *Jump Cut* No.6 (March/April 1975), pp.3-4; Wheeler Winston Dixon, *Disaster and Memory: Celebrity Culture and the Crisis of Hollywood Cinema* (NewYork: Columbia University Press, 1999); and Kim Newman, *Millennium Movies: End of the World Cinema* (London: Titan, 1999).

2. Nick Roddick, 'Only the stars survive: disaster movies in the seventies', in *Performance and Politics in Popular Drama: Aspects of Popular Entertainment in Theatre, Film and Television 1800-1976*, ed. by David Bradby et al (Cambridge: Cambridge University Press, 1980), pp.243-69.

3. Roddick, pp.243-4.

4. Ibid., pp.243.

5. Ibid., p.244.

6. Ibid., p.244.

7. Ibid., p.257.

8. Ibid., p.p.160-1.

9. Ibid., pp.259-60.

10. Ibid., p.252.

11. Maurice Yacowar, 'The Bug in the Rug: Notes on the Disaster Genre', in *Film Genre: Theory and Criticism*, ed. by Barry Keith Grant (Metuchen, New Jersey, and London: The Scarecrow Press, 1977), pp.90-107 (p.97).

12. Judith Crist, quoted in John Walker, ed., *Halliwell's Film Guide* 11th Edition (London: HarperCollins, 1995), p.20.

13. Michael Ryan and Douglas Kellner, *Camera Politica: The Politics and Ideology of Contemporary Hollywood Film* (Bloomington and Indianapolis: Indiana University Press, 1988), pp.52-3.

14. Lawrence Shaffer, 'The Good Dumb Film', *Film Comment*, Volume 9, Number 5 (September/October 1973), pp.52-5 (p.52).

15. Ibid., p.52.

16. Ibid., p.55.

17. Ryan and Kellner, p.54.

18. Yacowar, p.97.
19. Richard Dyer, 'American Cinema in the '70s: *The Towering Inferno*', Movie, Issue 21 (September 1975), pp.30-3 (p.31).
20. Ibid., p.31.
21. Ibid., pp.31-2.
22. Ibid., pp.32-3.
23. Ibid., p.32.
24. Ryan and Kellner, pp.56-7.
25. Roddick, p.254.
26. Ibid., p.254.

Urban Legend: The 1970s Films of Michael Winner
Xavier Mendik

Suffice it to say that if *The Chase* had been directed by a Michael Winner or a J. Lee Thompson, it is probable that, however resonant the project, it would never have caught my attention.
Robin Wood *Hollywood From Vietnam to Reagan* (p.13)

Death Wish enacts its moral ideology of purity on the representational plane. The narrative is fairly univocal, the cinematography is unsullied. The decisiveness of the isolated subject's will, the purity of his motives, is thus reinforced.
Michael Ryan & Douglas Kellner *Camera Politica: The Politics and Ideology of Contemporary Hollywood* (p.94)

Redressing the 'Reactionary'

In the period where Hollywood films were reclaimed as knowingly cynical and contradictory, at the point where the American mainstream was seemingly involved in an inward, in-depth examination in self-critique, there was Michael Winner. The British director moved fully into the American film scene in the early 1970s and produced a series of significant films that ranged from nihilistic and offbeat westerns to complex political thrillers and gritty urban crime dramas. These centred on psychologically floored or morally compromised individuals forced to choose between defending existing legal structures or revelling in a brutal desire for (near criminal) retribution. In the course of their violent quests, Winner's films of the era focus on individuals whose status as 'outsiders' proves fundamental to the disruption of order within the fictional communities they depict. This brief introduction to Winner's work makes clear that I view his 1970s American cinematic output as an important body of work. However, I am also interested in exploring the extent to which critical evaluations of Michael Winner's work has been hampered by a longstanding perception of his work as containing a right-wing and reactionary inflection.

Indeed, on first appearance, it may seem anomalous to include a chapter on Michael Winner in a volume so heavily geared towards the positive reconsideration of seventies cinema. This is because key theoretical accounts of the American film during the era have traditionally ranged Winner's work against the positive cinematic advances that were currently underway. For instance, Robin Wood inferred that the director should be placed in the reactionary camp when he constructed his polemical account of the ideologies behind the seventies American image (reproduced in the volume Hollywood From Vietnam to Reagan). More damaging are the comments of Michael Ryan and Douglas Kellner, whose groundbreaking study *Camera Politica* linked the director's work to a moral backlash against the liberal counterculture of the 1960s. Even more recent accounts such as Peter Lev's *American Films of the Seventies: Conflicting Visions* re-evaluates some previously marginal 1970s movies while continuing to situate Winner's work as an unsavoury extension of the right-wing crime thrillers popular during the decade.

Arguably, Michael Winner is by no-means the first British director to experience adverse publicity following a transition to the American scene. However, it is notable that at the same time his own position and output were being derided, the genres in which he was working (Westerns, political thrillers and crime dramas) were being reclaimed as offering progressive critiques of 70s America. Thus, when Robin Wood derides directors' like Winner and Thompson, he is critiquing those filmmakers whose work appears to offer a 'coherent' ideological position against the voices of radical dissent struggling for expression during this decade. These marginal forces can be identified as "the growing force and cogency of radical protest and liberation movements-black militancy, feminism, gay liberation."[1] Commenting in his Hollywood: From Vietnam to Reagan Wood identifies "Hollywood in the 70s the period when the dominant ideology almost disintegrated."[2]

For Wood, American film of the era can be seen as bearing the traces of recent social turmoil from the United States humiliating retreat from the Vietnam war and the spectre of domestic political corruption to issues of stateside racial violence and inequality among marginal sexual and ethnic groups. In this confused and a-moral environment, the values of the dominant order were so profoundly challenged that they facilitated a 'return of the repressed' or vocalisation of the marginal social and sexual groupings that the status quo would otherwise like to contain.

Wood most famously considered this subversive feature in his account of the seventies horror movies, which he noted often depicted the monster as a social or sexual Other, reflecting long-held fears surrounding the destructive impulses of groups such as women, ethnic minorities and the proletariat. Unlike previous periods in which the monster represented a force that was both punished and expelled from the narrative in its final stages, Wood notes that in many seventies horrors, the terrifying figure of the monstrous Other is often left unrestrained.

Beyond its depiction in the horror genre, Wood also identified a subversive representation of the Other in more mainstream Hollywood films. Here, he identifies the category of the 'incoherent text', which is neither liberating nor repressive, but instead reveals many of the ideological contradictions and textual tensions at play in the narrative. In this respect, the incoherent text can be defined as:

> Films that don't wish to be, or appear, incoherent, but are nonetheless, works in which the drive toward the ordering of experience has been visibly

Death Wish 2

defeated.[3]

Importantly, Wood notes that the strength of such works remains the fact that they deny any cohesive position on the social and sexual subject matter under review. Rather, the Other loses its troubling distance from society's mainstream and instead becomes a troubling reflection of what often passes for normality.

Once again, this curious position reflects the troubled period from which these narratives emerged. It also explains why the 'incoherent text' is often accompanied by startling images of violence as well as an overwhelming sense of nihilism and negativity. For Wood, this reflects the fact that while catastrophic events such as Vietnam, Watergate and civil unrest fundamentally shook the public belief in the state and social institutions, it did not lead to their replacement or the extremes of social revolution envisaged by the counter-culture of the 1960s.

If the incoherent text is thus defined by a contradictory (and essentially negative) impulse, it seen by Wood as functioning to blur the boundaries between normality and abnormality as well as using established genre codes as a way of critically reflecting on contemporary events within America. For instance, his account of *Taxi Driver* (1976), Wood indicates the extent to which the quest of the film's crazed hero Travis Bickle mimics the Western figure of the lone gunman/avenger whose violent actions reconstitute a legal and moral order. However, as Wood notes, Bickle's role remains far more ambiguous than that of the classical Western hero, who is traditionally defined as separate from the depravity of their prey. Rather, *Taxi Driver* presents an incoherent vision of its hero as both victim and aggressor, legal agent and lethal executioner. As Wood states:

> ...the central incoherence of *Taxi Driver* lies in the failure to establish a consistent, and adequately rigorous, attitude to the protagonist. We can see the film in relation to both the Western and the horror film. With the former, Travis is the gunfighter-hero whose traditional function has always been to clean up the town; with the latter; he is the psychopathic monster produced by an indefensible society. The latter option appears fairly unambiguously dominant through most of the film, but the former is never totally eclipsed. The film cannot believe in the traditional figure of the charismatic individualist hero, but it also cannot relinquish it, because it has nothing to put in its place. [4]

It is this increasing ambivalence toward the validity of the hero's quest that is also present in key examples of Michael Winner's 1970s work. Far from being reactionary, these texts contain the grain of 'incoherence' that writers such as Wood applaud in the more challenging Hollywood films of the decade. These are works in which "incoherence is no longer hidden and esoteric: the films seem to crack open before our eyes."[5] As with Wood's discussion of the splits within Travis Bickle's psyche, Winner's often constructs contradictory protagonists as a way of drawing unsettling parallels between the chaotic and the civilised, the legal and illegal, whose depictions point to a longer and more disturbing series of conflicts behind contemporary American crises.

Indeed, it seems relevant that in the same era the revisionist Westerns were being reclaimed for offering a nihilistic readings of its mythical roots, Winner produced two downbeat entries into the genre that undercut accepted readings of an American past while offering a mirror to recent national ills. For instance, *The Law Man* (1970) depicted the introspective and yet psychotic legal figure of Maddox (Burt Lancaster), whose relentless quest to bring a group of near-sympathetic killers to justice exposes the potential for violence that underpins the most tranquil and civilised areas of the American West. In so doing, *The Law Man* poses important questions of legality, retribution and personal responsibility, while its depiction of an apparently peaceful community whose boundaries and values can easily tip over into chaos provide an incisive comment on the internal conflicts of America during the 1970s.

With *Chato's Land* (1972), the links to recent American turmoil was made even more explicit. The film initiated Winner's long running association with the actor Charles Bronson, whom is cast here as a Native American that kills a racist sheriff in self-defence and then goes on the run to avoid a cavalry posse sent to hunt him down. With its theme of bigotry and white oppression being seen as a trigger to violence, *Chato's Land* reversed many of the racial connotations that would otherwise equate non-white with barbarism. In light of the many atrocities being committed in non-European lands by American troops during the period, the film has rightly been connected to cynical interpretations of the Vietnam war, particularly by French critics sympathetic to Winner's 1970s work. For instance, writing in *Le Monde*, Claude Fleouter commented that an:

> ...observation of the Vietnam war and atrocities committed there has lead Michael Winner to see and discover the same violence in the old West. In this respect, *Chato's Land* is a remarkable Western, told and filmed with skilful precision.[6]

In his review of the movie for the Parisian journal *Le Nouvel Observateur*, Jean-Louis Bory also picked up on the film's racial theme, concluding that *Chato's Land* was "valid for all those who have ever suffered humiliation."[7] The writer also identified an unsettling link between the actions of Chato and his attackers, noting how the normally peaceful Indian leads the pursuing cavalry out into uncharted lands before picking them off in particularly savage ways. For Louis-Bory, this reveals the ease with which "the hunters become the hunted",[8] while also pointing to the alternations and overlaps between the moral and immoral as well as the savage and civilised outlined by Wood's analysis of the incoherent text.

It seems little surprise that the construction of the seventies hero as contradictory protagonist resulted in what Wood saw as a process of doubling which functioned to connect characters from opposing camps and thus erode the distinctions between them. In the case of *Taxi Driver*, Wood argues that Travis Bickle's psychosis and penchant for perversion clearly links him with the diseased urban landscape he is so desperate to purge.

This doubling feature is also present in Winner's cinema and works to link otherwise opposing characters or characteristics to an extent that the distinct moral and ethical values that might otherwise separate them are undercut. In the case of *The Law Man*, this effect is achieved by repeatedly connecting Lancaster's character to the forces of brutal illegality, a trait that is underscored by the text's iconic and dramatic codes. The film begins with the image of a town in chaos as a gang of workers associated with the landowner Bronson (Lee J. Cobb) shoot up the neighbouring town of Bannock during a drunken spree.

After the group has departed, the camera pans back to reveal the body of an innocent civilian who has been killed during the crossfire. The credit scene that follows introduces Maddox's character into the fiction as a source of threat rather than an agent of legality. Shot in silhouette from a low-angled perspective he towers over the film frame as if a demon, the scene initiating his construction as a figure of potential violence. Indeed, when Maddox rides into the Bronson dominated town of Sabbath, intent on bringing the gang to justice, the villagers initially mistake him for a bounty hunter, before branding him as "a killer" as he begins to assassinate the gang in a series of brutal gun battles.

Maddox's sinister connotations are reiterated visually in the film by his repeated framing behind the curtains and windows of locals too terrified to meet him at street level. Sabbath's aged Marshall Cotton Ryan goes as far as to comment that the locals view the lawman "as a disease" rather than a focus of order. Indeed, even Bronson (who initially seeks to resolve the matter peacefully by getting his men to return to Bannock to face trial) brands Lancaster's character as "a murderer" after he dispatches the landowner's surrogate brother, Harvey. Maddox's penchant for unrestrained violence is actualised in the "bloodbath" that Judith Christ argued made up the film's closing scene.[9] Here, he guns down the remaining members of the gang, even shooting a terrified cow-hand in the back after he turns and flees into the arms of his wife (and Maddox's former lover).

This act of aggression, uncharacteristic for a mainstream film's central lead is mirrored by Bronson's actions during the scene. Cradling the body of his dead son and surrounded by the corpses of his men, Bronson chooses to blow his own brains out with a gun rather than face Maddox in a shoot out. The film thus eschews the generic expectation of the climactic battle between 'hero' and 'villain', indicating Winner's willingness to play with Western narrative codes in order to emphasise the moral ambiguity of the landscape he depicts. Following Maddox's departure, the final image of the film depicts the town in long shot with its inhabitants now safe to return to the streets and gather up the bodies of their dead. In so doing, the narrative provides a symmetrical reply to the disorder of the opening scene of the film. However, the gestures of resolution are applied in an ironic fashion with order coming at the expense of the destruction of the town's 'civilising' forces and the restoration of stability being premised on a violent display of strength of the American legal arm. As Winner has himself commented on this closing scene:

> After all this excitement the town just carries on. It has enveloped this little drama and now everyone will go back to exactly where they were before. This is exactly what happens in life. Nixon got chucked out, everybody got very excited about it, and three weeks later everyone is carrying on as before.[10]

If the film (and the director's own comments) lead to a cynical interpretation of legal force and the evolution of the civilised West, then these contradictions are not lost on Maddox himself. Indeed, rather than just depict his lawman as an insensitive brute, the significance of Winner's depiction lies in the melancholic and introspective attributes that he gives to this character. Although Lancaster's character remains wedded to an inflexible vision of personal responsibility (summed up by his statement that "without the law you are nothing"), he is also aware of the violent contradictions that surround his own role. As he discloses to one potential assailant, a lawman can be defined as "a killer of men. There are nicer ways of putting it, but it amounts to the same."

In many respects, Maddox remains becomes both an object of pity and a figure of terror, these incongruities being summed up in his key iconographical features: his skills as a gun hand/killer and his abilities as a flautist. Indeed the film frequently shifts between scenes of Lancaster's character dispatching an opponent to him focused in a moment of near meditation over his musical instrument. Understood in the light of the wider forces of restraint and release at battle in seventies America, these images can be seen as conflating the signifiers of extreme authoritarianism associated with Nixon's right-wing agenda alongside a deep-seated yearning for personal freedom and spiritual liberation associated with the counterculture movement. The fact that these tensions remain unresolved indicates Winner's protagonists as operating in a chaotic environment where emancipation is denied. As Kevin Gough-Yates has commented, Winner's characters "fight and kill in attempts to regain the moral equilibrium of the past, now forever gone even in themselves. They too are casualties of the time in which they live."[11]

Urban Legend: Rape, Revenge and Rightwing Misreading

If critical reaction of Winner's work effectively muted a positive re-reading of their features, opposition to his work was nowhere more evident than in the reception of his controversial 1974 rape and revenge drama *Death Wish*. The movie cast Charles Bronson as Paul Kersey, a middle class professional whose liberal views on social injustice are radically altered following the violent rape and murder of his wife and the mutilation of his daughter.

In response to the polices' inability to catch the gang responsible for the act, Kersey begins to stalk the subways and slum areas of New York searching out muggers and criminals whom he violently dispatches. With its theme of a law-abiding citizen who is forced to take the law into his own hands, *Death Wish* appeared to strike a cord with an increasingly militant and reactionary white, middle-class of seventies America. Upon first appearance, these reactionary tendencies would seem to be confirmed by the film's ending, when the police unofficially release Kersey after discovering his identity as the vigilante killer, thus allowing him to pursue a quest against the urban poor in neighbouring American cities.

It is this right wing 'reading' which is certainly evident in the press accounts of the film at the time of its release. For instance, writing in the *New York Daily News*, Rex Reed isolated *Death Wish*'s ability to draw out "a controversial and violent reaction from both audiences and critics",[12] which he linked to a growing anti-liberal Stateside sentiment. As he noted, "Even the most militant liberals are applauding like kids at a Saturday afternoon Punch and Judy show."[13] Bruce Williamson's review for *Playboy* went even further, commenting that after viewing the film, "righteous citizens will surely fantasise about rushing outside to form a posse."[14] Other reviews of the era also linked the film to an authoritarian approach to tackling urban crime. For Fred McDarrah the film satisfied "all the fantasies of thousands of helpless New Yorkers.",[15] while Gene Shalit commenting on WNBC-TV, defined *Death Wish* as "a rouser for everyone who wants safer cities, what I call the fed-up generation."[16]

If the press reporting of Winner's film assisted in constructing it as a right -

wing narrative, it in part explains why theorists such as Michael Ryan and Douglas Kellner have linked *Death Wish* to a 'Hollywood counter-revolution' that marked a return to conservative and moral values during the era. Writing in *Camera Politica*, the pair argue that whereas 1960s American film can be defined as an era of cinematic experimentation and liberal political concerns, it was replaced by a decade of fictions which stressed the need to counter an otherwise chaotic world with an aggressive moral and legal order. This conservative move was seen in the filmic flourishing of 'rightwing' police dramas such as *Dirty Harry* (1971), as well as the emergence of vigilante 'rape and revenge' movies such as *Straw Dogs* (1973) and *Death Wish*. As Ryan and Kellner comment, by beginning of the decade:

> ...a meaner, more cynical discourse began to emerge as the dominant mode of Hollywood film. In 1971 alone, *The French Connection*, *Dirty Harry* and *Straw Dogs* articulate an anti-liberal value system that portrays human life as predatory and animalistic, a jungle without altruism.[17]

Ryan and Kellner have conceded that a return to enforced legal morality is not the only form of Hollywood recuperation seen in the era (other examples including a return to sentimental and 'unproblematic' love stories). However, what is significant is the way in which the Hollywood counter-revolution often used crime narratives as

Death Wish 2

"vehicles for conservative counterattacks against the liberalism that many conservatives blamed for crimes in domestic order brought about by the sixties."[18]

Not only was this trait evidenced by the repeated theme of liberal beliefs that allow violent criminals out of jail to commit further transgressions, it was also indicated by the way in which such "law and order" thrillers inverted the symbols and signifiers of 1960s counter-cultural revolution for threatening effect. For instance, Ryan and Kellner's analysis of *Dirty Harry* emphasises the detective hero's violent quest as premised on the ill-informed liberal court structures which allow a psychotic killer named Scorpio back on the streets after he claims that Detective Harry Callaghan (Clint Eastwood) has violated his civil rights. As the authors' note, with his long hair, prominent wearing of peace symbols and effeminate and 'unmanly' ways, Scorpio is clearly associated with the signifiers of the 1960s counter-culture.

While the narrative drive clearly validates Harry's brutish methods, other films that Ryan and Kellner identify in this cycle (such as *Straw Dogs* and *Death Wish*) depict the transition of passive, law abiding males into potent and disenfranchised killing machines. For Ryan and Keller, these protagonists, "regress from civility to bestiality, to be a man."[19] Inso doing, their violent transition indicates the ambivalence with which the 1960s social advances of marginal sexual and racial groups were viewed. Thus in the case of *Straw Dogs*, the film's theme of a meek college professor reacting violently to the rape of his wife reveals an underlying ambivalence towards female sexual liberation.

For Ryan and Kellner, "the woman in the film is portrayed as a treacherous sex kitten who betrays her wimpy husband Peter",[20] after her attempted seduction of a former lover turns into a gang rape. The film responds to the event by sanctioning Peter's violent revolt against this gang of locals who dominate the small town to which he has retreated. However, it is noticeable that the film also extends a form of punishment to Peter's wife whose presence is increasingly marginalised in the film's finale. Thus, it is noticeable that after a climactic battle with the local thugs, Peter deserts his partner and the ruins of his home, along with a local retard who has sought shelter with the couple. For Ryan and Kellner, the final shots of the pair driving away reconstitute the family unit in the form of an all-male utopia, devoid of any disruptive female presence.

While *Straw Dogs* uses a strategy of excluding woman as a way of dealing with problematic issues of female sexuality, Ryan and Kellner see *Death Wish* as isolating womanhood in the domestic space, while promoting masculinity within a violent public sphere. For the authors, the film can be seen as the most conservative of the 1970s crime dramas for its combination of "ironic cynicism with romantic sentimentalism."[21] Here, women are associated with idyllic locations (such as Hawaii where Paul and Mary Kersey undertake a vacation in the film's pre-credit scene). These picturesque spaces are counter-posed to the grim and violent urban space of the city (these are literally seen to dwarf the couple as they ride in the back of a New York cab in the opening of the narrative).

It is a quest to recreate these hallowed and unthreatening spaces (and the memories of the women they evoke) which transforms Paul from a liberal to into life-taker. As Ryan and Kellner note, it is actually Paul's visit to a "sunbelt rightist"[22] in another idyllic location which implants the protagonist's desire to become a vigilante after being given a silver Colt pistol as a present. Upon his return to New York, Kersey receives the holiday photographs of him with his dead wife and this recollection becomes the final trigger in his violent transformation.

Implicit in Ryan and Kellner's critique of the film's division of idyllic and unsafe spaces is the fact that Kersey's extermination campaign has a distinctly racial edge to it. The pair comment, "Paul separates from others by exercising violence against them",[23] noting that the movie visually separates Bronson's character from the predominantly black muggers in the film-frame as if to underscore the moral, racial and socio-economic distinctions between them. In his recent book *American Films of the 70s: Conflicting Visions* Peter Lev has drawn similar conclusions, noting that there is "no ambiguity" surrounding the film's view of Kersey's quest:

> About the only complexity in *Death Wish* lies in the way Kersey stalks his prey. He appears to be a victim, ripe for plucking, but he is instead a ruthless predator. The title *Death Wish* seems to mean "a desire to kill."[24]

Despite such criticisms, what remains underexplored by both accounts is the disturbing degree of overlap that emerges between Kersey and his prey. Indeed, the film extends the view of violence as underpinning the civilising and social order found in earlier Winner movies such as *The Law Man*, by drawing parallels between professional and urban underclass fears surrounding economic servitude. These connections are established early in the film when Paul returns to his profession as an Architect and is informed by his colleagues about the spiralling crime wave that has occurred during his visit to Hawaii. When one of Kersey's companions comments that more cops is the answer to urban disorder, his superior replies that it would only make peoples taxes too high. His comments about the potential for economic insecurity are juxtaposed by a close-up of a cash till register which the camera pulls back to reveal as being located in a (distinctly downtown) local supermarket where Mary Kersey and her daughter, Carol are shopping. The link between these two sequences proves pivotal to Bronson's quest as it is this location where the gang of muggers meet the Kersey women before following them home to their apartment to rob them. Although much of the controversy surrounding *Death Wish* centres on the brutal rape and assault of the Kersey women, the focus of their humiliation remains economic rather than sexual. Indeed, when one of the muggers comments that he "hates rich cunts" he points to a financial disdain that is confirmed when they gang inform their hostages they will not be harmed if they have money. Equally, the siege only degenerates into sexual violence when the gang discover that the Kersey's do not have the disposable income associated with their presumed standard of living.

By juxtaposing these two scenes, *Death Wish* establishes a pattern where fears around economic insecurity become a troubling factor that links the professional to the proletariat and indicates a process of doubling between the middle-classes and the muggers. This paranoia around capital is further underscored in many of the character's encounters following the assault on his family. For instance, when he visits his wife in hospital, Kersey is shocked to discover a poor urban dweller whose wounds are left unattended because of his low social standing.

Thus, rather than isolating him from his social prey as Ryan and Kellner might suggest, Paul Kersey is gradually exposed to the harsh realisation of his vulnerability within the brutal economic regime of seventies America. From observing crime victims left unable to pay their rent, (as well as comic vagrants whose incomes have been reduced by the abduction of 'paw-painting' poodles), to the hero's own fears about funding the future health care of his daughter, the film reveals economic desolation as spreading across all levels of the social strata. When Kersey uses a sock full of dollar coins to lash out against one potential attacker, the scene represents not the triumph of one dominant class over the other, but rather the protagonist's literal and nihilistic realisation of the violent power underpinning capital relations. (A similarly ironic statement linking capitol to violence is given in the scene where looters outside Kersey's apartment disturb his television viewing during a bank advertisement claiming to liberate the lives of its customers). For Michael Winner, Paul Kersey's increasing economic empathy towards the disadvantaged was central to the effect he wished to create in *Death Wish*. As he has stated:

> When we made *Death Wish*, things statistically told you that muggers the muggers were 99% black and Hispanic. This was because of these people had been unfairly put down through decades of slavery and imposition, and I have to say that in a strange way I don't blame them. When you are that frustrated you will go to any lengths to survive. How often can you have your family beaten down with out reacting? If that happened to us, how would we react? There is no question that money has become their key motivation. And you can't blame them, because what money represents to them is the desire to lead a free life. You can buy space, you can travel, by the clothes you want, it gives you access to a consumer society - Money is freedom.[25]

Arguably, the director's own sentiments were overshadowed by the majority of those press reviews of *Death Wish* that sought to link the film to a right-wing agenda. Only Richard Natale's review of the film recognised the degree of contradiction in Winner's film, commenting that "It calls to the surface the deeply inbred racism, sexism and violence of the white urban middle-class."[26]

Paradoxically, it is Kersey's vigilantism that gradually separates him from his traditional middle class bonds (as indicated by his repeated isolation at chic parties and work functions) and pushes him closer to the urban dispossessed of the city. As if to underscore Kersey's growing connection with the ranks of the dispossessed, it seems pertinent that as the narrative progresses, Bronson's character even begins to emulate the 'ghetto' dress codes of his prey as he goes on evening journeys to the violent areas of the city. The fact that Kersey evades police capture by using the same network of passages that allowed the muggers entry to his apartment in the first place reiterates his connection with these criminal factions. Indeed, it seems pertinent that the most violent encounter that Kersey experiences in the film comes from the forceful, physical interrogation he endures at the hands of the police investigating the vigilante killings.

The Outsider Within: Ritual Violence Hits the Ghetto.

If Kersey's violent actions place him in a closer relationship to the muggers than critics have previously acknowledged, then it also has ramifications for the narrative's depiction of race. Although the dominant readings of *Death Wish* view the film as a violent white reaction against ethic urban crime, a closer consideration of the differences between Brian Garfield's original 1972 novel and Winner's cinematic rendition reveal a number of significant factors. As Terence Martin has noted in his article 'From Redskin to Redneck: Atrocity and Revenge in American Writing', Garfield's novel is premised on a distinctly racial assault on Paul's family. As he states:

> Before she subsides into a vegetable-like condition, Paul's daughter says that two of the three men may have been black-provocative details, to be sure, though they have no importance on the ensuing narrative(56). Contributing to her emerging trauma is the daughter's memory of the three assailants giggling and laughing throughout the violent ordeal.[27]

In the novel, it is it this violent assault which turns the "nominally Jewish liberal into an avenging angel",[28] while the narration even quotes the protagonist as saying "I should have been a Nazi" during his grim extermination campaign.[29] Elsewhere, Martin has noted that these ethnic aggressors are referred to as "animals and savages, making revenge all the easier to justify",[30] while their actions are unfairly generalised to that of wider racial groupings by police investigating the case. Although Martin notes that these racial factors are minimised by Paul's subsequent, undirected campaign, they still provide a significant narrative trigger that is absent from Winner's film. Here, it is noticeable that the trio of muggers invading the Kersey home are actually white, as well as carrying strong associations with white extremism. Not only do they decorate the hero's home with swastikas, but also one of the trio sports a skinhead and military style boots associated with racist paramilitary organisations. This act establishes a pattern whereby sources of actualised threat become associated with white rather than black attackers in the film. (Indeed, prior to his first killing, several scenes in the film play on Paul's misplaced fear that an attack will come from black characters he meets, when in fact his first violent encounter comes from a white junkie in Central Park).

While it would be simplistic to under-emphasise some of Kersey's violent encounters with black muggers in the latter part of the film (as indicated in his extermination of two thugs in a subway), these in no way represent evidence of a racially motivated campaign. Indeed, Winner plays on the casting of lead male Charles Bronson as a way of complicating colour divisions. Specifically, the actor carried the past

The Stone Killer

persona of recent roles enacted for the director. These included the non-white, vengeful Indian Chato, as well as the pro-black, liberal cop investigating a series of mob related assassinations in Winner's 1973 film *The Stone Killer*.

What is interesting about this latter example is the way in which authorities wrongly blame black militant activity for a series of outrages that are revealed as being borne out of a longer feud between rival underworld gangs. The background to this violent conflict is described by the film as an illegitimate fusion of Jewish and Irish gangs during the 1930s, with the blurring of racial and communal differences between these communities provoking a violent revenge plot that bleeds over into contemporary America. This factor proves significant to a wider understanding of Winner's 1970s American work, which is repeatedly governed by the theme of violence breaking as out when the differences between distinct groups or individuals have been eroded.

Evidence of this trait is seen in the ambivalent overlap between 'savage' and 'civilised' characters in Westerns such as *The Law Man* and *Chato's Land*. Winner's 1972 political thriller *Scorpio* finds an aged assassin (Burt Lancaster) seeking safety with former Soviet opponents after being double-crossed by his American political masters. (One Russian even informs the hero that in the ambivalent political climate of the 1970s, language "is the only difference between the American model and the Soviet model" of operations.) With latter films such as *The Stone Killer* and *Death Wish* it is not merely a transgressive mixing of different communities that provokes disorder, but the inability to structurally separate them which prevents the containment of chaos. If this strategy reaches its logical conclusion with Paul Kersey's assimilation of a violent persona comparable to that of the prey of *Death Wish*, it also evidences the strain of 'contaminated violence' that Rene Girard has noted in declining ritual and non-western cultures. In the book *Violence and the Sacred*, Girard has argued that both modern and traditional societies are haunted by the spectre of violence and savagery. This always occurs when distinctions and boundary markers between self and other, insider and outsider are eroded, in so doing, Girard points to the fact that the common bonds which bind people together are "nothing more than a regulated series of distinctions in which the differences among individuals are used to establish their "identity and mutual relationships."[31]

Girard exemplified the importance of boundary markers to the limitation of violence in ritual communities with reference to the fate of the Kaingang Indians of Santa Katrina. When the group were forced to move from their natural surroundings to a reservation, the established boundaries central to the creation of their culture (such as the ability to distinguish themselves from hostile neighbouring groups) were eroded. This loss of social distinctions resulted in the Kaingang's inability to 'externalise' the rivalries and hatred normally retained for outsiders. As a result, the community

The Stone Killer

collapsed in an orgy of self-destruction and violence.

Rather than rejecting the fear of internal violence haunting ritual communities as a 'primitive gesture', Girard argues that this attempt to limit and 'externalise' violence and is itself replicated by industrial society. For instance, the judiciary functions to limit the violence of continued reprisal by privileging the legal machinery with the ultimate power over acts of transgression. However, these legal and moral boundary markers are often threatened when contemporary society experiences intense political or social turmoil. When these divisions between self and other, insider/outsider are eroded chaos ensues, whether its location in Santa Katrina or seventies America.

In the chaotic and a-moral environment of Nixon's America, Michael Winner's films provide a fascinating document of a nation whose sense of moral and social boundaries have been destroyed in just this fashion. It seems more than coincidence that Paul Kersey actually shoots directly into the replica of the American flag that decorates the jacket of one mugger who attacks him on the New York subway. This startling image leads weight to the view that *Death Wish* and the other films Winner produced during the decade offer a cynical and nihilistic vision of the American scene, rather than enforcing a conservative reading of their protagonists actions. As a result, they cast doubt upon not only these specific characters, but also the wider social values that they embody. As Terence Martin has concluded in relation to the hero's quest in *Death Wish*, "What remains in doubt is the destiny of a character who subverts civilised codes to punish those who subvert civilised codes."[32] In so doing, Winner's films offer a challenging and unsettling account of a nation's social, racial and economic failings.

Notes

1. Robin Wood, *Hollywood From Vietnam to Reagan*. (New York: Columbia University Press, 1986), P49
2. Ibid., P69.
3. Ibid., p.47
4. Ibid, p.53.
5. Ibid., p.50.
6. Claude Fleouter *Le Monde*, cited in Kevin Gough-Yates (ed) *The John Player Lecture Series: Michael Winner- Director*. (London: National Film Theatre, 1974), p.46.
7. Jean Louis-Bory cited in Gough-Yates (ed) p.45.
8. Ibid.
9. Judith Christ, '*The Today Show*, NBC , New York', cited in Gough-Yates (ed), p37.
10. Michael Winner quoted in interview with the author.
11. Kevin Gough-Yates, *The John Player Lecture Series: Michael Winner- Director*, p.75.
12. Rex Reed, cited in Gough-Yates (ed), p.61.
13. Ibid.
14. Bruce Williamson, cited in Gough-Yates (ed), p.61.
15. Fred McDarrah, *Village Voice*, New York, cited in Gough-Yates (ed) p.62.
16. Cited in Gough-Yates (ed) p.62.
17. Michael Ryan and Douglas Kellner, *Camera Politica: The Politics and Ideology of*

Contemporary Hollywood. (Bloomington and Indiana: Indiana University Press), P.39.

18. Ibid., pp41-42.

19. Ibid., p.40.

20. Ibid., p.39.

21. Ibid., p.90.

22. Ibid., p.89.

23. Ibid.,, p.91.

24. Peter Lev *American Films of the 70s: Conflicting Visions.* (Austin: Columbia University Press, 2000), p38.

25. Michael Winner quoted in interview with the author.

26. Richard Natale, *Women's Wear Daily,* cited in Gough-Yates (ed) p.62.

27. Terence Martin, 'From Redskin to Redneck: Atrocity and Revenge in American Writing', http://clcwebjournal.lib.purdue.edu/clcweb01-2/martin01.html, p.4.

28. Ibid.

29. Garfield, cited in Martin, p.4.

30. Ibid.

31.Rene Girard, *Violence and the Sacred.* (Baltimore:John Hopkins University Press), 1993. p49.

32. Ibid., p.9.

"Justifiable Paranoia":The Politics of Conspiracy in 1970s American Film
Paul Cobley

The Meanings of Paranoia

More than any other group of films, I would argue that the set of narratives which constitute the 'paranoid thriller' are emblematic of 1970s America. One needs only to think of the number of movie thrillers on the theme of paranoia directed at establishment structures and individuals from the period which have become 'classics' in spite of variable reviews on their first outings: *Executive Action* (1973); *Serpico* (1973); *Three Days of the Condor* (1975); *All the President's Men* (1976); *Marathon Man* (1976); *The Boys from Brazil* (1978); *Capricorn One* (1978); and *Winter Kills* (1979).

The reasons for the close link between such paranoid thrillers and the American 1970s seems, at first sight, quite simple. American society in the period witnessed certain paranoia-inducing developments (such as the growth of surveillance) and, conveniently, the thriller genre has been, from its inception, devoted to a paranoid interpretation of events which might otherwise seem innocent. However, while there is a grain of truth in such formulations, they are, in fact, more of a hindrance than a help to the task of historically analysing popular texts. They act as short-circuiting devices which not only close down historical interpretation but also overlook the specificities of paranoia.

By focussing on two films from the same year, *The Conversation* (1974) and *The Parallax View* (1974), this article seeks to observe some of the particularities of social paranoia in the seventies and, by so doing, pave the way for a reconstruction of a historical account for these texts. First and foremost, it should be said that the notion of a paranoid style in American politics was not new even in the 1970s. In one of the most famous essays in the field of American political science, Richard Hofstadter describes paranoia in politics as an oratorial style which relies on the notion of a conspiracy against "a nation, a culture, a way of life."[1] What is crucial to Hofstadter's analysis is that paranoia, although often politically right-wing, is a strategy which can be employed by a number of actors within the breadth of the political spectrum; the threat envisaged in the paranoid style is, for him, always one concerning the core of American life.

The specific points of emphasis for paranoia in the period which must be taken into account in the era under review involve the assassinations of the 1960s, the

The Parallax View

invasion of privacy entailed by the growth of surveillance and the general undermining of individual freedom by agents of corporatism. Common to all paranoid texts of the period is a concern with the deceptiveness of appearances, the way that the familiar becomes threatening. Yet, what is crucial about the paranoid text in the seventies is that it is the site of a complex and contradictory political struggle. Nixonian and anti-Nixonian paranoia enjoyed a symbiotic relationship.

As early as 1970 *Newsweek* reported the discovery of a massive covert army surveillance operation focussed on "political activists"[2]; similarly, it became known in Washington at a later date that Nixon had compiled his own 'Enemies list' of "leftist" organizations that he intended to move against under the guise of the IRS.[3] A significant proportion of the population were at risk from surveillance operators or could at least be perceived to be so. The paradoxical scenarios in which government covert operations, all the way up to the secret bombing of Cambodia, became self-justifying was summed up in a famous military announcement during the Vietnam war which illustrated the contradictory logic of annihilating a small town: "It was necessary to destroy Ben Tre to save Ben Tre."[4]

Conversely, the paranoia of the administration and its covert operatives directly engendered the paranoid feelings of their opponents; and the key arena for this struggle was the press. The case of the Pentagon Papers and, later, Watergate, were to make this clear: the press and the media were aligned against those forces that threatened them. Where the Nixon administration might see the media as 'enemies', for the population in general the media were able to take on heroic status in their stand against political bullying. Many commentators conflated Woodward and Bernstein, the two reporters who chased the Watergate story, with the *Washington Post* in general.[5] Furthermore, as Ungar notes, "Enrolments in schools of journalism and communication skyrocketed."[6] None of this is to say that reporters were genuine free agents of liberty or that the importance of capital did not play a part in the media's *raison d être*;[7] however, at this time, the short-term ideological configuration which characterized American political events thrust the First Amendment into the foreground of hegemonic struggle. Clearly, the Nixon administration feared the media and targeted individual journalists such as Jack Anderson and Daniel Schorr for persecution.[8] As a result, the 'press' and 'conspiracy' became almost synonymous, albeit in different ways, for both sides.

The Parallax View

Loren Singer's novel, *The Parallax View* (1970) was published two years before the first act of the Watergate scandal. However, the narrative can be considered as one of the chief paranoid stories of the early seventies. Much of this can be attributed to the film version starring Warren Beatty which was released in 1974. However, the film contrasts greatly with the novel in a number of ways. Firstly, its plot explicitly identifies

The Parallax View

one of the sources of paranoia: where the book conjured up an image of assassination in the opening pages by replaying a newsreel of one which is privately watched by the main character and his colleagues, the film actually stages assassinations. As we have noted, assassinations in the period had a resonance in American life that went far beyond anything that a thriller could supply on its own.

The other major change from the novel is that the main character of the film (Graham in the novel, Joe Frady [Beatty] in the film) is a press reporter. Given the resonance of the role of the media in the paranoid mindset which we have mentioned, this is an important development; but it is also crucial to the way the film plays out the plot. The first scene opens with a shot of the Space Needle in Seattle. Built for the World's Fair of 1962 and rocket-like, it is a potent symbol of the New Frontier ethic of the Kennedy era. Representatives of the news media gather at the Needle's base as Senator Carroll and his wife enter the scene in a buggy (preceded by female Chinese dancers dressed all in red). A newscaster called Lee Carter (Paula Prentiss) puts a question to the senator and then the media party follow the latter to the cordoned area that leads to the lift of the Space Needle. Amongst the media people is Joe Frady. He attempts to gatecrash the media party by telling a security man that he is with Lee; she denies it and thus he is excluded from the scene of the assassination.

As drinks are passed round at the reception in the top of the tower, Senator Carroll makes a speech, extolling the virtues of the day-Independence Day-and his Independent status in the present campaign. He then adds, "Sometimes I've been called too independent for my own good . . ." and it is at this moment that he is shot dead. The assassin is chased by secret service men and falls off the top of the tower; a cut to a shot of the tower with a man in the foreground concludes with the man walking away, smiling. At the very outset, then, the narrative offers the possibility of a number of different readings of the assassination: as a media event, as precipitated by the political stance of 'independence', as connected with the Kennedy era, as an act co-ordinated by a number of people and as an event whose details remain untold.

In the opening titles which follow this scene the music on the soundtrack (by Michael Small) supplements a very long shot of a committee sitting on a legal bench. Above the chairman, there is a large American eagle and the camera zooms very slowly towards the panel of men. While this takes place and the title music plays, the titles unfold and the words of the chairman of the committee become audible. He is saying that the committee s conclusion is that the assassin responsible for Senator Carroll's death worked alone. Not only is there a possible reading of the committee as representing the Warren Commission (who worked on the Oswald case, drawing similar conclusions), but also the elements in the presentation of this scene imply that the committee is not telling the truth of the matter. This lighting is echoed most blatantly in the affairs of the Parallax organization: when their recruiter comes to meet Frady in his bedsit, the shabby place is lit almost identically; when the man comes a second time, close to the planned assassination, there is almost complete darkness in the bedsit, such murkiness implying conspiracy and cover-up. When such juxtapositions of the music and/or lighting recur in the text a reproduction of this reading is encouraged. *Capricorn One*, made four years later, so palpably recreates these lighting effects that it is difficult not to interpret the film as a tribute to its paranoid predecessor.

One of the first scenes in the film has Frady being harassed by policemen three years after the assassination. Frady's boss, Bill (Hume Cronyn), arrives to restrain Frady and deliver him from the police station. Back at their office, it becomes clear that Bill is the editor of a provincial newspaper and Frady is a journalist. The conversation makes clear that Frady has been regularly attempting to expose scandals and make a name for himself as an investigative journalist, an activity that Bill finds tiresome: "We're in the business of reporting the news not, creating it." Frady is thus now explicitly an investigative journalist on the brink of an exposé, a fact that would have specific meanings for contemporary audiences. It is easy to forget, for example, that *The Parallax View* was released in America approximately six weeks before the resignation of President Nixon, and directed by Alan J. Pakula two years before he made *All the President's Men*. Watergate notwithstanding, the role of the reporter in exposing aspects of Vietnam and the Pentagon Papers was, of course, already well established.

What sends Frady off on his quest is the knowledge he gathers that various witnesses to the Carroll assassination have all died within the last three years. Initially he is unwilling to accept that a conspiracy is afoot until he is visited by Lee Carter. She is clearly distraught and appeals to Frady, as an ex-lover, to investigate her claim that somebody is trying to murder her. He is very cool about the business: he suggests that this is not the first time she has displayed neurotic symptoms, that the deaths of their colleagues all have rational explanations. The scene that follows this one takes place at the morgue: Lee's body is on a slab and the end of the scene involves the camera drawing out slowly to show Frady nearby, regarding the corpse thoughtfully while the music which accompanied the committee plays on the soundtrack. The audience would not have to do too much work to fill in the gaps, but while the scene provides the catalyst for Frady's investigative crusade it also enables a reading of his integrity.

Frady begins to search for other witnesses of the Carroll assassination and eventually catches up with one, Austin Tucker (William Daniels). The latter is very nervous and wary of Frady, believing that the journalist is only out to blackmail him. Tucker says "Stop acting like you're on the *New York Times* or something" and refuses to speak to Frady except within the safety of his yacht. As the boat pulls out from the dock there is another long shot accompanied by music. Before too long, the boat has exploded, killing Tucker and his bodyguard but not Frady. Similarly, when the protagonist has penetrated the Parallax organization he uncovers a bomb plot involving an airbus. A suitcase is in possession of a man Frady has seen at the Parallax building; Frady follows him to the airport. The man is the same one who appears in a photograph of the Space Needle reception shown to Frady by Tucker; he is also the new sandwich boy who calls on Bill at his office minutes before the latter dies. The man gives the suitcase to luggage handlers who prepare it for loading onto the plane carrying a senator. As the trolley carrying the case moves toward the aircraft, the camera follows it slowly while the music once again plays on the soundtrack. Like the famous glass of milk in Hitchcock's *Suspicion* (1941), apparently innocent objects become heavily charged with fear of a conspiracy. Frady is no longer the deluded loner; his paranoia is justifiable.

A reading of these element in the conspiracy, then, produces two foci of paranoia in the narrative. The first is that appearances are rarely innocent; the second is an extension of this in that figures of authority are likely to entail danger. Frady throws doubt on the splintered bureaucratic nature of government agencies, saying to Bill:

> If you wanna use the FBI or CIA you don't have to infiltrate the whole agency to do it. At first I thought these killings were related only to the Carroll assassination. It's much bigger than that. Whoever's behind this is in the business of recruiting assassins.

Very shortly after making this statement, and as he infiltrates the assassination plot, Frady visits Parallax in order to receive an initiation which verges on indoctrination. In the text s noted set piece, Frady is seated in a darkened auditorium where he watches a large cinema screen. A montage of images is repeatedly shown, with increasing frequency. This is supplemented by music and each set of images is proceed by the captions ME, COUNTRY, HAPPINESS, LOVE, MOTHER, and GOD. The familiarity of many of the images is constantly mitigated by their juxtaposition with other images and captions. Some are apparently innocuous (pictures of sun rays), some are not so innocent (pictures of Hitler at Nazi rallies). However, in the context of the Parallax organization all the images become ideologically charged in different ways.

In the final scene of the film, which juxtaposes the veneer of legitimate politics with the darkness behind the scenes, something similar happens. A band and majorettes are rehearsing in a large hall which will be the site of a massive reception for Senator Hammond. As Hammond enters on a golf buggy, the band practices marching tunes and a group of young people in tiered seats turn over large cards in unison to show a composite picture of Washington, Lincoln, and then Hammond. Meanwhile, in the dark and shady rafters of the building Frady is waiting, having followed some Parallax operatives only to lose them at this point and become trapped. There then follows a close-up of three composite faces made consecutively by the cards. (It is difficult to make out the faces but two are Caucasian and the last is not. Is it an extra-diegetic comment - the assassinated Kennedy brothers and Martin Luther King?) A shot from the rafters suddenly kills Senator Hammond in his buggy, although it is clear that the unarmed Frady is not responsible. Somebody then spots Frady from below but he has noticed that directly opposite him there is an open door; as he looks, the screen is completely dark except for the very bright light in the doorway. Frady runs for the door and suddenly a silhouette with a gun appears and shoots into the camera as it faces the door. If Frady's assassin is shady, he is, in a neat reversal, also somehow bathed in the light of legitimate America represented below.

The very last scene of the film acts with the first to provide a frame: the committee is once again in session in identical circumstances. The chairman pronounces that "There is no evidence of a conspiracy in the murder of Gerald Hammond" and the camera zooms out slowly once more, supplemented by music and the end titles.

The Perpendicular View

The reviews of *The Parallax View* seem overwhelmingly negative. The paranoia expressed in the film was seen as either insufficiently specific or simply an example of the kind of conspiracy fears that suffuse many thrillers. In the review which appeared in the *New Yorker*, Penelope Gilliatt expressed her exasperation:

> Organised murder for a political purpose, or one man's madness? Film afterfilm now provides a bloody fantasy on the theme of an assassination conspiracy veiled for reasons muddled by filmmakers' wish not to nourish any particular popular enmity.[9]

Gilliatt's main complaint seems to be that the film is *too* hooked on the idea of conspiracy or that the conspiracy is not specific enough. The film for her is saying too little: "The fallaciously titillating statement is merely that the arcane series of accidents is the work of 'conspirators.'"[10] To this she adds the more explicit point that "No question is allowed of there being any defined political enemy."[11] Her reading is difficult to grasp immediately as the events of the narrative seem so definitely related to contemporary political upheavals, especially so many years later.

Yet it need hardly be stated that the narrative does not necessarily have to name the villain in order for the readers to make their own conclusions. This seems to be what Pakula is implying in a statement contained in the movie s publicity: "Real terror does not come from any ghoul but out of the audience's fantasy terrors."[12] Pakula makes it clear that he sees the film as:

> ... the exploration of secret plots and dangers and manipulations that may exist within a society where so much has been buried and made secret in the name of preserving stability. The fact that it dealt with plots that would fulfil even the most paranoiac was attractive to me.[13]

While *Time* was, like other publications, negative about the film as a whole, it also recognized that it shared themes in common with other contemporary thrillers which it would be difficult to ignore. Schickel writes:

> The paranoid thriller is an expanding genre in the movies and popular fiction. The idea is to start from a thinly fictionalised version of a political tragedy like one of the Kennedy assassinations and build on it a thickly embroidered explanation that caters to the suspicion that such murders are plotted by a malevolent Establishment. It is apparently comforting for many people to believe that the course of the world is changed more by rational planning, however evil, than it is by irrational individual actions.[14]

His misgivings about *The Parallax View* are quite different from Gilliatt's. For Schickel, paranoia in itself is-even in the face of Watergate-simply paranoia. The dilemma which he poses for the resolution of paranoia seems to have no knowledge of Woodward and Bernstein as a frame of reference; he adds:

> If the hero can break the conspiracy unaided, it cannot be much of a conspiracy. If, on the other hand, the conspiracy is all powerful, then the audience is robbed of the basic pleasure of identifying with the protagonist's triumph over the odds.[15]

For Gilliatt, then, the paranoia is not specific enough while for Schickel it pretends to be too specific in trying to make thrillers topical. Neither critic will allow that readers might be of a mind to do the work for the text.

If we compare contemporary American reviews with two of their British counterparts, of differing political hue, the contrast economically dramatizes the possibility of two main readings of paranoia in the text. The *Spectator*, for instance, calls *The Parallax View* "a genuine thriller of the post-Watergate age",[16] while at a different point on the political spectrum, the *New Statesman* refers to the plot of the film by declaring "Watergate substantiates that: one is not paranoid."[17] Thus, the 'semiotic environment' of the film is curious: there is overwhelming evidence of the way that establishment conspiracy is on the agenda of American political life and the narrative offers numerous opportunities for an assessment which is in tune with this. Yet the reviewers of the film, in the United States at any rate, seem intent to discourage such readings.

Her reading is difficult to grasp immediately as the events of the narrative seem so definitely related to contemporary political upheavals, especially when considered many years later.

The Conversation

The situation which obtained in the semiotic environment of *The Conversation* was somewhat different. *The Conversation* (1974) was an awaited and heralded film by *The Godfather* director, Francis Ford Coppola. Based on Coppola's original screenplay, the film features Gene Hackman as Harry Caul, "The best bugger on the West coast." Caul is an obsessive freelance surveillance operative who is, at the beginning of the film, supervising a team who are trying to record a conversation. The film does not contain conventional thriller action sequences such as chases and gun-play; instead, it relies on a great deal of dialogue, supplemented by visual set pieces, to effect its narration. It is possibly this fact which has made *The Conversation* ripe for complex critical exegeses of its 'meaning.'[18]

The all important opening of the film commences with a long, high shot of Union Square in San Francisco. There is a very slow zoom on people in general in the square, but the most volatile of the people seems to be a uniform-clad mime artist

The Conversation

whose movements mark him out from the rest of the people milling around. This is the time and place where Harry makes his recording and seemingly uncovers a murder plot. Harry's view of the subsequent events then dominates: his dreams, his premonition of murder, an inner scream, etc., are all part of the narrative. Harry is observed throughout the film and it is his job to observe; but it is also clear that he is almost totally prevented from seeing what he wants to see. His actual observation of the murder is witnessed by way of a microphone he fits in the adjacent room of the Jack Tar hotel and by way of a bloodied hand seen through translucent glass. When this happens, he immediately turns on the television and increases the volume before retreating between the covers of a bed. This is a crucial moment because it demonstrates Harry's 'exterior status, an existence based on the world of sound and an exteriority from that very realm of vision that so concerns the audience.

That Harry is an 'outsider' is, in other ways, unsurprising, especially given Hackman's screen persona in the early seventies. The two roles in which Hackman had appeared prior to *The Conversation*, in *The French Connection* (1971) and *The Poseidon Adventure* (1972), cast him as the central character but one who is definitely exterior to mainstream life. Moreover, this 'intertextual' exteriority of the main narrative figure is common to the paranoid thriller. The narrative of *The Conversation* constantly reveals Harry to be an outsider of a slightly different kind to previous roles: he has no social life and simply does not fit in with the people he meets. Also, Harry's clothes, his unfashionable plastic mac, his sparse apartment, his moodiness and eccentricity, all lend him an affinity with the protagonists of other paranoid narratives. Indeed, in the world in which he operates, there are good reasons for his exteriority: after Harry has already shown himself time and again to be a loner afraid of people interfering with his private life, he allows Meredith (Elizabeth MacRae) to seduce him, only to find that she has stolen the tapes of the Union Square conversation while he slept.

In this way, Harry's exteriority offers something other than an opportunity for the audience to experience repulsion or disdain. Discussing the tapes in the surveillance van opposite Union Square he says "All I want is a nice fat recording", the surveillance-obsessive's version of the common worker's desire for "a nice fat pay packet." Harry's previous lack of scruples is well outlined by a fellow surveillance operative, Bernie Moran (Allen Garfield), who is professionally intrigued by one technical innovation that Harry has used but which has caused three deaths on the East coast. But, soon after, Harry begins to listen to the contents of the Union Square tape, and then to act upon it. On visiting the building of the Director (Robert Duvall) who has commissioned him to make the tape, he is first met by Martin Stett (Harrison Ford) who informs him that the Director is not available and that he will take the tapes from Harry. A scuffle for the package ensues and it is clear that Harry has now developed scruples that go against his simple desire for a nice fat recording. In a prostitute's parlance he has started to "come with the customers."

The Conversation

The fatal words in the narrative are those spoken by Mark (Frederic Forrest) in Union Square: "He'd kill us if he had the chance." The paranoia engendered in one camp by paranoia existing in an opposing camp which we have seen to be a part of the logic of Watergate is here reproduced. When Harry finds out that he has made a mistake about the identity of the murder victim he becomes completely paranoid. In the final scene of the film he receives a call from Stett who replays over the phone Harry's own saxophone playing of a moment earlier; Harry then strips his entire apartment and searches for the bug. Although Harry's reaction seems extreme, *The Conversation* makes such paranoia justifiable. Somebody *is* out to get him, he has witnessed their work and he knows that he is being observed. Once again, the most familiar of environments, in this case Harry's home, becomes the most threatening.

Interrupting *The Conversation*

The Conversation received more positive reviews than some of the other 'paranoid' films of the era, although this can be attributed to the middle-brow publications' nod to Coppola's auteur status. In publicity for the film, Coppola's statements also served to efface a direct connection with contemporary politics:

> I had no idea of what was to come in 1973. White House plumbers, Watergate, Ellsberg files, of course were unfamiliar phrases to me, even now I'm not completely sure of how these names and events relate to this film, despite so many coincidences and prophecies.[19]

That *The Conversation* advertised itself, following the critical praise for *The Godfather*, as something more than a popular film, is incorporated into the reviews. The historical transience of possible readings is mitigated for reviewers by the fact that *The Conversation* seems to be, for them, something more than 'of the moment.' John Simon of *Esquire*, in his own way, plays down contemporary references by dubbing the film a "quasi-documentary about wire-tappers at work."[20] Rather than noting the possible specific investments accruing to surveillance for the audience in the early seventies, he treats eavesdropping as a purely cinematic device.[21]

In contrast to her comments on *The Parallax View*, Penelope Gilliatt in the *New Yorker* seems more willing to countenance tenuous connections between the film and contemporary events. She points out that "Francis Ford Coppola began the script in 1966, long before we learned our repulsive familiarity with bugging, telephone tapping, and tape recordings tampered with so that they mean the opposite of what the original said."[22] Yet, she also hints at further dimensions to the phenomenon of surveillance in the concurrent climate when she writes of Harry in the earlier part of the film that he "prefers to think of himself as the employee of a Private Party, concealing from himself that his Private Party may be anyone, including the President."[23]

The reviewers studiously avoided facile equations of the historical period and the text of the film. Rather than treating the film in terms of topical meaningfulness of its content they supplemented or replaced such readings with commentary on the formal aspects of the film. The comments of Jay Cocks in *Time* illustrate the tendency nicely:

> *The Conversation* is a film of enormous enterprise and tension. It also gains, because of Watergate, and added timeliness, but it does not depend on it. More than anything it is a film about moral paralysis, a subject that does not need headlines to lend it importance.[24]

Cocks praises the film's formal attributes, he notes potential points of contemporary investment whilst playing them down and attributes what he sees as the film's success to the timeless nature of its theme. This is a common motif in criticism which desires to see its object as a work of 'art.' However, in light of historical events and the other paranoid films released in the period, it remains difficult to believe that audiences would accept the encouragement to view *The Conversation* as a narrative somehow transcending its period.

Conclusion

What I have attempted to examine in this discussion of the paranoid thriller in the 1970s is the idea that the term 'paranoia' as it is utilized in the description of such texts cannot be understood simply by defining it as an eternal psychological mechanism. Rather, as the films under review have indicated, paranoia is historically specific. Such specificity cannot be examined in thrillers by a scrutiny of the text's mechanisms alone. Before the corpus of texts which we have called paranoid thrillers came to prominence in the 1970s there were a number of narratives with almost identical properties: the most famous dates back to 1915, *The Thirty-Nine Steps* by John Buchan. Other famous examples can be found in Hitchcock s films, especially *The Man Who Knew Too Much* (1934), *North by Northwest* (1959) and the non-fictional narrative, *The Wrong Man* (1956). The difference between these early texts and those of the seventies, of course, is in the nature of the conspiracy. Above all, it is important in the later narratives that there is a *corporate, establishment* conspiracy.

Far from being texts with immutable reactionary-'sick'-mechanisms (as Ernest Mandel's definition of the genre would have it),[25] the paranoid thrillers demonstrate that, in the early 1970s there was every reason to presume that paranoia was an understandable mindset with regard to the vicissitudes of governments and corporations. If Watergate and Vietnam had not made this an abundantly plausible response, then smaller agencies such as police departments could reinforce such views. Pauline Kael notes that:

> We have no word, as yet, for justifiable paranoia - that is, for the sane person's perception of a world become crazily menacing - and in terms of behaviour there may not be much difference between living in terror of actual enemies and living in terror of imaginary enemies, particularly if the natural

enemies represent the whole system of authority.[26]

Interestingly, she is referring here to the story of Frank Serpico, the undercover policeman who exposed widespread corruption among the NYPD.[27] And this is the key point: paranoia can be said to exist as a mindset in the seventies on a number of levels of the power structure of American society but it is repeatedly represented through the acts of the *establishment* and *authorities*. It would be difficult to characterise this mindset as hysteria, but at the same time it must be remembered that distrust of authority structures was probably abnormally acute in comparison with other periods, and not without justification. If anything, then, the paranoia that characterizes the texts we have discussed is symptomatic of a more serious questioning of the role of authorities in American society. For Jameson (echoing Mandel), this fact is just a sop to liberalism and is not an institution of real change; he writes:

> It is indeed as though the major legacy of the sixties was to furnish a whole new code, a whole new set of thematics-that of the political-with which, after that of sex, the entertainment industry could reinvest its tired paradigms, without any danger to itself or to the system... [28]

This view, though bland and obvious, is irrefutable. Yet the fact that it is irrefutable is not to say that texts do not contribute to political struggle whether they do so with or without discernible long term effect. On the one hand, texts with a political content rarely effect change single-handedly; on the other, the early seventies was manifestly a period when the texts of Woodward and Bernstein had led directly to the removal of an incumbent president.

Furthermore, mainstream Hollywood cinema was being forced to respond to social forces no matter how instrumental or contained such a response might be. As 'the outsider' became increasingly visible in mainstream films from *Easy Rider* (1969) onwards, films had to redraw the lines regarding who existed on the margins of American society. In the same way, the paranoid thrillers offered audiences the opportunity to ask the questions "Who is paranoid?" and "Is it justified?" Clearly, a film such as *The Conversation* is much different from *Capricorn One*; similarly, *The Parallax View* contains events much different to those of *Serpico*. Yet, these texts can become grouped together in terms of the likely regimes of reading in which they might have existed in the contemporary period, and the likely questions that audiences might have asked of them. And these, of course, are not questions which the films alone would provoke audiences to ask.

Notes

1. Richard Hofstadter, 'The paranoid style in Amercan politics' in 'The Paranoid Style in Amercan Politics' and Other Essays (New York: John Wiley and Sons, 1964), pp.3-40 (p.4: pp.7-10).
2. Newsweek, 4 May 1970 p.35
3. William A. Dobrovir et al, The Offenses of Richard M. Nixon: A Guide to His Impeachable Crimes

3rd edn. (New York: Manor Books, 1974), pp.23-27.

4. Michael Herr, *Dispatches*, (London: Pan, 1978), p.63.

5. See for example, Frank Mankiewicz, *Nixon's Road to Watergate* (London: Hutchinson, 1973), p.190.

6. Sanford J. Ungar, *The Papers and the Papers: An Account of the Legal and Political Battle Over the Pentagon Papers*, Rev. edn., (New York: Columbia University Press, 1989), pp.309-310.

7.cf. the story concerning the *Boston Globe* told by Nat Hentoff, 'Subverting the First Amendment: Nixon and the media', in *What Nixon is Doing to Us*, ed. by Alan Gartner et al., (New York: Harper and Row, 1973), pp.20-31, (p.21).

8. See Jack Anderson with George Clifford, *The Anderson Papers*, (London: Millington, 1974); J. C. Spear, *The Presidents and the Press: The Nixon Legacy*, (London and Cambridge, MA.: M. I. T. Press, 1989), p.134, pp.148-50; Ungar, p.305; E. Howard Hunt, *Undercover: Memoirs of a Secret Agent*, (London: W. H. Allen, 1975), p.183; Daniel Schorr, 'Secrecy and security', in *Crisis in Confidence: The Impact of Watergate*, ed. by D. W. Harward, (Boston and Toronto: Little Brown and Co.), pp.74-85, (p.82).

9. Penelope Gilliatt, 'Review of *The Parallax View*', New Yorker, 24 June 1974. p.106.

10. Ibid., p.106.

11. Ibid., p.106.

12. Publicity Brochure for *The Parallax View*, (C.I.C., 1974), p.3.

13. Ibid., p.3.

14. Richard Schickel, 'Paranoid Thriller', *Time*, 8 July 1974, p.71.

15. Ibid., p.71.

16. Duncan Fallowell, 'Review of *The Parallax View*', The Spectator, 12 October 1974, p.23.

17. John Coleman, 'Review of *The Parallax View*', New Statesman, 4 October 1974, p.32.

18. Kaja Silverman, *The Acoustic Mirror: The Female Voice in Psychoanalysis and Cinema*, (Bloomington and Indianapolis: Indiana University Press, 1988), pp.87 ff.

19. Publicity Brochure for *The Conversation*, (C.I.C., 1974).

20. John Simon, 'Review of *The Conversation*', Esquire, (June), 1974, p.40.

21. Ibid., p.48.

22. Penelope Gilliatt, 'Tapped Telephones in Desk Drawers, Bugging Gadgets in Buckets of Fish Bait', *New Yorker*, 15 April 1974, p.104.

23. Ibid., p.104.

24. Jay Cocks, 'The Sounds of Silence', *Time*, 15 April 1974, p.78.

25. Ernest Mandel, *Delightful Murder: A Social History of the Crime Story* (London: Pluto Press, 1984), p.74.

26. Pauline Kael, 'The Hero as Freak', *New Yorker*, 17 December 1973, pp. 107-108, (p.107).

27. Paul Cobley, *The American Thriller: Generic Innovation and Social Change in the 1970s* (London: Palgrave, 2000), pp.101-9.

28. Fredric Jameson, 'Class and Allegory in Contemporary Mass Culture: *Dog Day Afternoon* as a Political Film', *Screen Education*, no. 30, (Spring 1979), pp.75-94, (p.78).

Part Two: The Ethnic Other in Action
By Xavier Mendik

Fast, funky and furious, the explosion of kung fu and blaxploitation cinema announced the mainstream arrival of ethnic superstars during the seventies. Although Chinese and African-American action superstars had long established ethnic bases of fan appeal, they had hitherto failed to provide the impact on white American audiences achieved by 1970s icons such as Bruce Lee, Pam Grier and Tamara Dobson. However, this translation from marginal to mainstream appeal complicated the depictions of race and sexuality that both genres offered. From the continued controversy over Bruce Lee's downgraded star billing in *Enter the Dragon*, to claims that blaxploitation accentuated its more flamboyant characteristics for wider audience acceptance, these representations frequently split both critical and fan opinion. In the second section of *Shocking Cinema of the Seventies* we consider both the characteristics and controversies that surrounded various examples of 'ethnic' action cinema.

Our examination begins with a star study of the kung fu legend Wang Yu, the subject of Leon Hunt's article 'One Armed and Extremely Dangerous: Wang Yu's Mutilated Masters.' Here, the author highlights the way in which Wang Yu (often painfully) reconstructed his body in an attempt to carve out a career beyond the shadow of Bruce Lee. Although the actor initially made his name in a series of roles as a doomed Chinese knight, he will be best remembered for a series of surreal kung fu capers, which pitted his damaged body against opponents with other worldly powers. As Hunt notes, this trend towards self-mutilation was initiated in *The Chinese Boxer*, where Wang Yu plunges his hands into a cauldron of iron filings in order to prepare them for combat. By the time of *The One Armed Boxer* series Wang Yu's heroes were cast as having only one arm to punish, but this still had to be damaged, mutilated and 're-trained' in order to defeat the assortment of non-Chinese nationals that had destroyed his Kung Fu school. As Hunt notes, the theme of male punishment and disembodiment running through Wang's film extend to the construction of their villains. Thus, in *The Master of the Flying Guillotine*, the one armed hero is ranged against a blind monk whose favoured weapon of a decapitating hatbox appears to be an extension of his own body. As Hunt concludes, the fact that these surreal productions employed such manner of other worldly characters and fighting styles in part reflects the fact that Wang Yu was *not* Bruce Lee and his skills as a fighter were in fact very limited. (This seems confirmed by the over-reliance on camera tricks and special effects during the fight scenes of his films). However, what Wang lacked in authenticity and technique he made up for in a grim determination to push his body to extremes, thus anticipating much of the savagery that was to accompany Hong Kong cinema in decades to come.

Alongside kung fu, the other key cycle to depict the ethnic Other in action was blaxploitation. Although this genre has recently gathered a strong cross-cultural appeal (primarily among teen audiences), its initial 1970s focus was marked by a distinctly ethnic focus (both in terms of the make up of its production personnel as well as its appeal to urban black audiences). The extent to which blaxploitation cinema subverted established 'white' cinema values remains a contentious point for film and race theorists alike. While these unresolved debates do explain why blaxploitation cinema has frequently been interpreted as an extension (and inversion) of classic American crime cinema, this examination has frequently overshadowed the consideration of related cycles. In his article 'Possessed By Soul: Generic (Dis)Continuity in the Blaxploitation Horror Film' Steven Jay Schneider offers an overview of the still undertheorised cycle of blaxploitation horror. Here, the author accounts for the production of 15 films produced between the years of 1969 and 1976, which either fully or partially fused a focus on ethnic concerns within a more traditional horror narrative. Having established the existence of a corpus of works that can be defined as blaxploitation horror, Schneider devotes the remainder of his article to interpreting the racial and gender dynamics behind this cycle. In so doing, Schneider questions the apparently radical nature of blaxploitation horror raised in Harry Benshoff's important article 'Blaxploitation Horror Films: Generic Reappropriation or Reinscription?' Here, Benshoff argued a case for the progressive nature of the cycle based on the depiction of their black monsters as sympathetic characters whose motives are frequently justified as a response to white racism. However, Schneider argues that rather than producing a legion of radically motivated monsters, blaxploitation horror at best represents "compromise formations" which require analysis beyond their obvious depictions of terror. Through analysis of films such as *Ganga and Hess* and *The Beast Must Die*, Schneider reveals that sympathetic, politically aware 'monsters' were by no means the preserve of all blaxploitation horror. Equally, such ambivalent depictions cannot be separated from wider changes occurring in 1970s horror cinema (a point further explored further in part three of this volume). Through a closing analysis of the controversial *Exorcist* clone *Abby*, the author also concludes with a call for more research into the issue of sexism implicit in ethnic film patterns such as blaxploitation horror.

Whereas the contradictions around black "compromise formations" dominate Steven Schneider's analysis, it is the concept of "co-optation" that concerns Christopher S. Norton & Garrett Chaffin-Quiray's work on the *Cleopatra Jones* films. In their article 'Jonesing James Bond: Co-optation and the Rules of Racial Subordination', the authors link this notion to the seventies marketing of Tamara Dobson as a black female secret agent. For Norton and Chaffin-Quiray, the concept of co-optation represents far more than mere blaxploitation filmic parody. Rather, it is a way of relaying complex themes around black power and sexuality emerging within 1970s America. In *Cleopatra Jones*, the traits of James Bond can be seen in the heroine's status (as a secret agent called into service by her nation), codes of dress (where sharp tailored suits were replaced by sexy furs and fedoras) and an emphasis on gadgets as a means of defeating opponents. However, for both authors, Dobson's rendition is significant for the way in which it subverted many of the sexist values implicit in blaxploitation and Bond, as well as locating transgression to white characters. Although the latter point remains embedded in the radical tradition of black genre cinema, they occur in Dobson's films at the point where Roger Moore's performance as Bond is reconstructing the black Other as a source of threat. As is indicated towards the end of the article, the Bond film *Live and Let Die* is itself a co-optation of blaxploitation cinema through its use of urban locations, drug fuelled imagery and the casting of established 'ethnic' action stars such as Yaphet Kotto and Gloria Hendry. As Norton and Chaffin-Quiray conclude, the film functions as a form of recuperative white fantasy where the threat of black power and corrupting sexuality can be both identified and contained through Bond's mythical powers.

As with previous chapters in this section of the volume, I.Q. Hunter's article deals with the racial tensions that emerge from the hybrid mixing of colonial and ethnic genre forms. In his chapter 'Hammer Goes East: A Second Glance at *The Legend of the Seven Golden Vampires*', he concerns himself with re-evaluating a genuine cinematic oddity: Britain's only kung fu vampire film. Although the film has been dismissed as the most chaotic of the *Dracula* cycle of films that Hammer produced, Hunter identifies a "structural elegance" in the way in which the narrative blends British and Hong Kong genre elements. While the film's curious composition reflects the transnational personnel that created it, it shares many of the complexities surrounding other kung fu co-productions (such as Bruce Lee's *Enter the Dragon*). Specifically, the uneasy fusion between the East and West produces a tension between the colonial and the ethnic Other which *Legend* attempts to deal with through the established struggle between Dracula and Van-Helsing. As Hunter notes, the fact that the film begins with an image of the vampire invading the body of his corrupt Chinese disciple indicates the extent to which the film equates evil and perversion with Western aristocracy. Paradoxically, Hunter also notes that *The Legend of the Seven Golden Vampires* also draws on mythical constructions of the 'exotic' and the savage East as part of its construction of the Chinese landscape. Although critics of the film tend to see it as an aberration from the rest of the Dracula cycle Hunter notes that these colonial tensions are played out in Hammer's familiar arena of sexual desire. For instance, he notes that the narrative strikes a liberal cord in its depiction of an interracial relationship between a Chinese fighter and the film's heroine Vanessa Buren. However, as if to underscore the a-typical nature of this coupling, it seems significant that Hammer dramatically kills off this heroine after both Buren and her lover become infected. The film appears to end on a conservative note, falling back on Van Helsing's ability to restore order for the Chinese (through Hunter's definition of him as a "mobile colonial advisor"). However, rather than seeing the tensions that the film raises as specific to Hammer, they once again point to the complex and contradictory depictions of the ethnic Other during the seventies.

One-Armed and Extremely Dangerous:
Wang Yu's Mutilated Masters
Leon Hunt

"Actually, Bruce Lee wasn't really my type. I preferred Wang Yu."
Stanley Kwan, *Yang + Yin: Gender in Chinese Cinema* (1996).

Who was the first kung fu star? Older Chinese audiences would doubtless agree on Kwan Tak-hing, the actor who played Wong Fei-hung in over seventy black-and-white Cantonese films. But western kung fu cultists are more likely to pick Wang Yu, whose trend-setting *The Chinese Boxer* (1970) predated Bruce Lee's *The Big Boss* (Lo Wei, 1971). Like David Chiang, Ti Lung, Lo Lieh and Angela Mao-ying, Wang's films were widely seen internationally and he had enough of a profile to be relaunched in a 'crossover' film, *The Man From Hong Kong* (Brian Trenchard-Smith, 1975). I'll be examining Wang's cult and critical reputation, his cinematic strategies for overcoming limited martial arts skills, his frequent on screen mutilation and the attempt to launch him as 'the new Bruce Lee.'

Before (and after) Bruce Lee

In his film *Yang + Yin: Gender in Chinese Cinema*, director Stanley Kwan recalls that adolescent visits to kung fu films were less about fighting than the "spectacle of male bodies in action, very often half naked." If his preference for swimming/water polo-champion-turned martial arts star Wang Yu over Bruce Lee seems surprising, an on screen publicity shot of an impossibly boyish Wang confirms that Shaw Brothers studios aimed to deliver "the most eye-blistering male beauty ever tossed on screen."[1] Lee and Wang embodied different versions of the martial arts star. Lee was 'authentic', the shape of things to come, paving the way for Sammo Hung, Jackie Chan, 'superkickers' like Huang Jang Lee and John Liu. Wang was the first of Shaws 'superhunks', cast for his looks first and martial skills second. Ostensibly brought in to make Mandarin cinema more 'masculine', one commentator nevertheless suggests that these bodies were both masculine and feminine-"(f)rom the waist up he's exposed iron, from the waist down... concealed silk."[2] While this partly reinforces an Orientalist 'feminisation' of the East, it does capture the way Shaws traded in male bodies. For instance, when Wang Yu left for Golden Harvest, Shaws simply found another actor with the same name.

By the mid-'70s, however, the original Wang's looks had gone, he had about two facial expressions and some would say only one or two more kung fu moves. So, what do kung fu fans remember (and love) him for? The following film titles might offer a clue: *The One Armed Swordsman* (1967), *Return of the One Armed Swordsman* (1969), *The One Armed Boxer* (1971), *Zatoichi and the One Armed Swordsman* (1973), *The One Armed Boxer vs. The Flying Guillotine* (1976), *One-Arm Chivalry Fights Against One-Arm Chivalry* (1977), *Two One-Armed Heroes* (1977) and *One Armed Swordsman Annihilates the Nine Disciples of Chu* (1979).

Wayback Wang: The Background to Lee's Shadow

Wang signed to Shaws in the mid-'60s, at the same time as Lo Lieh. They appeared together in *Tiger Boy* (Zhang Che, 1966), *Golden Swallow* (Zhang Che, 1968) and Wang's directorial debut, *The Chinese Boxer* (1970). Lo remained at Shaws and blossomed into an impressive character actor, notching up some memorable villains; most notably, the mobile-pulsed, testicle-retracting white-eye browed monk Bai Mei in *Executioners From Shaolin* (Lau Kar-leung, 1976). Wang, meanwhile, cast a covetous eye at Lee's from-out-of-nowhere success. Bruce had turned down Shaws' prehistoric contracts in favour of Golden Harvest's flexibility, and Wang also decamped to Golden Harvest. While *One Armed Boxer* (Wang Yu, 1971) and *Beach of the War Gods* (Wang Yu, 1973) are barely distinguishable in style from Wang's Shaws films, Golden Harvest did give him a Lee-like shot at international stardom and renamed him 'Jimmy Wang Yu.' Wang's career declined, and he spent the remainder of the '70s with mainly Taiwanese independents, but he seems to have attracted most attention via what I shall discreetly call his business activities. Tony Williams has even referred to him "the George Raft of Taiwanese cinema."[3]

Wang Yu belongs to a time both before and after Lee, and his career encompasses four overlapping images. In his earliest films, he is the rebellious, often doomed, Knight Errant of *wu xia* (martial chivalry) fiction, a figure who can be traced to novels like *The Water Margin* or more recent ones by Louis Cha. His most critically celebrated role was as Silver Roc in *Golden Swallow*, a swordplay film dusted off and repackaged for the kung fu market as *Girl With the Thunderbolt Kick* in the early '70s. 'Poetic', 'anarchic', psychologically complex (credited with a death wish),[4] Silver Roc has rather more on his mind than avenging his teacher or proving that Chinese Boxing is better than Karate.

The second role emerges in *The Chinese Boxer*, which injects the nationalistic bravado into the kung fu film that Lee was to develop in *Fist of Fury* (Lo Wei, 1972). It's sometimes seen as a coarsening of Wang's heroic persona,[5] but it did establish the genre's dominant conventions for the next few years; rival schools, a 'special technique' and Sino-Japanese conflict (*King Boxer*, *One Armed Boxer*, *Hapkido*). These two roles co-exist in the early '70s-Wang continued to play swordplay roles even as kung fu dominated the market. *Beach of the War Gods* pits Ming Dynasty hero Hsiao Feng against Japanese invaders so that he can embody both righteous heroism and the kind of macho xenophobia ("You Jap bastards!") that was de rigeur by then. While Japan-bashing films like *Fist of Fury* and *Hapkido* draw on a colonial matrix, Wang's films just melt down into a 'you wipe out my school, I'll wipe out yours' series of contests. In *Chinese Boxer* and *One Armed Boxer*, the main villains are Chinese and the Japanese are mercenaries-for-hire rather than potential invaders; in the latter, they are only one of a collection of Asian/non-Chinese stereotypes. Ackbar Abbas has suggested, in any case, that the anticolonialism of films like *Fist of Fury* "cannot be taken too literally" and give the impression of having "no idea who the 'enemy' really was."[6] Only Lee was tackling western fighters in the early '70s. Wang's 'exotic' villains seemingly comprise the non-Chinese races of Asia (Japan, Thailand, Tibet, India), as though eager to differentiate the newly modern Hong Kong from its immediate rivals and neighbours by caricaturing them as savages and brutes.

Wang's third role emerges in *The Man From Hong Kong*, propelled by the search for a 'new' Bruce Lee to paper the cracks in Hong Kong cinema's precarious position in the global market. Finally, while the genre 'matured' from the mid-70s in the early films of Lau Kar-leung, Sammo Hung and Yuen Woo-ping, Wang 'developed' by pushing the excesses of the early '70s in more baroque directions. Wang's cult/fan reputation rests largely on the paracinematic delirium of films like *Master of the Flying Guillotine/One Armed Boxer vs. The Flying Guillotine* (Wang Yu, 1975), allegedly one of Tarantino's favourite films.[7]

Thus, Wang's career seems to have enjoyed two very different evaluations. In the first, he is a star of the late 1960s, that moment when Hong Kong cinema conquered South East Asia (but not yet the rest of the world) with its Mandarin-language swordplay films. However, by the 1970s, this system was compromised by a "limited acting range, unconventional looks and comparatively unimpressive physical skills."[8] According to Tony Rayns, he "belongs to an earlier era, an era of stoic, individual heroism and of special- effects-assisted martial feats."[9] Wang was Zhang Che's discovery, and, by implication, his creation. His *One Armed Swordsman* (Zhang Che, 1967), is driven by Zhang' well-documented obsession with *yang gang* (male attributes).[10] For Rayns, Wang's '70s career finds him 'trapped within' Zhang's homoerotic/masochistic 'schema', unable to reinvent himself in spite of his departure from Shaws.[11] But the transcultural success of early '70s kung fu rather complicates or postpones this 'decline and fall' narrative: Wang's roles as a "limb-challenged death machine",[12] are firm favourites with 'old school' kung fu fans. For British fanzine *Eastern Heroes*, *One Armed Boxer* is a "labyrinth of exhilarating entertainment" which can "make most martial art movies look mediocre in comparison."[13] 'Serious' critics of Hong Kong cinema prioritise *Golden Swallow*, but *The Essential Guide to Hong Kong Movies* also gives a top-scoring five-fist rating to *The Master of the Flying Guillotine*:

> Wang Yu's awkward martial arts style may not make him the prettiest of fighters, but his sheer innovative genius in his fight choreography makes his films timeless classics, and the many ways in which battles are fought often seem to be breaking the boundaries of normal martial art techniques.[14]

Contrasting aesthetic agendas are not, in themselves, unexpected when it comes to a genre like the martial arts film. But where one might expect kung fu skill

The Man From Hong Kong

to be offset against thematic/narrative richness, fans and critics seem united in their assessment of Wang's martial skills. Some of his detractors are decidedly more blunt-"his techniques are awful and ugly... agonizingly long fights with flailing arms"[15]-but the *Essential Guide* does acknowledge Wang's "awkward martial arts style."

Thus, his 'innovative genius' is defined by his overcoming such physical shortcomings, just as his characters overcome their limb loss. With this in mind, Rayns' notion of the 'trap' is useful, but not as the point of closure he offers-rather, as the subject of Wang's later films, with the trap in question being the body of the kung fu star. For Yvonne Tasker, the kung fu film is about "the *constitution of the body through limits*" (her emphasis),[16] a particularly resonant idea in this context. This ties in with the second thing Wang's observers agree on, namely his spectacular masochism-"he not only undergoes the pain involved in loss of the limb, but also that torture attendant on building his remaining limb into a doubly strong instruments of revenge."[17] It doesn't always end there-at the end of *One Armed Boxer*, Yu Tien-lung is missing an eye as well as an arm, blackened and bloody, both triumphant and abject. In contrast to the unified, armoured body discerned by Tasker, Wang Yu's heroes are frequently invincible but incomplete, permanently mutilated and alone. These are therefore kung fu films about inadequacy.

Invincible/Incomplete

"So, the One-Armed Swordsman is only a one-winged chicken!"
Master of the Flying Guillotine

In *The Chinese Boxer*, Lei Ming (Wang) asks his Confucian teacher to explain the differences between kung fu and karate. Chinese Boxing, he is told, disciplines the mind as well as the body, with its aim is to "develop good citizens." Karate, by contrast, is "aggressive ... very hostile... directed to only one end and that is to kill, or if not to kill then to cripple." Nevertheless, it is very powerful because a "Karate expert's hands are fantastically strong." There's a mixture of arrogance and envy in this scene- after all, Lei Ming can only defeat Lo Lieh's bleached-blonde karate expert by making his hands "like iron." This denigration-and misrepresentation-of Japanese culture is accompanied by a longing for the kill-and-cripple spectacle it ostensibly attributes to a savage other. It's well known, in any case, that Mandarin cinema reinvented itself by borrowing aesthetic practices and technicians from Japanese cinema.[18] Lei Ming is injured and left for dead when the villains wipe out his school, and he fights back with a mixture of 'Iron Fist' and weightless kung fu. Lei plunges his hands into a cauldron of iron filings to strengthen his hands, and practices his leaps with heavy weights attached to his legs. In one scene, he sits gazing at his (gloved) hands: empowered but alienated from the rest of his body, as though reconstituting them as weapons makes them no longer a part of him.

By the time of *One-Armed Boxer*, the 'Iron Fist' narrative was seemingly so familiar that the plot could be reduced to maximum fighting (three in the first ten minutes) and maximum pain for the hero. "What are you doing at my table?" one character demands in the opening scene, and that's all the motivation anyone needs to fight. When Yu Tien-lung burns his remaining arm in a fiery cauldron, Wang rolls his eyes, bites his tongue, looks close to losing consciousness. This time there would be no lectures on disciplining the mind - in *One Armed Boxer*, it's all down to the body. The film is often remembered for its exotic gallery of fighters: the fanged and feral 'Man from Okinawa' Han Tui (Lung Fei); two Tibetan lamas, one trained in the Iron Fist, one in the internal arts (when he closes off his pressure points, someone appears to inflate a life jacket inside his robes); a (blacked-up) Indian Yogi who circles his opponents dizzyingly on his hands; two Thai boxers and comparatively restrained Taekwondo and Judo experts.

Wang has already endured a beating from his teacher (for fighting the rival school), and is sporting a bandage on his head from a vicious fight with Han Tui's two students before the fanged master himself tears off his arm during a battle at the school. He is the only survivor, but returns both with an unbreakable arm and the disconcerting ability to spring up, jack-in-a-box-like, from a horizontal position. But his piece de resistance comes in his battle with the Indian master. He manages to circle him on one finger before blinding him with the same finger: "Standing on one finger!/Damn him!" grumble the villains at this ostentatious performance. The film works at two levels which epitomise Wang's films from here on. Most of his adversaries are superior on screen fighters,-the 'Tibetans' are especially good-so Wang triumphs with camera tricks and special effects (reverse motion, slow motion, trampolines). But the staging of the action supports this by pushing the tournament in a direction where the body which most exceeds itself will win. David Bordwell has characterised Hong Kong action as a "carnal cinema" of sensory and corporeal excitation-a symphony of pulses, rhythms, amplified (e)motion and dynamic bursts of action punctuated by moments of stasis that the spectator's body simply can't resist.[19]

This is also very close to the film-viewing dynamic proposed by Steven Shaviro, whose central referents are 'tactile' genres like pornography and the slasher film in which the spectator's body is defined by its "capacity for being affected."[20] Shaviro's proposed dynamic is masochism and thus a refusal of a 'fixed self': "The agitated body multiplies its affects and excitations to the point of sensory overload, pushing itself to its limits: it desires its own extremity, its own transmutation."[21]

In 'body' genres, those which simultaneously represent and facilitate corporeal extremes-such excitations and transmutations are also likely to find their equivalent on screen. The kung fu hero's body can offer images of both plenitude and inadequacy, the latter most frequently eliminated by rigorous training and newly mastered techniques. But the genre has a history of mutilated heroes, from disabled swordsmen in Louis Cha's novels to 'crippled hero' films like *Crippled Avengers* (Zhang She, 1978) and *Crippled Masters* (Joe Law, 1982). While the 'Avengers' are played by the all-too-whole 'Venoms' team, Masters features disabled martial artists in the two leading roles, but both triumph by forming a 'collective body' to defeat the villain. While Masters conjures visions of an alternative universe where Tod Browning worked at Shaws, Avengers is the culmination of Zhang Che's dismembered heroes-its Chinese title is *Incomplete*.[22]

Wang Yu's masochism is usually equated with his stoicism. The 'father' of Wang's pain is Zhang Che, who in turn locates him in the wu xia hero's sacrificial tradition. In 'Heroic' fictions, there is a thin line between losing an arm and giving it up. In *New One Armed Swordsman* (Zhang Che, 1970), Lei Li (David Chiang) severs his own arm when he is defeated by the villain's three-section staff. He leaves it pinned to a tree, and an ellipsis finds its skeleton still there (months? years?) later as a reminder of his retreat from the martial world. Chiang's graphic trophy of a dead part of himself recalls the fact that for many ritual theorists automutilation is often a marker of the entry into adult society. In *New One Armed Swordsman*, it is the first stage in Chiang's transformation from cocky duellist into someone who will fight for something. In *One Armed Boxer*, Wang Yu's arm loss is partly expiation for his teacher's death, but also marks his transformation from pupil to master.

There is one significant difference between these two sacrifices, however. Chiang's Lei Li-like so many Zhang Che heroes-is recuperated and/or validated by his love for another male hero, in this case Ti Lung's Feng. There is more than a touch of narcissism about this homosocial love affair-the dashing Feng is Li's carefree, younger self-and it is his gruesome death (cut in half) which pulls our one-armed hero back into action. Wang, by contrast, is, as Rayns observes, "resolutely solitary."[23] He avenges his dead teachers in *Chinese Boxer* and *One Armed Boxer*, scarcely seems interested in anything in *Master of the Flying Guillotine* (despite the narrator's assurance that he is a Ming rebel), and does not bond, even when recruiting patriotic swordsmen in *Beach or the War Gods*.

A throwaway comment by Bey Logan brings the focus of these works back to the star as a <u>physical</u> commodity-"Wang was always more effective with one arm than two, except, perhaps, during his swimming career."[24] How to transcend, or make a virtue of, comparative physical limitations as the post-Lee kung fu film places more and more emphasis on pro-filmic skill and 'real' (recognisable) Chinese Martial Arts? *The Master of the Flying Guillotine* takes notions of physiological alteration to the furthest extreme in Wang's filmography. The film is supposedly a sequel to *One Armed Boxer*, but is actually set in an earlier historical period (Qing Dynasty as opposed to early Republic). Historical accuracy is not high on the film's agenda-Qing/Ming conflict had largely replaced Sino-Japanese face-offs by the mid-70s, but the film isn't big on period detail. Wang seems to be a composite of his kung fu and *wu xia* heroes-the English dub misnames him the one-armed swordsman in one scene. *Master* is choreographed by Lau Kar-leung and his brother Lau Kar-wing, and features some recognisable fighting styles: Eagle Claw, Mantis, Snake, Monkey, 'Iron Robe', some northern kicking techniques-but mixes them with the exoticism favoured by Wang. The film features another Indian martial artist, this time blessed with extendible arms. Central to the narrative, though, is its titular weapon, described memorably as "a sort of Frisbee attached to a chain, which would transform into a head-slicing cakebox when thrown at a hapless victim."[25]

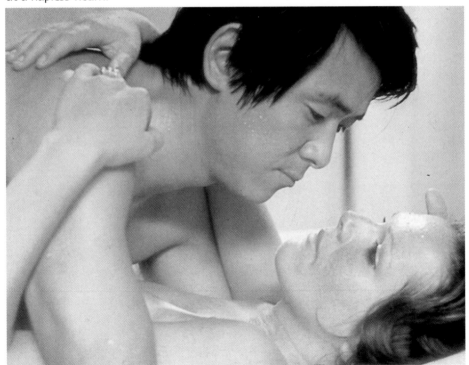

The Man From Hong Kong

This time Wang is the object of revenge: he has killed the disciples of the Flying Guillotine's 'Master', Fung, a blind kung fu expert working for the Manchus. Fung vows to behead every one-armed man he meets, including an unwisely boastful drunk and a contestant in the tournament drives what little plot there is. Blind martial artists, especially with white eyebrows, are no more uncommon to the genre than one-armed heroes, and these two incomplete masters are born to tussle. If the original *One Armed Boxer* compensates for loss by strengthening the remaining arm, *Master's* strategy lies in finding ways of extending the body. Fung's guillotine is akin to the villainous son's metallic arms in *Crippled Avengers*, a semi-prosthetic attachment. As fanzine descriptions suggest-hatbox, frisbee, "a quilted tea cosy on a chain"[26] -the guillotine is a pretty polymorphous implement to begin with. The soundtrack invests it with what sounds like the retort of a Winchester rifle as it strikes. It is both an extension of Fung's body-we see close-ups of his eyebrows twitching before a strike-and a lethal force in its own right. "The strength of the guillotine lies in its impetus", Yu Tien-lung (Wang) explains, "Once it's built up speed, it's almost impossible to stop it."

The film is built around two parallel tournaments: an 'official' one staged by the Eagle Claw School (seen by Fung as a possible lure for Yu) and the climactic one in which Wang must take on a powerful Thai kicker, the Indian fighter, Japanese Wayakuma (blades concealed in tonfa clubs) and, finally, Fung. Significantly, Wang takes no part in the first contest-the one featuring 'real' kung fu-and, in fact, doesn't so much as raise a fist during the first half of the film. The only indication of his skill is a demonstration of weightless kung fu (achieved through breath control): he can now walk up walls and stand on ceilings, as he indicates to the fighters at his school. The moment he enters the struggle, he is injured by the guillotine, cue close-ups of Wang in agony-and the film shifts gear.

As this description should make clear, there are explicit parallels once again between Yu Tien-lung and Wang Yu-both look tired, bored, trading on past glories before reluctantly taking on one more collection of baroque martial artists. When the Indian fighter mockingly suggests that "the one-armed swordsman is only a one-winged chicken", it is starting to look as though he might have a point. But he makes the mistake of destroying the altar to Kwan Ti, Chinese God of War (or "Saint Kwan" as the English dub calls him) and the glove is off. Avoiding his opponent's sweeping, elongated arms, Wang 'extends' his own arm with his belt, ties one of his opponents limbs to a pillar and breaks it.

If the original *One Armed Boxer* adheres to notions of sacrificial excess *Master* is, if anything closer to Bakhtin's non-classical body; transcending borders, outgrowing itself, refusing to fully differentiate itself as a static, unified, 'classical' whole.[27] Wang's body 'sprouts' a blade to defeat Wayakuma, but his most striking tactic is the use of, and fusion with, elaborately constructed rooms designed to exploit his opponents' weaknesses. He defeats the Thai fighter in a metal-floored room built over a fire, triumphing as his adversary's bare feet blister and burn. The climactic fight with Fung

The Man From Hong Kong

takes place first in a circle of bamboo, the poles standing in for, and deflecting the blade from, Wang's head. Subsequently, they face off in a customised funeral home equipped with bird cages and spring-loaded axes concealed in coffins. As Wang moves across the ceiling, throwing stones at the coffins to trick Fung into releasing the axes, he is fully incorporated into his own creation. Wang's approach to fight choreography -never better than in this scene-is the child of necessity (his 'awkward' fighting style, which now seemed to be what the one-arm motif meant). But it anticipates the '90s kung fu film's blurring of the line between pro-filmic performative skill and 'cinematic' virtuosity. In *Master of the Flying Guillotine*, it is technology (and cinematic 'mastery') which makes the kung fu star 'complete.'

Caged Mantis: The Man From Hong Kong

> In my country... we have a sport. We take the giant praying mantis and put him in a cage and make him fight for his life with his own kind. I thought you would enjoy such sport." *The Man From Hong Kong*

If a number of Wang's films are explicitly about loss-of a limb (or similar injury), of one's mentor and friends, then *The Man From Hong Kong* partly responds to both the loss of, and the challenge posed by, Bruce Lee. It belongs to the 1973-5 period of international co-productions designed to launch Hong Kong stars in the west and replicate the success of *Enter the Dragon* (Robert Clouse, 1973). Shaws, for example, collaborated with Hammer Films (*Legend of the Seven Golden Vampires*, *Shatter*) and various Italian and Spanish companies (*Blood Money*) to produce hybridised vehicles for David Chiang, Ti Lung and Lo Lieh. *Man* was Golden Harvest's collaboration with the Australian Movie Company and resembles *Enter the Dragon's* division of labour: western writer and director (Brian Trenchard-Smith), Chinese choreographer (Sammo Hung) and star (Wang Yu), the latter billed equally with a western co-star (George Lazenby). The film is usually judged a failure,[28] although Bey Logan notes the way its mixture of martial arts and gritty, stunt-filled action anticipates Jackie Chan's *Police Story* series.[29] There is a world of difference, however, between Chan's genial boy-next-door and Wang's taciturn, humourless Inspector Fang Sing Ling, beating up suspects, extracting confessions by taping a grenade in Lazenby's mouth or ramming the car of a trapped henchman. "What are you going to do?" he is asked at one point, to which he replies, "More!" Wang's suffering also makes for an illuminating comparison with Chan's.

'Loss' haunts Chan's career in a manner less extreme on screen, but with more serious implications in the realm of the real. Indeed, the self-endangering action star is partly anticipated by Wang Yu's life-threatening stunts in *The Man From Hong Kong*. (For instance, he almost died during the film's hang-gliding sequence). Chan and Wang both had Lee's legacy to contend with, and both have been characterised as masochists, but clearly of very different kinds. Chan is a Deleuzian masochist: "twisting the law by excess of zeal."[30] "I live for pain", Chan is quoted as saying. "Even when I was young I loved pain."[31] This taste-so the story goes-was acquired via the discipline of Opera teacher Yu Jin-Yuen, both through physical punishment and the disciplining of his performing body. His early films re-enact this discipline in excruciating training sequences or humiliation at the hands of superior fighters. But Chan's suffering always respects the unity of the body, and seems bound up instead with his persona's ongoing postponement of adult sexuality (his eternal boyishness).

In *The Man From Hong Kong*, Fang is routinely slashed with knives and axes, blown up, and most seriously injured during a fight in a martial arts school, after which he slips into a self-induced semi-coma, slowing his heart rate to stop the bleeding. Inspector Fang of Hong Kong Special Branch travels to Australia to extradite a Chinese drugs courier (Sammo Hung). Here, he is drawn into the Federal Narcotics Bureau's pursuit of 'Mr. Big' Jack Wilton (Lazenby), a villainous smoothie with a penchant for Chinoiserie in his bachelor pad. Fang's modus operandi is to batter, crush, hack and blow up every human obstacle until he gets to Wilton-"This country's got a small population", observes an Australian cop, "and he's getting through them very fast." What's most immediately striking, however, is that, to date, Wang is the only Hong Kong action star allowed to travel to the west with his libido intact. The neutered Asian hero hinges both on western representations of "the East as a site of a mystical, sexual knowledge"[32] and concomitant anxieties about "the irresistible, dark, occult forces of the East" which have equated Asian male sexuality with frequent representations of sadism, rape or captivity.[33] In contrast with Bruce Lee's asexual character in *Enter the Dragon*, *Man* seems to draw on 'Blaxploitation' conventions for its Chinese Superstud: he has seduced one Australian woman before even leaving Hong Kong and seduces another while recovering from his injuries. ("A Man is a Man is a Man", insists the song on the soundtrack, as though auditioning for an aftershave ad).

This is not to say that the film's racial politics (any more than its sexual ones) are 'progressive.' It makes self-conscious jokes about both love scenes, reinforces stereotypes about the brutal "Far East" and attributes his motivation to some inscrutable Eastern code: "To understand... you would have to be a Chinese", he says, as though that's all we need to know. Hong Kong is reduced to its usual tourist guide signifiers: skyscrapers, harbour, Victoria Peak, marching colonial police and characterised as "Beautiful, squalid, exhilarating and frightening-all the traditional contradictions of the East in one city." Yet amidst the jokes about Asian flu, yellow streaks, *55 Days at Peking* and Chinese torture, there are some intriguing reminders of Fang's colonised status. Wilton (Lazenby) taunts him for his English : "All your officers have to speak English, don't they?", while spelling out the cultural-colonial implications of his own linguistic skills:

> My business takes me to the East regularly. I find the Chinese make the best servants. I understand your culture, and your language, Inspector, and your martial arts. Especially those.

Lazenby's short-lived fame as James Bond (echoed on the soundtrack

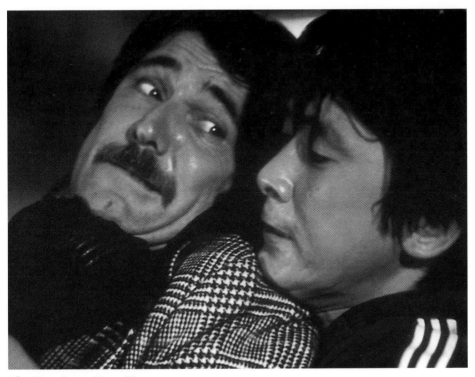

The Man From Hong Kong

The Man From Hong Kong

accompanying his scenes) is quite resonant here, the colonial playboy is now the villain, the colonised ethnic underdog the hero. Like *Enter the Dragon* (which uses Bond less subversively), *Man* is a combination of both new and old representations of Chinese masculinity, of both Chinese Superman and the Yellow Peril.

In many ways, Man reinvented Wang Yu (and the kung fu hero) and it is fun to see him driving a Mercedes and generally being rather flash. But the film still has to work with the star's inbuilt limitations. According to choreographer Sammo Hung, "Wang was never a martial artist in the way that Bruce Lee was... basically it was just street fighting."[34] Hung was one of the pioneers in injecting martial arts scenes into modern-day action films, combining flashy kung fu moves with 'gritty' street fighting and bone-shattering stunts. He also has a reputation for making the most limited fighters look good on screen. Given that even Lazenby looks convincing in the fight scenes, it should come as little surprise that Wang looks more formidable than usual. The martial arts school fight uses under cranking and an impressive stunt team (Lam Ching Ying, Yuen Kwai) to offer a traditional surround-the-hero-but-wait-your-turn kung fu fight. But Hung largely works with Wang's limitations, locating him within a more 'realist' milieu (none of his fights are won easily) and suggesting (again, like Chan) not so much a martial arts master as a hero with some martial arts skill who wins through endurance, bravery and determination. This impression is reinforced by Wang's stunts (hang-gliding, climbing up or hanging from buildings).

Such 'Everyman' action heroes flourished in the eighties, after Hong Kong's economic miracle, but it is near-impossible to imagine Wang in kung fu comedy.

Moreover, in many ways, the solitary kung fu hero died with Bruce Lee, replaced by the team, unit or family.' Even Chan has increasingly fused into the 'Jackie Chan Stunt Team.' The sacrificial *wu xia* hero returned in a different genre, the 'heroic bloodshed' film, most persuasively incarnated by Chow Yun Fat, a hero who suffers as greatly as Wang ever did-crippled, blinded, retarded by a head injury. As Julian Stringer argues, Chow incarnates both control/cool and hysteria/suffering,[35] but both are expressed through his virtuosity as an actor. More importantly, like Zhang Che's heroes and in contrast to most of Wang's, he suffers and/or dies for somebody/something. As Stringer notes, "a Chinese fulfills himself within the network of interpersonal relationships... the words 'single' and 'alone' have the connotations of 'immoral' and 'pathetic'" [36]

Wang's lack of physical gracefulness and taciturn persona make it easy to see why his stardom was short-lived. But it's equally easy to see why his cult reputation endures; largely ignoring generic trends and often finding ingenious ways to compensate for his limitations as an actor and a fighter, he remains a stubbornly perverse figure. He barely seems part of the same national cinema as Jackie Chan, John Woo and Tsui Hark (or even Bruce Lee and late Shaw Brothers) and yet in many ways

The Man From Hong Kong

the actor anticipates so much of 'Hong Kong action' to come.

Notes

1. Karen Tarapata, 'Chick Flicks: Shaw Brothers' Kung Fu Films', in *Hollywood East: Hong Kong Movies and the People Who Make Them*, ed. Stefan Hammond (Lincolnwood, Illinois: Contemporary Books, 2000) pp.82-3 (p.83).

2. Ibid., p.83.

3. Tony Williams, 'A Tribute to Jimmy Wang Yu', *Asian Cult Cinema*, Issue 24 (3rd quarter 1999), pp.18-20 (p.18).

4. Stephen Teo, *Hong Kong Cinema: The Extra Dimension* (London: BFI, 1997) p.100.

5. Ibid., p.104.

6. Ackbar Abbas, *Hong Kong: Culture and the Politics of Disappearance* (Minneapolis: University of Minnesota Press, 1997) p.30.

7. Rick Baker and Toby Russell, *The Essential Guide to Hong Kong Movies* (London: Eastern Heroes, 1994) p.96.

8. Bey Logan, *Hong Kong Action Cinema* (London: Titan, 1995), p.19.

9. Tony Rayns, 'Wang Yu: The Agony and the Ecstasy', in *A Study of The Hong Kong Martial Arts Film*, ed. by Lau Shing-hon (Hong Kong: Urban Council of Hong Kong, 1980), pp.99-100 (p.99).

10. Teo, p.102.

11. Rayns, p.99.

12. Hammond, *Hollywood East*, p.81.

13. John Brennan, 'The Man From Hong Kong', *Eastern Heroes*, Volume 2, Issue 1 (1994), 8-11 (p.10).

14. Baker and Russell, p.96.

15. Ron W. Lim, 'The Martial Artist's Guide to Hong Kong Films',
http ://www.ronlim.com/martial.html.

16. Yvonne Tasker, 'Fists of Fury: Discourses of Race and Masculinity in the Martial Arts Cinema', in *Race and the Study of Masculinities*, ed. by Harry Stecopoulos and Michael Uebel (Durham and London: Duke University Press, 1997) pp.315-336 (p.317).

17. Verina Glaessner, *Kung Fu: Cinema of Vengeance* (London: Lorrimer, 1974), p.98.

18. Sek Kei, 'The Development of 'Martial Arts' in Hong Kong Cinema', in *A Study of The Hong Kong Martial Arts Film*, ed. by Lau Shing-hon (Hong Kong: Urban Council of Hong Kong, 1980), pp.27-38 (p.31).

19. David Bordwell, *Planet Hong Kong: Popular Cinema and the Art of Entertainment* (Cambridge, Massachusetts and London: Harvard University Press) p.244.

20. Steven Shaviro, *The Cinematic Body* (Minneapolis and London: University of Minnesota Press, 1993) p.59.

21. Ibid., p.59

22. Bordwell, p.249.

23. Rayns, p.99.

24. Bey logan, p.15.

25. Hammond, p.81.

26. Baker and Russell, p.96.

27. Mikhail Bakhtin, *Rabelais and His World* (Bloomington, Indiana: Indiana University Press, 1984), p.318.

28. Williams, p.20.

29. Logan, p.87.

30. Gilles Deleuze, *Masochism: An Interpretation of Coldness and Cruelty* (New York: Zone Books, 1971/1989) p.88.

31. Bordwell, p.58.

32. Tasker, p.328.

33. Gina Marchetti, *Romance and the 'Yellow Peril': Race, Sex, and Discursive Strategies in Hollywood Fiction* (Berkely, Los Angeles and London: University of California Press, 1993), p.28.

34. Logan, p.87.

35. Julian Stringer, 'Your Tender Smile Gives me Strength: Paradigms of Masculinity in John Woo's *A Better Tomorrow* and *The Killer*', *Screen*, Volume 38, number 1 (Spring 1997), 25-41 (p.35).

36. Sun Longji, quoted by Stringer, p.39.

Possessed By Soul: Generic (Dis)Continuity in the Blaxploitation Horror Film

Steven Jay Schneider

Blaxplo's Blind Spot: Race-Horror at the Margins

Between the years 1969 and 1976, no fewer than eight films were released in the United States which can be unproblematically classified under the hybrid heading of 'blaxploitation horror.' These included films with such transparent titles as *Blacula* (1972), *Blackenstein* (1973), *Scream Blacula Scream!* (1973), and perhaps worst/best of all, *Dr. Black, Mr. Hyde* (a.k.a. *The Watts Monster*, 1975). Unproblematically, that is, once working definitions of both 'blaxploitation' and 'horror' are laid down, and once the qualifications for membership in this most unlikely of subgenres (*not* the mere sum of its parts) are elaborated. Furthermore, as we shall see, an additional eight films released during this period may be identified as either 'proto-' or else 'quasi-' blaxploitation horror, leaving us with a total of sixteen in all.

Despite being similar in their production values, marketing philosophy, plot lines, and thematic concerns (and period of production), blaxploitation horror remains one of the most overlooked, underappreciated, and insufficiently theorised of cinematic subgenres. But this sorry state of affairs appears to be changing. An essay by Harry M. Benshoff in a recent issue of *Cinema Journal* examines the various ways in which these films "[might] have addressed the specific fantasy needs of the black social imaginary", and in particular, how "the generic tenets of 'normality' and 'difference' [are] refigured (if they are) when viewed through the lens of a marginalized racial collective."[1] Perhaps not surprisingly, considering the ambivalence, ambiguity, and downright confusion of outlook/message/statement prevalent in both the blaxploitation and horror genres taken independently of one another, Benshoff seriously qualifies his argument in favour of blaxploitation horror's progressive potential:

> Ultimately...blaxploitation horror films mounted a challenge to the Other-phobic assumptions of the genres more common reception. However, while appearing to critique white racism in America, most of these films were

unable to withstand the genre's regular demonisation of gender and sexuality, which are arguably more deeply embedded as monstrous within both the horror film and the culture at large.[2]

There is much of value in Benshoff's essay. His appreciation of socio-historical context, his comprehensive knowledge of the horror genre, and his sensitivity to issues of gender and sexuality are to be commended. On the whole, however, the piece suffers from a number of strategic and methodological weaknesses. For one thing, Benshoff fails to distinguish between blaxploitation horror-'proper' (i.e., those central cases described as "unproblematic", above) and what we have chosen to call 'proto-' and 'quasi-' blaxploitation horror (i.e., those cases which lie on the fringes of our manifest subject area); thus, his investigation is not fine-grained enough to identify certain issues concerning the evolution and narrative-stylistic specificity of the subgenre in question.

For another thing, Benshoff surveys too small a sample, making mention of only twelve blaxploitation horror films in total (keeping in mind the previous criticism), and discussing but seven of them in any detail. This leads him to overlook characters, scenes, and pro-filmic events capable of serving as evidence for or against particular claims. Then again, although he touches on some recurring themes (e.g., the representation of voodoo as alternative/authentic African-American religion), Benshoff ultimately eschews a thematic investigation in favour of an allegorical one, attempting to show how blaxploitation horror "reappropriated the mainstream cinema's monstrous figures for black goals, turning vampires, Frankenstein monsters and transformation monsters into agents of black pride and black power."[3] The disadvantages of focusing on blaxploitation horror *monsters*, to the near exclusion of almost everything else concerning these films, will become clear as we proceed.

Finally, Benshoff's two-part thesis (quoted above) is at least partially mistaken on both counts. First of all, to the extent that blaxploitation horror films "mounted a challenge" to the genre's "Other-phobic assumptions", this was par for the course during the time of their release. Simply stated: blaxploitation horror does *not* stand in marked contrast to the rest of '70s horror cinema for turning things around and being especially progressive, even radical, in its figuration of monstrosity, Benshoff's remark about the genre's "more common reception" to the contrary. Now this might sound more reactionary, or at least politically incorrect, than it really is. Because what needs to be emphasised here are the *continuities* between blaxploitation horror films and the rest of 70's horror cinema, which on the whole tends to alternate (often in the very same picture) between the ideologically progressive and conservative. Rather than simply viewing blaxploitation horror monsters as "black *avenger*[s]...justifiably fight[ing] against the dominant order",[4] we are better off viewing them as compromise-formations, as sites of uneasy negotiation between conflicting, even contradictory, impulses, pressures, and concerns. (It should be noted, at one point Benshoff acknowledges that while "blaxploitation horror films may have attempted to reappropriate the genre for racial advancement, the genre's deeply embedded structure still worked to reinscribe racist tropes." But the reason he gives in support of this claim-that blaxploitation monsters tended to be "more animalistic" than their white counterparts-will be shown to be largely false).[5]

The second half of Benshoff's thesis, that the positive racial messages emblematised in and by the monsters of blaxploitation horror were offset by the subgenre's "regular demonization of gender and sexuality", is also problematic. As noted above, whatever racial messages may have been so emblematised, uniformly positive/progressive they most certainly were not. Furthermore, there is no way of separating out blaxploitation horror's treatment of gender and sexuality from its treatment of race: these modalities were inextricably tied up with one another (a trend which continues in the race horror films of today). *Contra* Benshoff, the blaxploitation horror subgenre cannot be adequately theorised in terms of monsters who were at once racially progressive and sexually reactionary. Not just because the monsters in question are too complex and confusing (both culturally-and ontologically-speaking) to admit of such an analysis, but because a great deal more was at stake in blaxploitation horror films than the politics of (monstrous) representation.

Proto, Quasi and Plain: Categories of Blaxplo Horror

For the purposes of our current investigation, I have limited myself to the following working definition of the genre under review. Blaxploitation films were low- to mid-budget commercial productions released in the United States between the years 1969 and 1976 (approximately). They possessed some degree of African American creative input (via actors, directors, crewmen, or more rarely, producers); which specifically targeted African American audiences (through ad campaigns, distribution strategies, and the celebration of various aspects of '70s black culture, including Afrocentricism, jazz music, Black Nationalism, and ghetto style). Also they typically presented stronger, more successful, more militant images of black men and women triumphing over white, frequently racist, adversaries (thus making genre films the favoured format).[6] By around 1975, the blaxploitation craze was essentially over, having burned itself out on formulaic sequels which saw the genre's once-proud black action heroes and heroines deteriorate into comic book caricatures of their former selves.

The late '60s-mid '70s was also a time when American horror cinema temporarily reinvented itself, as a number of films made by young auteurist directors either commented self-reflexively on the genre's outdated conventions (e.g., *Targets* [Peter Bogdanovich, 1968], *Sisters* [Brian DePalma, 1973], *Martin* [George Romero, 1978]), or else utilised the genre's familiar tropes to dramatise (in distorted, nightmare fashion) various social ills (e.g., *Death Dream* [a.k.a. *Night Walk*, Bob Clark, 1972]), *It's Alive* [Larry Cohen, 1973], *The Hills Have Eyes* [Wes Craven, 1977]). But whether the antagonists in this post-*Psycho*, post-*Peeping Tom* (both 1960) era were supernatural monsters or homicidal maniacs, whether they were truly malevolent or just plain misunderstood, it was the sheer fact of their existence which placed these films squarely in the horror category. Again similar to the blaxploitation genre, albeit for different reasons, this period of self-aware, socially conscious, and commercially successful horror cinema came to a close as the decade wound down.

Blacula

As I indicated earlier, whether a candidate blaxploitation horror film truly warrants classification under this hybrid heading is *not* simply a question of its fusing together features from its constituent genres. Although the following five conditions- (I) less than top-notch production values; (ii) some degree of African American creative input; (iii) the targeting of African American audiences; (iv) strong black characters; and (v) the existence of a monster-may be *necessary* for a film to qualify as 'blaxploitation horror' (assuming it was released in the United States during the appropriate era), even taken together they remain insufficient. For it could be argued, and quite plausibly, that while films such as *The Omega Man* (1971), *Welcome Home Brother Charles* (a.k.a. *Soul Vengeance*, 1975), and *Black Voodoo* (a.k.a. *Nurse Sherri*, 1976) satisfy all five of these conditions, the fact is that they bare only a tangential (or 'quasi-') relationship at best to blaxploitation horror-proper. So what are they lacking? How do blaxploitation horror films differ from both proto-and quasi-versions of the same? Answering this requires the positing of two additional conditions: (vi) the presence of an African American protagonist, whether male or female, and (vii) the presence of a monster who is-or *was*, at one time or another-African American (or else just African) him or herself.

The eight films alluded to earlier which satisfy all seven of the conditions necessary (and jointly sufficient) for unproblematic classification under the hybrid heading of 'blaxploitation horror' are, in order of their respective release dates: *Blacula*; *Blackenstein*; *Scream Blacula Scream!*; *Abby* (a.k.a. *Possess My Soul*, 1974); *Sugar Hill* (1974); *The House on Skull Mountain* (1974); *Dr. Black, Mr. Hyde*; and *J.D.'s Revenge* (1976). Of the remaining eight candidate films, three of them-*A Change of Mind* (1969); *Watermelon Man* (1970); and *The Thing With Two Heads* (1972)-may be identified as proto-blaxploitation horror. What makes this trio of race-reversal films 'proto-' as opposed to '-proper' has primarily to do with the fact that, although the reversals in question are greeted with horror by the victims and their respective families (especially in *The Thing With Two Heads*, for obvious reasons), none of the victims can be considered 'monsters' in any but an ironic sense of the term. That is to say, to the extent that these men are treated (or what is worse, to the extent that they treat *themselves*) as monsters, this merely serves to expose that insidious strain of racial prejudice which remains more or less concealed so long as everything-and everyone-remains in its proper place/body.

The final five films under examination here must be considered 'quasi-', rather than 'proto-', blaxploitation horror, since each of them presents viewers with an ostensible monster, however sympathetic he/she/it may be. However, each of them fails to satisfy at least one of the *other* conditions required for genuine blaxploitation horror membership. Before turning briefly to these films, it should be noted that just because they are quasi-, this does not mean they are in any way inferior by their very nature, or that they will have no role to play in the discussion which follows. Quite the contrary, as we shall see.

Ganja and Hess (a.k.a. *Blood Couple*, a.k.a. *Black Vampire*, 1973) and *The Beast Must Die* (a.k.a. *Black Werewolf*, 1974) are quasi-blaxploitation horror films for the same reason, although this reason is pretty much all they have in common. This is because marketing and promotional campaigns aside, from the standpoint of cinematic-narrative discourse neither film can be said to target a specifically African American commercial audience. *Ganja and Hess* (directed by black auteur filmmaker Bill Gunn), despite its traditional horror iconography, is far more art or experimental film than blaxploitation film. The eponymous leads are a wealthy African American vampire couple who reside in a huge mansion, replete with black servant, outside the city. Dr. Hess Green (Duane Jones, best known for his role as Ben in Romero's *Night of the Living Dead*, 1968) is an esteemed anthropologist researching how an ancient Nigerian tribe were wiped out by a blood disease ten thousand years before. However, his obvious disdain for contemporary black culture, in addition to his white bourgeois materialist lifestyle, mark him as a deeply flawed character. Manthia Diawara and Phyllis R. Klotman go so far as to argue that "the film indicts...Green's very wealth and class position as vampirism."[7] But it is *Ganja and Hess*' "deliberate art-house style"-including its pacing, editing, and use of sound-along with its "self-conscious thematic and narrative ambiguity"[8], which makes the film a radical (and potentially subversive) alternative to the usual blaxploitation horror fare. This led to its being suppressed in the United States by its none-too-pleased producers, even *after* receiving many favourable reviews.[9]

Paul Annett's *The Beast Must Die* also presents viewers with an aristocratic and unsympathetic black protagonist (Calvin Lockheart), only this time he is someone who shows no interest in anything African, and speaks with an upper-crust, semi-convincing British accent. Although *The Beast Must Die* differs greatly from *Ganja and Hess* insofar as it positions itself squarely within the category of genre filmmaking, the genre in question is not horror but mystery (of the 'whodunit?' variety). With one notable exception (the opening scene, which we shall have reason to return to below) the fact that both hunter and hunted in this picture are black skinned/coated is of next to no importance, and the protagonist's Europeanised speech and mannerisms makes him a poor choice for African American audience identification.

The 'quasi' definition of blaxploitation horror I mentioned earlier also extends to works such as *Black Voodoo*, *The Omega Man*, and *Welcome Home Brother Charles*. Although two of the main goodguys in *Black Voodoo* are African American (a temporarily blind ex-football great, and the pretty orderly who just happens to be his biggest fan), the film's monsters-a disembodied cult leader seeking revenge against the doctors who failed to save his life, and the nurse whose body he inhabits in order to commit his heinous crimes-are both white. In *Omega Man*, the monstrous albino plague victims are of diverse racial backgrounds, but now the hero is a white man (Charlton Heston, no less) who sacrifices himself, Christ-like, in the film's final scene. Last but certainly not least, we come to *Welcome Home Brother Charles*, an ultra-low budget production written and directed by African American filmmaker Jamaa Fanaka while he was still attending U.C.L.A. Marlo Monte stars as Charles Murray, a reticent black man who is nearly castrated by a racist cop, then sent to prison for a crime he did not commit. While there, he gets subjected to a series of bizarre medical experiments which greatly increase the size and facility of his genitalia. In the film's signature scene, Charles sneaks into the suburban home of his antagonist's partner, quickly seduces the man's wife, and strangles him with a super-elongated, python-like penis. Despite its obvious exploitation of racial stereotypes, and its numerous aesthetic and technical shortcomings (the sound, for example, is so murky as to render much of the dialogue unintelligible), *Welcome Home Brother Charles* is a complex, ambitious, inspired film with subversive potential, insofar as it transforms (via the logic of *reductio ad absurdum*) a myth of black male freakishness into a fantasy of black male revenge. But the reason it falls under the heading of *quasi*-blaxploitation horror, rather than blaxploitation horror-proper, is that its monsters are without a doubt the hyper-racist police officers who are ultimately to blame for victim/hero Charles' unnatural condition.

Black Monsters

Having done the conceptual groundwork necessary in order to distinguish blaxploitation horror-proper from its proto and quasi cousins, we may finally turn our attention to the *monsters* of the subgenre. Here, it is important to evaluate Benshoff's claims concerning their progressive potential, and exposing the limitations of an investigation which places too much emphasis on monstrous metaphors and not enough on frequently recurring (one might even say obsessive) thematic concerns.

Benshoff's main contention is that the monsters of blaxploitation horror-the male ones in particular-were effectively 'reappropriated' so as to serve the goals (or at least fulfill the wishes) of African American audiences; at one point, he writes that "unlike the classical Hollywood horror film narrative, there is no need to punish or destroy the monsters. In fact, the reverse is true: the monsters kill the racist agents of 'normality', and the audience is expected to cheer these developments."[10] One primary means by which this "reappropriation of the monster as an empowering black figure" was accomplished involved "the softening, romanticising, even valourising of the monster."[11] Without a doubt, there is some truth to Benshoff's claims. Be that as it may, he still has not told us anything of interest about the blaxploitation horror subgenre *in particular*, as opposed to '70s horror cinema *in general*. And to make matters worse, despite his subsequent attempts at qualification, Benshoff's argument is over simplistic, relying far too heavily on an analysis of the first, best known, and most commercially successful blaxploitation horror film, William Crain's *Blacula*.

While it is certainly the case that *some* blaxploitation horror films refigure the (male) monster as tragic hero/victim (*Blackenstein*, in which an African American soldier returns home from Vietnam a quadriplegic before undergoing risky DNA experiments), romantic hero (*Blacula*, to be sure, and its less accomplished sequel, *Scream Blacula Scream!*), or avenger of white racism (*Sugar Hill*, *Welcome Home Brother Charles*), plenty of *other* blaxploitation horror films were more than satisfied keeping their male monsters distinctly unromantic. Equally, many of these 'black monsters' and none too interested in combatting racial prejudice (e.g., *The House on Skull Mountain*, *J.D.'s Revenge*, and such quasi-cases as *The Omega Man*, and, arguably, *Ganja and Hess*). In these latter films, the monster may indeed be black, but he is no less monstrous because of it. Thus, we may conclude that there is insufficient evidence to justify Benshoff's blanket claims in favour of blaxploitation horror's positive reappropriation of the monster, even the male ones. In one respect, the situation with blaxploitation horror was much like that of *non*-race oriented horror in the '70s, insofar as a number of these films possessed monsters who were sympathetic (e.g., *Sisters*, *Dawn of the Dead* [1978], *It Lives Again* [1978]), or at least justified in their extreme behaviour (e.g., the 'rape-revenge' cycle which flourished towards the end of the decade); while plenty of others had monsters who were just plain evil (including *The Omen* [1976], *Alien* [1979], and the decade's numerous 'revenge of nature' films, such as *Frogs* [1972], *Jaws* [1975], and *Squirm* [1976]).

Towards the end of his essay, Benshoff doubly qualifies his argument in favour of blaxploitation horror's progressive potential: first, he claims that most of the films in this subgenre, "like blaxploitation films in general, tend to uphold male-dominated (hetero)sexuality, and participat[e] in the genre's usual demonisation of women and nonpatriarchal sexualities." Secondly, he claims that "the lingering racist discourse of Negro bestiality...is evident in these films' makeup codes."[12] In support of this latter assertion, Benshoff cites the figures of Blacula/Mamuwalde (William Marshall), who, "when he gets his blood lust up...becomes almost lupine, with a hairy face and brow, a trope usually not used for more debonair white vampires", Abby Williams (Carol

Speed), who "also has facial hair and a deep voice", and *Blackenstein*'s Eddie Turner (Joe De Sue), with his "hairy hands" and Boris Karloff-inspired box top afro.[13] Benshoff might also have listed *The Beast Must Die*, in which a black woman (Marlene Clark, previously Ganja in *Ganja and Hess*) about to transform into a wolf is initially identified by the thick black hair which sprouts up on her arms.

Should the depiction of a few blaxploitation horror monsters as animalistic lead us to conclude that the subgenre as a whole, despite its efforts at progressive reappropriation, inevitably reinscribed racist tropes (e.g., that black people are more bestial or primitive than white people)? Certainly not. A more thorough and sensitive look at the data reveals the often extreme lengths makeup artists and other creative personnel went so as *not* to depict black monsters in stereotypical, much less racist, terms. In fact, the most one can claim about the monsters of blaxploitation horror as a group is that their physical monstrousness tended to be a function of either racial ambiguity or, to use Noel Carroll's phrase, "categorical contradictoriness."[14]

Let us begin with a few obvious examples, before making our way to some of the more controversial ones. First are those blaxploitation (including proto and quasi blaxploitation) horror films whose monsters are interracial, bi-racial, or otherwise ambiguous in their race-related physical characteristics. In *Omega Man*, the monstrous mutants who have temporarily taken over the planet (or at least California) are pale-skinned, robe-and sunglass-wearing zombies whose diverse racial origins, not to mention cultural heritages, get collapsed under the cult-like rule of a diabolical demagogue. True, viewers can still tell the difference between black and white victims of the plague, but this is more a contingent fact about the film's shabby production values than evidence of any concerted effort at preserving racial distinctions (the powder sprinkled on Rosalind Cash's afro simply does not cut it).

In *Dr. Black, Mr. Hyde*, the protagonist-a well-to-do African American doctor named Henry Pride (Bernie Casey)-is transformed by an experimental serum into a "white-skinned, blue-eyed killer who goes on [a] rampage in Watts."[15] As in *Omega Man*, audiences were not fooled by the black doctor's Caucasian countenance nearly as easily as were the film's gullible characters. As Isabel Pinedo has quoted, "although black[s] refer to the killer as 'a white dude', he looks more interracial than white, thus casting doubt on the claim the monster is racialised as white."[16] Unlike *Omega Man*, however, it is hard to believe that the monstrous Dr. Pride's interracial incarnation resulted from a lack of finances or effort; the man in charge of makeup, after all, was Stan Winston, who would gain a reputation as the best in the business four years down the road with *Alien* (1979). A more likely answer is that those behind the film wanted an African American version of Mr. Hyde, one who would invoke the monster's familiar fears of regression to a more primitive/uninhibited state of being (in previous film versions of the tale, Mr. Hyde was depicted as spider-like [1920] and ape-like [1931]) *without* promoting racist stereotypes of Negro bestiality. An ash-coloured psychopath with excessive facial clefts and an oversized forehead was the best Winston could come up with. It is worthwhile comparing the zombies of *Omega Man* and the post-metamorphosis Henry Pride with the *pre*-metamorphosis state of bigoted insurance salesman Jeff Gerber [Godfrey Cambridge] in Melvin Van Peeble's *Watermelon Man*

(1970). Although the latter film, ostensibly a comedy, traces Gerber's tortuous path from disgust to acceptance of his black roots, viewers are apt to find his initial appearance in 'whiteface' both disturbing and unconvincing, or perhaps simply disturbing *because* of its unconvincingness.

A number of other blaxploitation horror films managed to eschew traditional racist representational strategies by depicting the monster as racially ambiguous, although the means they employed to achieve this end were various, and did not always involve makeup resulting in an exaggeratedly interracial appearance. In *The Thing With Two Heads*, the monster is not so much interracial as *bi*-racial, in that the head of a dying white bigot gets transplanted onto the body of a black convict currently serving out a sentence on death row. Here it is not the mere two-headedness of the resulting Siamese which is intended to provoke terror (and laughter), but the 'unnatural' and inseparable union of races/faces. In *Scream Blacula Scream!*, despite the fact that an African American Renfield character is added to the mix, Blacula's victims now include a number of Caucasians who return from the dead as vampires, right alongside their black brethren. A similar bi(racial)furcation of the monster takes place in *The Beast Must Die*, when we discover at film's end that the black werewolf under attack all along was *not* the African American woman with hairy arms (mentioned above), but an Anglo Saxon male who just happened to infect her. Even *Blackenstein* introduces us to a second, white patient of Dr. Stein's, one whose side-effects from a series of animal DNA injections (including a leg which looks like that of a giraffe) are far more bestial than Eddie Turner's.

And what of Abby Williams, a female blaxploitation horror monster whom Benshoff claims is *doubly* reinscribed, in that, after her possession by the West African Yoruba spirit Eschu, she is depicted in terms both racist (through "facial hair and a deep voice") and sexist ("[her] appetites are figured as grotesque and in need of eradication"[17])? It is true that once possessed, Abby adopts a more traditionally masculine deportment, becoming increasingly aggressive and forsaking the security of monogamy for the thrills of casual sex. But like her white prototype, Regan MacNeil (Linda Blair of *The Exorcist* [1973]), her 'bestiality' is primarily *behavioural* rather than physical. Only a couple of times during the course of the picture is Abby depicted with patches of bushy hair on her skull and brow, and then only via insert shots; most of the time, her clothing, language, and conduct code her as a hyper sexual/'loose' woman. And whenever she speaks in an unnaturally deep voice, it is obvious that Eschu (a male god) is the one doing the talking. In short, any claim to the effect that *Abby* promotes racist stereotypes via its physical rendering of the (here female) monster simply does not hold up under scrutiny.

The charge of sexism in this film is more difficult to defend against, considering that the main symptom of Abby's possession is her wanton sexuality, a symptom which is contained and eventually discharged by an African/Catholic priest (*Blacula*'s William Marshall, this time in the role of saviour). But just as with Diana Hill (Marki Bey) in *Sugar Hill*, Abby's turn from demure good girl to deadly seductress can easily be read in positive terms, as a form of *empowerment*, despite any messages to

Sugar Hill

the contrary. Darius James goes so far as to label Abby's former identity as a "closed-kneed minister's wife" a "masquerade",[18] and Benshoff himself admits that Diana/Sugar's Afrocentric hyper sexuality is a "sign of...power" *as well as* of "monstrosity and violence."[19] The most important point to make here, however, is that any analysis of female blaxploitation horror monsters (or of female characters in blaxploitation films generally) which attempts to discriminate sharply between issues of race and issues of gender is bound to neglect the extent to which 'black woman-*qua*-black woman' stood as its own, unique representational category. This is one which possessed its own, unique set of problems, challenges, and concerns.

Blaxploitation Horror: New Traits of Terror

The above discussion indicates that if we want to discover anything of interest about the blaxploitation horror subgenre *per se* it is not adequate to base an analysis on blaxploitation horror *monsters*. These form far too heterogeneous and racially ambiguous a lot to justify any general claims concerning their allegorical import. As the above survey attempts to show, these monsters are not so much metaphors as *anti*-metaphors, figures who represent a self-conscious-and for the most part successful-effort on the part of their creators (including writers, directors, actors, and makeup artists) *not* to promote any particular socio-political agenda. A more fruitful approach to take to this subgenre is one which identifies and investigates those central themes and issues which turn up again and again in a wide selection of blaxploitation horror films, and which turn up very *in*frequently (for obvious reasons) in horror films lacking a discernible racial component. Before concluding, we can at least try and pave the way for future studies by making mention of a few (related) themes central to the blaxploitation horror subgenre, themes which also reappear in a number of contemporary race horror films.

1. In at least six of the films here under investigation (*Abby*, *Sugar Hill*, *The House on Skull Mountain*, *Watermelon Man*, *The Omega Man*, and *Welcome Home Brother Charles*), the prospect of interracial coupling is explicitly raised and addressed. In not *one* of them is the heterosexual union between black person and white person (whether actual or still merely potential) represented in unproblematic terms. Considering the decade, this is none too surprising: studies indicate that, between the years 1970 and 1980, black-white marriages in the United States increased by roughly 125%, from a mere 65,000 couples to more than 165,000.[20] The anxiety experienced in both population groups as a result of this dramatic increase in size and visibility was reflected in blaxploitation horror films in a number of different ways. In *Abby* and *Sugar Hill*, for example, potent black women use their charms-both sexual *and* supernatural-to seduce white men, albeit for instrumental purposes only: Abby/Eschu cruises a white guy at a bar while searching for victims, and Diana/Sugar flirts with the gangster boss responsible for her boyfriend's death as a way of facilitating her revenge. The

Candyman

genders are reversed, but not the pragmatic (as opposed to romantic) motivation, in *Welcome Home Brother Charles*, as Charles' phallic powers include the ability to hypnotize white housewives and make them his sexual slaves.

Although the possibility of an equal, loving interracial relationship at least gets considered in *The Omega Man*, the film operates so as to undercut this possibility through bad jokes ("If I was the only boy in the world, and you were the only girl… Well, I'm the only boy!") and convenient turns in the narrative (the first kiss between Dr. Neville [Heston] and Lisa [Rosalind Cash] gets interrupted by a surprise attack; Neville dies before the couple get a chance to consummate their relationship). Similarly, in *The House on Skull Mountain*, the budding romance between white anthropologist Andrew Cunningham (Victor French) and black heiress Lorena Christophe (Janee Michelle) is spoiled by the strange-but-true fact that the two are actually cousins. *Watermelon Man* at least affords an interracial couple the opportunity to go to bed together, but significantly, the white woman Gerber sleeps with is *European*, not American, and once her desire to engage with him only as a sexual plaything (rather than as a fellow human being) is brought into the open, she shows her true colours by accusing him of rape.

It was not until the release of Wes Craven's *The Serpent and the Rainbow* in 1988 that a race horror film managed to depict a black-white relationship in romantic, mutually satisfying terms. But by far the most complex and extended treatment of this theme occurs in Bernard Rose's *Candyman* (1992). In this film, the eponymous monster is a black man who was tortured and killed in the late 1800's for impregnating the daughter of a white landowner. A century later, Candyman (Tony Todd) returns for the soul-and body-of his reincarnated lover. Concerning the relationship between Candyman and Helen Lyle (Virginia Madsen), Pinedo asserts that "as the interracial romance of the past once conjured up disgust and loathing in the white mob, so the suggestion of intimate contact with Candyman conjures up body horror in the audience."[21] Pinedo is here recapitulating the work of Judith Halberstam, who in 1995 wrote that "ultimately…, horror [in *Candyman*] stabilises in the ghastly body of the black man whose monstrosity turns upon his desire for the white woman."[22] Claims such as these are supported by the fact that, upon kissing Helen for the first time, Candyman's mouth and coat open to reveal a multitude of swarming bees.

As is so often the case with both blaxploitation and contemporary race horror films, however, an alternative, even contradictory interpretation to what is perhaps the most obvious one may reasonably be proffered. Considering how much Candyman suffered as a result of hooking up with a white woman in the first place, it comes as something of a surprise to discover that-like Imhotep (the original Mummy) and Blacula/Mamuwalde before him-Candyman hunts his prey *not* out of hatred or revenge, but out of a desire to (re-)unite. In order to lure Helen to his fortress-tenement, he kidnaps a black infant, thereby providing the final member of an (admittedly dysfunctional) interracial family, and sending a message-to audiences, as well as to those in the film-that *nothing*, not even the most horrible of deaths, will prevent such families from coming into being. As with *Welcome Home Brother Charles* and *Sugar Hill* (at the conclusion of which a bride-seeking Haitian demigod carries off the scantily-clad girlfriend of Sugar's antagonist), white male fears of a black man-beast come to take away their women are exposed and critiqued in *Candyman*, precisely *because* of the way such fears are hyperbolically, even monstrously, concretised. What we have here is an African American-initiated 'return of the repressed' with a vengeance. Indeed, it must be noted that, at least according to Freud, such returns inevitably bring with them concomitant releases of anxiety.

Two additional themes prevalent in both blaxploitation and contemporary race horror films which are well worth exploring in detail, but which we can only make mention of here:

2. The sundry ways in which traditional African religions, voodoo especially, are figured as compatible with (rather than exclusive of) Christian forms of worship, Catholicism in particular. Hardly a blaxploitation or race horror film has been made which does not at least touch on the subject. Prime examples include *Scream Blacula Scream* (in which voodoo is referred to as an "exceedingly complex science"), *Abby*, *Sugar Hill*, *Black Voodoo*, *The House on Skull Mountain*, *Ganja and Hess*, *The Possession of Joel Delaney* (1972), *The Serpent and the Rainbow* (in which a black doctor asserts that "there is no conflict between my science and my faith"), *The Believers* (1987), *Headhunter* (1990, in which a Professor of "Pan African Studies" admits to "mov[ing] freely between cultures"), *Vampire in Brooklyn* (1995; another Craven job, albeit a less accomplished one), and the third "tale" in the Spike Lee-produced *Tales From the Hood* (1995).

3. Various takes, some a great deal more self-aware (or at least more sensitive) than others, on the familiar racist fear of modern white 'civilisation' being infiltrated/infected by 'primitive' black interlopers. For example, the opening of *The Beast Must Die* follows a desperate and isolated black man as he tries to escape a small army of whites who are hunting him down in a forest with incredibly sophisticated technology, including sound sensors, hidden cameras, and hi-powered rifles. Eventually, the black man makes his way towards a clearing, only to find himself on the well-manicured lawn of what appears to be the property of an Anglo Saxon aristocrat. As he runs towards the party of white people sitting just a few yards away, shots ring out, and in full view of everyone assembled, the man falls dead to the ground. But not really. We quickly learn that the black man-who remains very much alive-is actually owner of the land upon which he has just been 'killed': the entire hunt was a sort of survival game (with blanks for bullets), and the entire cadet of soldiers all work for him. What we discover here, once again is that blaxploitation horror films can be a great deal more complex and interesting than their critics have allowed.

Notes

1. Harry M. Benshoff, 'Blaxploitation Horror Films: Generic Reappropriation or Reinscription?', *Cinema Journal*, Volume 39, Number 2 (Winter 2000), 31-50 (p.31).
2. Ibid., p.31.

3. Ibid., p.37.

4. Ibid.

5. Ibid., p.42-43.

6. Ibid., p.33. See also Ed Guerrero, *Framing Blackness: The African American Image in Film* (Philadelphia: Temple University Press, 1993), pp.69-112.

7. Manthia Diawara and Phyllis R. Klotman, 'Ganja and Hess: Vampires, Sex, and Addictions', *Black American Literature Forum*, Volume 25, Number 2 (Summer 1991), 299-314 (p.301).

8. Benshoff, p.43.

9. Diawara and Klotman, p.299

10. Benshoff, p.37.

11. Ibid.

12. Ibid., pp.40, 42.

13. Ibid., p.42.

14. Noel Carroll, *The Philosophy of Horror; or, Paradoxes of the Heart* (New York: Routledge, 1990), pp.42-52.

15. Isabel Cristina Pinedo, *Recreational Terror: Women and the Pleasures of Horror Film Viewing* (Albany: State University of New York Press, 1997), p.115.

16. Ibid.

17. Benshoff, p.41.

18. Darius James (a.k.a. Dr. Snakeskin), *That's Blaxploitation! Roots of the Baadasssss 'Tude (Rated X by an All-Whyte Jury)* (New York: St. Martin's, 1995). p.163.

19. Benshoff, p.42.

20. Roberta P. McNamara, Maria Tempenis, and Beth Walton, *Crossing the Line: Interracial Couples in the South* (Westport: Prager, 1999), p.5.

21. Pinedo, p.129.

22. Judith Halberstam, *Skin Shows: Gothic Horror and the Technology of Monsters* (Durham: Duke University Press, 1995), p.5.

'Jonesing' James Bond: Co-opting Co-optation and the Rules of Racial Subordination

Christopher S. Norton & Garrett Chaffin-Quiray

Configuring Co-optation

The impact of James Bond on all spy thrillers following *Dr. No* (Terence Young, 1962) and the success of *Goldfinger* (Guy Hamilton, 1964) cannot be overstated. These films were originally released at an historical moment when the economic dominance of Hollywood's studio system was being diminished by competing media, including television and alternative international cinemas. Hollywood's 'disconnection' with contemporary audiences and various socio-cultural changes (not the least of which being racial and gender-oriented strife), resulted in the successful formulae of the James Bond franchise being quickly taken up in film, television and popular literature. Partly this 'Bondian' influence has to do with 007's ability to master all manner of intrigue and resolve complicated narrative conflicts within a two-hour movie. Equally, this influence has to do with the methods used to resolve these narrative conflicts that affirm more traditional Hollywood myths through 007's ever-ready male libido and skill with using various machines and weapons, negotiating unusual social situations and enjoying an assortment of female partners. When turning to blaxploitation as another of Hollywood's attempts to recapture increasingly detached audiences in the early 1970s, it is no wonder that one finds Bondian tropes liberally sprinkled in the films to organize narrative action.

Produced near the end of the blaxploitation cycle, *Cleopatra Jones* (Jack Starrett, 1973) and *Cleopatra Jones and the Casino of Gold* (Charles Bail, 1975) are two excellent examples of Bondian influence on spy thrillers. They indicate how alternative approaches to popular cinematic genres depend on, and depart from, established conventions. This is both because the Jones franchise is a product of, and response to, the 007 formula, but also because the two Jones films respond to the newly re-established classical Hollywood values of the James Bond franchise by reflecting them through the lens of racial and gender difference. Whether it be the exotic and far-flung locales, ingeniously concealed and excessive weaponry, or how Cleo manages to escape from even the most implausible snares set by her nemeses, the Bondian sub-text is never pushed too far below the surface. Equally, Bond provides the guiding principle against which Cleopatra Jones expresses her diegetic mastery, while also providing direction for production staffers who would use her precedent to expand the expressive domain for 007.

By the mid-1970s, and as the figurehead of an increasingly popular espionage culture, James Bond would not be out-performed by an outrageously bedecked female black action hero. His persona would grow to absorb Cleo's most outrageous deviations from his formulae by co-opting her co-optation to affirm 007's dominance of the spy-thriller genre. Simultaneously, 007's rise to the top of the box office would also symbolise the return of a new, and economically stabilised, Hollywood studio system based on updated genres, franchise production, inclusion of the historic 'Other' in narrative action and new uses of topicality to organise story points and characterisation. With Roger Moore's first appearance as James Bond in *Live and Let Die* (Guy Hamilton, 1973), these Hollywood co-optations of blaxploitation find Bond dispatching a number of voodoo practicing and heroin smuggling black gangsters who wallow in the style made popular by blaxploitation movies, among them the Cleopatra Jones cycle. The term co-optation signifies a strategy of appropriation that operates beyond a simple borrowing of tropes or even homage. It incorporates a level of critique and response to the very things it cites. Together, these films display a remarkably tangled web of co-optation strategies as they apply to race in the cultural backdrop of Hollywood.

By recognising this web and then examining the period of blaxploitation as it applies to Hollywood, generally, and the spy-thriller genre more specifically, several over-riding themes of cultural production become self-evident. Not only has Hollywood co-opted black aesthetics, themes and images through its blaxploitation genre during a time of economic crisis and popular disconnection, but the Cleopatra Jones films have co-opted the male-dominated blaxploitation cycle in combination with the Bondian formula. Finally, though, texts like *Live and Let Die* co-opt blaxploitation, including the Jones films, to re-affirm the dominance of white-male-dominated spy-thrillers atop the box office treasure chest. This action returns the racial and gender-based Other to a more historically familiar position of missionary subordination.

The Emergence of Blaxploitation

Most discussions surrounding the birth of blaxploitation point to Melvin Van Peebles' film *Sweet Sweetback's Baadasssss Song* (1971) as the inspiration, and pivotal expression, for the formula. Regardless of the various late 1960s movies that began centering on black themes and aesthetics like *Cotton Comes to Harlem* (Ossie Davis, 1970), *The Liberation of L.B. Jones* (William Wyler, 1970) and even *Guess Who's Coming to Dinner* (Stanley Kramer, 1967), *Sweetback* represents a turning point in black-oriented films because it dismisses assimilation, views the dominant system as corrupt and then chooses to fight against it, both from the level of what it depicts and the methods used to produce that depiction.

As critics such as Donald Bogle, Ed Guerrero and Mark Reid have pointed out, *Sweetback* arose out of the Black Power movement of the 1960s when the rift between a white-dominated mainstream culture and black-expressed sub-culture was widening to allow space for truly alternative expressions of difference. This militant

Live and Let Die

spirit sprang from "the rising political and social consciousness of black people (taking the form of a broadly expressed black nationalist impulse at the end of the civil rights movement)."[1] It also capitalised on the splintering cultural values of the times that increasingly saw a simultaneous mainstream integration of cultural multiplicity and a strident expression of cultural distinction outside of that mainstream. "Otherness" and difference in the arts and media became centers of popular consumption and cultural affirmation in as much as the traditional systems of artistic expression hopelessly behind the times.

Viewed through the lens of an industrial history, blaxploitation arose at a critical juncture for Hollywood. From an all-time crest of commercial activity and weekly attendance in the mid-1940s to an all-time low point of commercial loss in the mid-1960s, mainstream Hollywood was in financial peril. Several of the major studios were losing millions of dollars on an annual basis forcing them to face the distinct prospect of bankruptcy for the first time in their history.[2] Other key studios were responding to the changing financial times by diversifying their interests into television production or by consolidating their assets through the sale of valuable film libraries, back lot acreage and the cancellation of contract talent. Hollywood's decline also stemmed from the divestiture and divorcement of film production from film distribution and exhibition channels that had solidified the hold of Hollywood on popular culture in the 1930s.

Sweet Sweetback's Baadasssss Song introduced the force of the Black Power movement to the screen as a counterpoint to the depiction of white hegemony partly because it was a wholly independent black production and because it centered its narrative action on the experiences of a black 'outlaw.' Writer, director and star Melvin Van Peebles made the film outside the conventional system by claiming it was a porn production so as to escape hiring a union crew, being forced to pay scale rates and, therefore, participate in the film industry his film was attempting to disrupt.[3] Not only did this decision stem from the shrewdness of his artistic vision to create a film styled with the contributions of black artists, including the musical group Earth, Wind and Fire, but it was his example of using financial limitation to his advantage. The result was a raw, angry and unpolished film that resembled the neorealist and New Wave movements popular in the times, if not the budding genre of pornographic and exploitation films. On a budget of $500,000 ($50,000 of which was contributed by Bill Cosby), Van Peebles shot the film in nineteen days and was picked up for distribution by Cinemation, an independent distribution channel then carving out business for itself from the space leftover by the Consent Decrees.[4] By the end of 1971, and despite its amateurish style, decidedly adult-oriented content, anti-white sentiment and a lack of mainstream studio backing, *Sweetback* had grossed nearly $10 million without the benefit of Hollywood's distribution system or exhibition alliances which was a huge success for the era.[5]

Live and Let Die

The success of *Sweetback* helped Hollywood leaders realise the power of the black ticket buying public, which accounted for more than 30 percent of the box office in major cities.[6] Hollywood quickly seized onto the profitability of the *Sweetback* formula and spawned a cycle of film's dedicated to black male and female characters. For instance, *Shaft* (1971), directed by Gordon Parks, marked the beginning of Hollywood's overt attempt to cash in on *Sweetback*'s success. Despite its black director and small budget relative to studio norms, the film was in fact financed by MGM, a fact which marks the movement of the Hollywood studios towards capitalising on emergent alternatives to its worn out genres and practices to re-affirm its position of commercial dominance. With regard to *Shaft*, Donald Bogle writes that, "This little picture, which its studio, MGM, thought might make a little money, instead made a mint–some $12 million within a year in North America alone–and single-handedly saved MGM from financial ruin."[7]

The financial success of both *Shaft* and *Sweetback* was not lost on anyone within the film community and in the four years following *Shaft* some 60 blaxploitation films were made. Some of the more remarkable examples from this movement include *Black Caesar* starring Fred "The Hammer" Williamson (Larry Cohen, 1973), *Hell Up in Harlem* (Larry Cohen, 1973), *The Legend of Nigger Charlie* (Martin Goldman, 1972), *Boss Nigger* (Jack Arnold, 1975), *Bucktown* (Arthur Marks, 1975), *Slaughter* starring ex-Cleveland Browns running back Jim Brown (Jack Starrett, 1972), *Black Mama, White Mama*, with a story by Jonathan Demme which he sold for $500 (Eddie Romero, 1972), *Coonskin* which was an animated dig at the entire cinematic history of black representation (Ralph Bakshi, 1975), *Blacula* (William Crain, 1973) and *The Spook Who Sat by the Door* which was not strictly blaxploitation inasmuch as it is a politico-cinematic exploration of Black Power taken to its ultimate conclusion (Ivan Dixon, 1973).

Despite these many examples and the general critical opinion that blaxploitation expresses a different tone on established generic principles, there are questions surrounding the idea of what constitutes a blaxploitation film. Confusion over the point stems from there being no pure example of the cycle when given the range of stories and genre conventions sampled in the movement which are as varied as mainstream films, although action and adventure inform every movie as basic structural devices. Violence and guns also appear in the films, as do central characters and aesthetic values co-opted from black artists and black cultural producers.

What differentiates blaxploitation movies from mainstream films of the 1970s, then, is the predominance of black characters in the narratives that stretch across most known genres to constitute a cinematic movement more than to establish a new genre on the basis of a coherent set of symbols, themes and conventions. Most blaxploitation films also use a "good/black versus white/evil allegory"[8] that equates whiteness with criminality and 'deviant' sexuality in much the same way the white-male dominated mainstream culture has historically used the reverse allegory to justify demeaning depictions of blacks in popular culture. This black versus white dichotomy was the defining element of *Sweetback* and the chief co-

opting measure of the movement that centered itself on previously marginalized people by, instead, marginalizing the white race typically represented at its centre. Writing on the subject Guerrero says that *Sweetback*, "tells the story of a "bad nigger" who challenges the oppressive white system and wins, thus articulating the main feature of the blaxploitation formula."[9] In turn, *Shaft*'s main antagonist comes in the form of the white mafia kingpin who kidnaps a black gangster's daughter and sets the film's narrative action in motion.

Following *Shaft*'s success, 1972 saw the proliferation of blaxploitation films and the further expansion of the cycle's focus. One of the most notable examples was the independently produced *Superfly* (directed by Gordon Parks Jr.). This elevated 'the life' of urban dwellers whose world revolves around drugs, sex, pimping, gambling and guns. It centres on a drug dealer named Young blood Priest (Ron O'Neal), whose goal is to retire from the street by scoring a million dollars of cocaine and living on the profits.

While related to other strands in the popular media of the time (especially the fiction of Iceberg Slim and Donald Goines), Priest's retirement comes at the expense of the black community. By setting up an overtly destructive act in flooding the black community with one million dollars worth of cocaine, Priest expresses the peculiarly American impulse to succeed through entrepreneurial risk and, in the process, he manages to outwit his white adversaries thus adhering to blaxploitation's general thematic structure. That his cocaine sale augers untold destruction within the community he comes from only serves to plant the seeds of discontent that would divide blaxploitation's predominantly black audience and eventually dissolve the movement altogether.

With *Sweetback*, *Shaft* and *Superfly* firmly in the popular eye, the period from 1972-1974 saw the bulk of blaxploitation production and the release of a new film in the cycle every few weeks. Expressing a mixture of concern and admiration on the movement, the cover of the October 23, 1972 issue of *Newsweek* features the face of John Shaft (Richard Roundtree) with the headline, 'Black Movies: Renaissance or Ripoff?' The accompanying article states that, "In an industry that has recently been producing little more than 200 films a year, fully one-fourth of those now in the planning stage are black."[10] However true this statement may be from the standpoint of movie subjects in the early 1970s, this black movie boom was not the result of blacks gaining control in the white controlled film industry. As Bogle points out:

> What became most disturbing was that while these movies appeared to be black (in concept, in outlook, in feel) and while they were feverishly promoted and advertised as such, they actually were no such thing. Many of the new black-oriented films were written, directed, and produced by whites [sic]. Worse, many of the new movies were often shot on shoestring budgets, were badly directed, and were technically poor. The film industry hoped simply to make money by indeed exploiting an audience need.[11]

This fact was not lost on audiences and critics of the films who sharply increased their criticism after *Superfly*. As quickly as blaxploitation rose to prominence by co-opting and adjusting the principles of established action genres, including the spy thriller, production of black-oriented, if not strictly blaxploitation, films fell off in number near the end of 1974. Addressing the reasons for this decline Guerrero writes:

> Another factor that contributed directly to the demise of blaxploitation was Hollywood's perception, near the end of 1973, that black audiences were tiring of the industry's cheap, endless reworkings of the crime-action-ghetto blaxploitation formula [sic]. Accordingly, the film industry realised that it did not need an exclusively black vehicle to draw the large black audiences that had saved it fromfinancial disaster. This important point was underscored when surveys showed that as much as 35 percent of the audience for the megahits *The Godfather* (1972) and *The Exorcist* (1973) was black.[12]

Blaxploitation did carry on past this threshold year of 1973 with such reflexive films as *Willie Dynamite* (Gilbert Moses, 1974). Still, the movement was largely over by the end of 1975 when considering the quantity and complexity of black dominated movies that could be clearly traced through the paternity of *Sweetback*, *Shaft* and *Superfly*.

Cleopatra Jones: Black, Beautiful, and Bond-ed

Coming as they did towards the end of the blaxploitation cycle, *Cleopatra Jones* (1973) and *Cleopatra Jones and the Casino of Gold* (1975) both interact with, and depart from, the formulae and themes of the movement. Along with Pam Grier's heroines in films like *Foxy Brown* (Jack Hill, 1974), Tamara Dobson's Cleopatra Jones embodies the female counterpart, and critique, of the previously male-dominated blaxploitation cycle. Both Jones films lack the graphic sex scenes that marked movies such as *Shaft* and there is none of the glorification of drugs so roundly criticised in movies like *Superfly*. In fact, and as a sort of counterpoint to *Superfly*'s montage of casual cocaine use, *Cleopatra Jones* shows a prolonged scene where Cleo and her boyfriend watch a man going through severe withdrawal symptoms.

Further adjusting the scope of the racialised good/black versus white/evil allegory present in blaxploitation movies from *Sweetback* onwards, both Jones films substitute white lesbian drug lords as their chief antagonists to centre on a feminised cinematic world set against a sexist, white mainstream. In addition, there is a well-constructed intertext between the Jones movies and the James Bond franchise. This connection puts *Cleopatra Jones* at a critical and historical juncture where her characterisation continues to expand the representation of blackness beyond the standard of male-centred blaxploitation films while also directly linking her with the Bondian spy-thriller genre to co-opt some of its themes for added commercial flare.

While released relatively late in the blaxploitation cycle, *Cleopatra Jones* displays many elements of previous blaxploitation films. It revolves around the black

Live and Let Die

character of Cleopatra Jones, a 'special agent' for the United States government who is sexually symbolised by her clothing and possessions and who is able to communicate within and across the black community with apparent comfort and ease. When necessary she is capable of violent, martial arts-laden outbursts of sheer force and destruction and she is filled with a heroic ability to oppose white people depicted as cartoonishly evil and anti-black in their specific narrative goals.

The film begins with Cleo globetrotting to Turkey where she oversees the destruction of poppy fields controlled by the lesbian drug lord, Mommy (Shelly Winters), who has been growing the crop for distribution in the black inner city. In response to the crop's destruction, Mommy becomes outraged and attempts to avenge herself on Cleo by having the police bust a drug rehab centre run by her boyfriend. Subsequently, Cleo continues to complicate Mommy's illicit business ventures that typically intend to target some section of the black community and as a result she continuously tries to have Cleo killed. By the film's end, Cleo dispatches Mommy and her agents and affirms the power of her black femininity over an evil, white (lesbian) foe that would destroy both her and the black community, for profit. As is the case with most spy thrillers after the success of the early Bond movies, *Cleopatra Jones* has borrowed much from 007. Quite obviously, Cleo is a special agent working to undermine the drug trade in the United States, she has an arsenal of specialised equipment and unusual weaponry and she is frequently forced to rely on the strength of her cunning and hand-to-hand martial abilities. At the time of its release the similarities with 007 were missed by no one as critics called Cleo "a black distaff James Bond."[13] Like Bond, who seldom tried to hide his identity by usually using his real name during introductions and relying on his being recognized as 007, Cleo is not a stealthy character trying to infiltrate the underworld by losing her identity. She never goes undercover and instead relies on her flamboyance and ability to be recognized to disrupt the plans of her enemies. Also like Bond, she drives a flashy car outfitted with hidden compartments containing machine guns and sundry other equipment specialized for her various adventures.

In many ways, Cleo's outrageous outfits are analogous with Bond's dinner jackets and playboy wardrobe. Her three-foot hat brims and flowing fur robes are treated with respect and awe within the film, just as Bond's refinements are looked upon as the height of good taste. Their wardrobes also connote their sexuality but to different degrees and along gendered patterns. While Bond is often decked out in refined clothing that connotes his English-ness and power as a man, Cleo's clothes connote her as sexually available through their fetishistic qualities. Her frequent use of fur also links her sexuality to black misrepresentations of animality.

Cleopatra Jones and the Casino of Gold is also an excellent example of the Bondian influence on the spy thriller. In this sequel Cleo has been ordered to locate two black government agents who were posing as heroin buyers in Hong Kong. The two agents are sent to contact an Asian drug lord named Chen (Bobby Canavarro), who is trying to take over the Hong Kong drug trade a white lesbian drug lord named the Dragon Lady (Stella Stevens). The Dragon Lady, in turn, busts up the drug deal and kills Chen who has betrayed her. She then takes the two agents captive until she can verify their credentials as drug smugglers and houses them in her casino where they are pampered in luxury by her Asian sex slaves (who also turn out to be her adopted daughters).This fact doesn't prevent the Dragon Lady from incestuous lesbian love scenes that further characterise her evil deviance. During the search for the two agents, Cleo escapes from several traps set for her by the Dragon Lady. She eventually pays a visit to her casino where she rescues the two agents and kills her foe to end the film.

The Casino of Gold reflects its Bondian influences in several ways. Through modes of characterisation the Dragon Lady is called 'Mr. Big', which is clearly a masculine title that calls attention to her lesbianism while also resonating with the villain in both the novel and filmed version of *Live and Let Die*. The title of the Jones sequel itself also recalls two words often associated with Bond in that gold is used throughout the 007 franchise as a recurring title phrase though, oddly, gold plays no part in *The Casino of Gold*'s narrative. Casinos also appear with regularity in most Bond films where gambling table serve to demonstrate his superior wit, refinement and luck. In *The Casino of Gold* similar elements can be attributed to Cleo, however an intertext with other blaxploitation films complicates matters in that gambling is used to further characterise the much-celebrated criminal life. When Cleo sits down at the gambling table, she not only recalls Bond, but also the craps games so prevalent in other blaxploitation films thus simultaneously aligning her with his whiteness and her own generic heritage. This intertext of gambling, along with misperceptions of racial animality keeps Cleopatra Jones aligned with representations of blackness, and specifically the kind of blackness showcased in blaxploitation movies.

The importance of Cleo's separation from James Bond, though, lies in the complicated arena of co-optation itself because Cleo is not simply a black female copy, but a black female response to James Bond who bends the conventions and formulae surrounding 007 to serve another end. While the Jones films have co-opted Bond, they avoid a total fusion of her character with that of Bond because this process is an outright critique of the Bondian ideology. On the subject of the Bond films of the 1960s, Tony Bennett and Janet Woollacott have posited that they exert their unique pleasures and affirmations of older generic patterns by:

> Drawing together and working upon a series of ideological tensions in relation to the nation, gender and the Cold War, they operated both to shift and stabilise subject identities at a time when existing ideological constructions had been placed in doubt and jeopardy, when, if you like, the articulating principles of hegemony were in disarray and alternatives had not been successfully established.[14]

To this list of nation, gender and the Cold War, race can easily be added since race was an existing ideological constructions that blaxploitation was putting into doubt and jeopardy in the 1960s and 1970s.

The Bond films of the 1960s and their progeny in *Live and Let Die* can be seen as efforts to stabilise white hegemony in the face of global nationalist tensions and rising black militancy easily characterized by blaxploitation's heroes and the representation of previously excluded Others. On this subject Bennett and Woollacott have stated that, "[T]he geographical and racial distribution of villainy is also such that the villain is always a member of a non-Anglo-Saxon race."[15] More specifically this attempt to re-stabilize white hegemony towards the end of the blaxploitation cycle is a direct response to the economic crisis of Hollywood in an era when studio produced movies missed their commercial mark while alternative productions like *Sweet Sweetback's Baadasssss Song* discovered previously untapped audiences.

By expanding the characterisation of villainy to include whiteness, and lesbian whiteness at that, Cleo's appropriation of Bondian influences draws direct intertextual links with the 007 franchise thereby re-directing criticism of its racist elements directly back to James Bond himself. These intertextual connections form a symbolic bridge between the films where responses and critiques pass fluidly in the continuum of a shared pop cultural heritage acting in the space of public reception. This 'conversation' in light of the simultaneously diverging and converging heritages of the two film cycles is how Cleo maintains her firm footing in representations of blackness. Cleo's linkage with blaxploitation and the spy thriller genre also contributes to a potent, if not consistent, critique of the James Bondian mythology while at the same time promoting the distinctions between them so as not to fully whitewash her with his white-hegemonic heritage.

Live and Let Die: Bring on the Black Guys

Live and Let Die was the eighth James Bond film and the first to star Roger Moore in the title role. It opens to find agent 007 travelling to the United States to investigate missing agents who were surveying Dr. Kananga (Yaphet Kotto), the prime minister of the mythical Caribbean island of San Monique. Black thugs, who are tipped off about his arrival by Solitaire (Jane Seymour), Kananga's white tarot-card reading slave, quickly target Bond who becomes entangled with Mr. Big, a Harlem drug lord who turns out to be Kananga in disguise. Bond travels to San Monique and then to New Orleans where he uncovers Kananga's heroine operation and, after a series of chases, kills Kananga, ending his plans to consolidate all heroin distribution in the United States.

The film departs from most Bond plots by placing its emphasis on a drug-related criminal underworld (a blaxploitation staple) and not on a plan to disrupt world power structures more typical of earlier Bond films. From the start *Live and Let Die* changes its narrative emphasis and draws itself up along racial lines that place blackness as the primary agent of evil and whiteness as responsible for putting things back in order. As an obvious reversal of the black/white dichotomy in blaxploitation movies this conventional racial coding of protagonists and antagonists is in keeping with a return to form of the Hollywood machine, built up as it is on normative themes and easily mastered generic signals.

Because *Live and Let Die* was released during the height of the blaxploitation boom, and because part of its narrative organisation responds to this cycle, the influence of blaxploitation is self-evident. Noticing these connections, popular periodicals around the release of the film contain articles with such titles as 'The New Bond: Shaft in Reverse'[16] and 'In *Live and Let Die*, The Bad Guys Are Black'[17] speculating about the inter-relationship of the Bond film and the blaxploitation cycle then currently in vogue. *Live and Let Die* contains many elements of blaxploitation that have been reversed to accommodate its white protagonist. Where blaxploitation often had its black characters sleep with white women, Bond sleeps with the black CIA agent Rosie (Gloria Hendry) who turns out to be working for Kananga, therefore equating a presumably good black character with villainy. *Live and Let Die* centres itself in the urban world (Harlem and New Orleans) so common in blaxploitation movies while connections exist between Mr. Big and *Superfly*'s Priest, although *Superfly* glorified its drug pushing hero while *Live and Let Die* has cast the same figure with the paint brush of evil. The casting of Yaphet Kotto as the villain in *Live and Let Die* brings up other intertextual links to blaxploitation and independent race films of the 1960s. Kotto appeared in *Nothing But a Man* (Michael Roemer, 1964) and such blaxploitation films as *Across 110th Street* (Barry Shear, 1972), *Truck Turner* (Jonathan Kaplan, 1974), and *Friday Foster* (Arthur Marks, 1975.)

Though it is easy to see the extant text of *Live and Let Die* through the prism of blaxploitation rather than interpret the movie from within its socio-politico-cultural context as one of many films, the movie's producers cannot fully escape the determinations of blaxploitation regardless of their seeming indifference. Harry Saltzman, the producer of most of the early Bond films, seems to make the case in an interview with *New York Magazine* that *Live and Let Die* has nothing to do with blaxploitation. Rather he argues that the film was produced in a kind of cultural vacuum but at the same time implies that it is a humorous version of the blaxploitation formula.[18]

Despite the reasonableness of the chronology of events Saltzman cites during the making of *Live and Let Die*, his remarks are hard to swallow when considering the film's blatant appropriation of blaxploitation tropes that could have been avoided had the film truly been designed before the rash of early 1970s black centred films. The film is littered with pimpmobiles, outrageous dress in the blaxploitation tradition and background music that could have been written by Curtis Mayfield (the composer for *Superfly*).

Saltzman's use of a chronology to defend the film misses an important set of facts. While blaxploitation may in fact have originated with 1971's *Sweet Sweetback's Baadasssss Song*, the social pressures that made Van Peebles's film possible predated it with the emergence of civil rights agitation and the rise of alternative media practices in the 1960s, including direct cinema and television journalism. Then there is the fact of various films like *The Liberation of L.B. Jones* that predate *Sweetback* and depict black people as active and charismatic protagonists fighting against a corrupt system.

It is clear that *Live and Let Die* is a kind of 'white fantasy' filled with xenophobic designs, overt racism and sexism and stereotypical representations of other cultures that would also fuel many other 1970s mainstream films. This fantasy involves killing black men, sleeping with black women, and restoring whiteness to a position of power on the screen. Linking these presumptions to blaxploitation suggests that this white fantasy is no doubt provoked by the explosion of black orientated films seen through the period. The fantasy of killing black men and sleeping with black women without recrimination are also linked to blaxploitation's depiction of white evil-ness and white women being subjugated by black men. Bennett and Woollacott speak to the fantastic aspects of the Bond novels by writing that, "Attempts to explain the appeal of the novels have thus usually been couched in terms of the scope they offer for the gratification of repressed desires or for the realisation, by proxy, of otherwise unattainable pleasures."[19]

While the repressed desires fulfilled in *Live and Let Die* are those revolving around white dominance of minority cultures and the indomitable power of white hegemony, in reality, these desires are not repressed at all but de-stabilised in the

midst of Hollywood's post-War economic crisis. That *Live and Let Die* allows these semi-repressed desires to be openly voiced, enacted and shared by the white spectator because is surprisingly reactionary position when given the perceived liberalism and expressive reconstruction of the entire blaxploitation era. Thus, the co-optation of blaxploitation aesthetics and themes in *Live and Let Die* directs the white fantasies of retribution and hegemony towards the more militant black figures found in blaxploitation movies, specifically, and the Black Power movement and its refusal to assimilate, more generally.

The Interplay of Texts

Considering how fast Hollywood integrates successful formulas into its ongoing production cycle, it is reasonable to assert that *Live and Let Die* sought to capitalise on the ongoing success of blaxploitation if for no other end than the financial rewards its producers wished to reap at the box office. But the appropriated material in *Live and Let Die* also responds to the very co-optation of 007 tropes found in the *Cleopatra Jones* films, just as co-optation in both of these texts serves to facilitate criticism of the Bond movies. Speaking about the role of women in *The Spy Who Loved Me* (Lewis Gilbert II, 1977) Bennett and Woollacott write, "The main ideological work thus accomplished in the unfolding of the narrative is that of a 'putting-back-into-place' of women who carry their independence and liberation 'too far' or into 'inappropriate' fields of activity."[20] Extending this statement to *Live and Let Die* and its treatment of blacks, the film responds to blaxploitation's going 'too far' with its portrayal of whiteness as evil and reacts to the display of blacks in 'inappropriate fields of activity' such as black men sleeping with white women. This response and reaction is rooted in the white xenophobic fantasy of retribution and is represented, figuratively at least, by the re-centring of Hollywood after the destabilisation of the 1960s and 1970s.

Live and Let Die responds to black militancy and the refusal to submit to hegemony that is the underlying concern of nearly every blaxploitation film. It allows white spectators to assert their desires and fantasies of white power that have been toppled in blaxploitation. To enact this fantasy *Live and Let Die* calls up the world of blaxploitation as the site of ideological contest through methods of reverse co-optation that re-set white hegemony on top of the social order. In this capacity, co-optation functions as a method for subverting oppositional voices that were given a specific industrial space and commercial vehicle through black-centred movies following *Sweet Sweetback's Badasssss Song* and continuing through the movement's feminized cycle in the films about Cleopatra Jones.

By overcoming black figures in *Live and Let Die*, James Bond reclaims his space of unrivalled supremacy that was co-opted in espionage blaxploitation and he returns his screen persona to a site firmly rooted in white hegemony. To perform this hegemonic switch the film uses precisely the same strategy as both Jones films by appropriating blaxploitation's aesthetics and themes to direct its white-oriented response towards its black-empowered target. Just as Cleo displays her separateness from 007 to avoid association with his cycle's various levels of racism, 007 separates himself from black militant characters by reversing the black/white binaries set up in the blaxploitation movement meant to re-centre the marginalized black voice within the American mainstream. *Live and Let Die* surrounds Bond with the elements of blaxploitation but separates him from their influence except as topical settings to re-assert his superiority as both a character and hegemonic persona.

Both Jones movies and *Live and Let Die* are involved in a reciprocal relationship of co-optation. Due to changing economic needs and industrial strategies aimed at appropriating successful formulas in a moment of real doubt about the future of American studio-based film-making in the 1960s and 1970s this reciprocal co-optation functions at a much deeper level. It directly speaks to fermenting racial tensions then gaining currency in the popular media, television and music, and sets up lines of filiation and opposition between marginal and centric voices vying with white hegemony for representational supremacy.

In this capacity co-optation serves as its own form of espionage. By first co-opting mainstream generic conventions and inserting black aesthetics and themes into them, blaxploitation digested the ideological structures of the James Bond franchise through the guise of Cleopatra Jones and then sought to disrupt its ideological hold on at least one form of popular entertainment. That this project was not an overt decision characterised by concerted action across some strata of cultural producers but was, instead, the by-product of a socio-cultural moment is a testament to the various influences informing the moment. Likewise, *Live and Let Die* regurgitated some of blaxploitation's tropes to disrupt the movement's aspirations towards re-centring the mainstream with an oppositional voice. By using co-optation as their secret agent, these films used the cover assignment of seeking financial gain to undermine each other's ideological structures and, in this mission, co-optation succeeds to reaffirm the period's basic ideological currents.

Notes

1. Ed Guerrero, *Framing Blackness: The African American Image in Film* (Philadelphia: Temple University Press, 1993), p.67.
2. Ibid., pp.82-3.
3. Donald Bogle, *Toms, Coons, Mulattoes, Mammies, and Bucks: An Interpretive History of Blacks in American Films* (New York: Continuum, 1995), p.238.
4. Ibid., p.238.
5. Guerrero, p.86.
6. Ibid., p.83.
7. Bogle, p. 238.
8. Guerrero, p.98.
9. Ibid., p.86.
10. Charles Michener, 'Black Movies: Renaissance Or Ripoff?', *Newsweek*, (23 October 1972), 74-81 (p 77).
11. Bogle, pp.241-42.
12. Guerrero, p.105.

13. Mary F. Mebane, 'Brother Caring For Brother', *New York Times*, Section 13 (23 September 1973), 6 (p.6).

14. Tony Bennett and Janet Woollacott, *Bond and Beyond: The Political Career of a Popular Hero*. (New York: Methuen, 1987), p.280.

15. Ibid., p.72.

16. John Bryson, 'The New Bond: *Shaft* in Reverse', *New York Magazine*, (25 June 1973), pp.38-41.

17. 'In *Live and Let Die*, The Bad Guys Are Black.' *New York Times*, section 11 (15 July 1973), p.6.

18. Bryson, pp.39-40.

19. Bennett and Woollacott, p.15.

20. Ibid., p.39.

Hammer Goes East: A Second Glance at *The Legend of the 7 Golden Vampires*
I.Q. Hunter

Introducing the Legend

The Legend of the 7 Golden Vampires (1974) is one of Hammer's most engaging oddities–British cinema's first and only kung fu vampire film. Like many of the studio's later films *Legend* has attracted little positive comment. Because critical interest has focused on the classics directed by Terence Fisher and starring Christopher Lee and Peter Cushing, the revisionist experiments of Hammer's decline have tended to be overlooked or even despised. This is not unreasonable. Some of the films, such as *Dracula AD 1972* (1972), would defeat the most committed advocacy. A few, however, are well worth sympathetic re-evaluation, not least for their bewildering mix of styles and genres–the feminist romp *Slave Girls* (1968); the SF western *Moon Zero Two* (1969); the indescribably camp and surreal *The Lost Continent* (1968). Of these bold and eccentric films *The Legend of the 7 Golden Vampires* is by far the most likely to appeal to the current postmodern–and cult–taste for transnational cinema and generic hybridisation.

In this essay I've chosen to read *Legend* in the light of post-colonialism (although its setting of mainland China is not itself a British colony), placing it in the context of Hammer's populist imagining of the Other. My argument is neither that it is a post-colonial film in the fullest contemporary sense of the term–a deliberate, politically subversive reworking of imperialist myths–nor that it rethinks the horror genre from the point of view of the Other. Indeed at first glance, as Leon Hunt points out, *Legend* seems an unambiguously colonialist and even racist movie.[1] My argument is that although the film does reproduce colonialist tropes, its response to Otherness is more subtle and sympathetic than a first glance reveals.

Horror Before Hybridity: Hammer's Golden Years

Hammer's vampire films are versions of Romantic Gothic which tell a familiar story about British repression and sadistic sexuality. Emerging in a period of Cold War tension and moral panic about youth, *Dracula* (1958) and its sequels offered a decadent, pop-Freudian interpretation of the vampire as dangerous, gentlemanly and sexually voracious. With their coherence of setting, secured by repeated use of the same sets and locations, these films have a consistency of moral perspective that David Pirie ascribes to Fisher's clear-cut, fairy-tale separation of Good and Evil.[2] In Fisher's Manichean universe, Good is firmly associated with bourgeois values and restrained sexuality and Evil with flamboyant eroticism and violations of order and good taste.

The bold simplicity of Fisher's early films, with their grand metaphysical struggles and confident nostalgia for Victorian certainties, lends them enormous aesthetic appeal. But their strict demarcation of Good and Evil was merely the formal conceit of an ageing and conservative genre, and already inadequate to changing sexual and ideological trends. While in Stoker's novel Van Helsing embodied the spirit of the modern age, in the 1960s it was Dracula who seemed the more contemporary figure –an amoral James Bond-like rebel against sexual orthodoxy, whose seductions liberated rather than despoiled his victims.

By the end of the decade Hammer conceded what Robin Wood called the "obsolescence" of the traditional vampire and began to satirise it in revisionist films like *Taste the Blood of Dracula* (1968) and *The Vampire Lovers* (1970).[3] *Taste the Blood*, for example, inverted the genre's conventional moral scheme, eliciting sympathy for the young vampires slaughtering their hypocritical Victorian fathers. Elsewhere, in more questionable fits of creative desperation, Hammer transported Dracula into the dying days of Swinging London (*Dracula AD 1972* [1972] and *The Satanic Rites of Dracula* [1973], in which by a curiously Marxist twist he became a property developer). The Dracula of these films was a monosyllabic red-eyed beast; far removed from the tragic "English aristocracy of Christopher Lee's Dracula", which, as David Thomson remarks, was Hammer's most original contribution to the vampire sub-genre.[4] Weary of travestying his greatest role, Christopher Lee left the series after *The Satanic Rites* and did not appear in *Legend*.

Despite their formal experimentation the later vampire films still worked within the conservative moral framework of traditional Gothic. With a few exceptions, like *Taste the Blood of Dracula*, the revisionism was entirely on the surface. Hammer did not subvert the reactionary subtexts of the vampire film but merely subjected them to degrading camp pastiche. Lesbianism, for instance, though enthusiastically exploited in *The Vampire Lovers*, retained Hammer's usual associations of transgressive sexuality–wickedness, contagion, offensiveness to British moral standards.

Dracula Goes East

The Legend of the 7 Golden Vampires was Hammer's last and most outlandish attempt to update its Dracula franchise. An opportunistic fusion of genres and cultural references, it combined Gothic horror with elements of Hong Kong cinema, newly fashionable in the West with the success of Bruce Lee's *Enter the Dragon* (1973). Indeed, this was not the only British genre film that went East in search of reinvention. The Bond film *The Man with the Golden Gun* (1974), set in Phuket, Thailand and Hong Kong, also sent its hero to the Orient in pursuit of a rogue Westerner. Casting around for new sources of finance and inspiration Hammer made a deal with Run Run Shaw of Hong Kong's Shaw Brothers company to make two films on location in Hong Kong: *The Legend of the 7 Golden Vampires* and *Shatter* (1974). Don Houghton's script was directed by a sceptical Roy Ward Baker ("It was a good idea, not that I had any real taste for it and I didn't really want to do it but I did it"),[5] but for the sake of authenticity the martial arts scenes were choreographed by Chang Cheh, one of the Shaw Brothers'

Chinese directors. Commercially, *Legend* was a great success and did 'fantastic business' in Britain and the Far East.[6] It was not released in the USA until 1979, when a heavily cut version called *The Seven Brothers Meet Dracula* appeared.

Although unquestionably bizarre, *The Legend of the 7 Golden Vampires* strives for structural and thematic coherence. The plot itself is fairly straightforward. On a Chinese lecture tour in 1904 Van Helsing is persuaded by Hsi Ching, one of seven brothers, to help exorcise an ancient evil from the Szechwan village of Ping Kwei. Dracula, having possessed the body of a Chinese disciple, has revived the cult of the Seven Golden Vampires, who are kidnapping young women from the village and draining them of blood. Arriving at Ping Kwei Van Helsing oversees the vampires' defeat in extended kung fu fight sequences before staking Dracula in the traditional manner. Hearn and Barnes rightly suggest that film works rather like a western. Its main structural inspiration seems to have been *The Magnificent Seven* (1960), in which villagers also seek help to defeat marauding bandits[7]–although this film in turn had drawn on Kurosawa's *Seven Samurai* (1954). As Pete Tombs remarks, in terms of horror there was "no real attempt to use indigenous Eastern elements."[8] Horror was not a major genre in Hong Kong cinema at this time. The main local cinematic source would have been Chinese ghost stories, but these romantic melodramas had little resonance in the West, the film's primary market. In fact, it was Hammer's arrival in Hong Kong, combined with the global success of *The Exorcist* (1973), that inspired the horror genre's revival in the colony between 1974 and 1977.[9]

The generic blending is symbolised in the prologue, when Dracula takes possession of Kah: "two genres in one body", as Hunt remarks.[10] Stephen Teo reads the scene as a metaphor of cultural colonisation, of Hong Kong cinema's complicity with the West:

> The debate about globalization has centred on the question of western hegemony, US cultural imperialism, and this scene could be seen as an indicator of how globalization proceeds from the idea of dominance and repression. Is Hong Kong cinema the bearer of the Western image? Are we really Draculas in disguise? If you scratch us, do we reveal our true selves – that of Hollywood culture in the present instance? Such is the polemic of this scene...[11]

As Teo suggests, *Legend* cannot be accused of unauthenticity to Chinese traditions, for Hong Kong cinema has always been 'contaminated' by the example of the West. *Enter the Dragon*, the immediate influence on *Legend*, was itself a hybridised crossover film. As Leon Hunt explains:

> *Enter the Dragon* was arguably the first transnational Chinese-American action film... What Hong Kong and *Enter the Dragon* share is a similar sense of hybridity, of uncertain ownership and cultural affiliation. The film is most frequently damned as in authentic, neither one thing nor the other–too cheap and tacky for Hollywood, too cynical and packaged for Hong Kong.[12]

The Legend of the 7 Golden Vampires

To appreciate these films we should think of genres not as coherent, deeply embedded cultural myths, whose essence a film either captures or betrays, but rather as open storehouses of images, clichés and surface details. These are public goods for lively imaginations to appropriate and recombine. From this (admittedly postmodern) angle *The Legend of the 7 Golden Vampires* can be seen to anticipate the impure, larcenous aesthetic of recent generic hybrids such as *Near Dark* (1987), *Blade* (1998) and *From Dusk Till Dawn* (1996).

Interestingly, although *Legend* seemed idiosyncratic at the time, its fusion of Gothic and martial arts anticipated the highly successful Hong Kong *jiangshi dianying* (cadaver movies), which began with *Mr Vampire* (1985) and its sequels.[13] Because these films were not aimed at international audiences, they were free to rework the Western myth of the vampire in conformity with local traditions of the 'hopping vampire.' As Stephen Teo notes, although "indebted to Hollywood and to Britain's Hammer films, the cadavers [of such films] were a venerable part of Chinese folklore."[14]

In trying to create a new myth at the same time as it revived the existing one, *Legend* achieves a certain structural elegance. It succeeds mostly by pairing characters and themes, often in order to find correspondences between the two cultures. Van Helsing is balanced by Dracula–each is an ageing patriarchal figure who represents a stereotype of the West, rational science in Van Helsing's case and corrupt decadence in

Dracula's. There are seven brothers to match the seven vampires. Kah is twinned with the head of the local Tong: both of them rule criminal clans, respectively of vampires and gangsters. There are two cross-cultural romances, one between Van Helsing's son, Leyland, and Mai Kwei, the brothers' sister, and one between Hsi Ching and Vanessa Buren, the Scandinavian widow who finances the expedition. Similarly, to broaden the vampire myth from its strictly Western origins, vampires are made equally vulnerable to crucifixes and shrines of the Lord Buddha.

With its thematic doubling, sense of ritual (a prologue takes place in 1804, the finale exactly a hundred years later) and classic quest narrative, *Legend* has a less ramshackle air than the other late Dracula films. Equally, it integrates the two cultures and genres to surprisingly good effect. Admittedly, the influence of the Hong Kong kung fu film is largely restricted to the staging of set-piece fight sequences. There are certainly none of the subtle mythic and nationalist overtones that King Hu and Bruce Lee discovered in the genre.[15]

Vampires, Virgins and Vixens: Reflections on Sexuality

Legend of the 7 Golden Vampires is careful not to represent the East as totally Other. It is true-and unsurprising in an exploitation film-that it occasionally falls back on racist clichés about the exotic East-shots of comically gruesome 'foreign' food (headless frogs etc.); the grinning Tong leader who 'loses face' when Vanessa Buren rejects him; Kah's torture of beautiful young women, which perpetuates the identification of the Far East with exquisite sadism. On the other hand, Van Helsing goes out of his way to emphasise that China has had a sophisticated civilisation for 3000 years (the film makes use of the liberal ploy of having a Westerner speak up for the East). There are crucial ambiguities in the film's sympathetic portrait of China, but it is certainly far removed from the crudities of the Fu Manchu films or Hammer's earlier *Terror of the Tongs* (1961), which centred on a grotesque Fu Manchu-like crime lord who perpetrates 'fiendish' and bizarre bone-scraping tortures.

Legend's liberalism falters, however, in the matter of cross-cultural sex. The film is far more comfortable with romance between an Englishman and a Chinese woman than between her brother and a Western, though unusually self-assured, female traveller. At first it leans cautiously towards sexual as well as cultural equality. The portrayal of women is unusually sympathetic for a Hammer film. Vanessa Buren (Julie Ege), the film's main erotic interest, is one of the feistier representatives of 'Hammer glamour.' Widowed, rich and Scandinavian (a coded reference at a time when Scandinavia meant unbridled sexuality) she is, as Leyland remarks, "a totally liberated female." "Danger and excitement are like food and drink to me", she announces, insisting that she accompany Van Helsing on the expedition she has financed. Unlike most women in Hammer films she is neither virginal and repressed (as British women tend to be portrayed) nor demonised for her independence and sexuality.

Women who transgress Hammer's conservative vision of femininity are invariably coded as evil monsters, whether they are lesbians, Dracula's over-aroused victims, or merely old and sexless as in *The Brides of Dracula* (1960) and *The Gorgon* (1964). At times Hammer goes so far as to separate women into two archetypal categories: dark and dangerous, and blonde and passive. This scheme is at its most ruthless in *One Million Years BC* (1966) and *Slave Girls* (1967), in which hair colour ordains temperament, tribal allegiance and even location on the evolutionary scale. *Legend*, however, marks something of a change and its women characters are more appropriate to the early 1970s. Vanessa Buren manages a combination rarely seen in a Hammer film–blondeness, foreignness, virtue and 'liberation.' Mai Kwei, too, marks out new territory. Although at times a stereotype of the passive 'Oriental' woman–as when she is rescued from the vampires–she also takes part energetically in the fights against the Seven, anticipating the rise of the strong female kung-fu protagonist in local cinema. Yet in the end *Legend* does not deviate from Hammer's conventional representations of gender and fights shy of depicting sexual relations between a Chinese man and a white western woman, implying that such transgressive liaisons lead to tragedy. Vanessa Buren is bitten by a vampire–paying the price for her adventurousness–after which Hsi Ching kills her and then himself. Mai Kwei survives, however, presumably in some relationship with Leyland Van Helsing.

Legends of the Other

Most important in the film's recasting of the cultural associations of the vampire is its association of Dracula with the West rather than the East. In Stoker's novel Dracula is a symbol of Eastern infection, but in *Legend of the 7 Golden Vampires* he is emphatically an invader from the West. Hammer always downplayed the 'foreignness' of both Dracula and Van Helsing. Foreignness was an issue only when the arch-vampires were women, as in *Countess Dracula*, *The Vampire Lovers* and *Lust for a Vampire* (1971), where lesbianism was a sign of dangerously liberated continental sex. The 1958 *Dracula* suppresses any indication that either Van Helsing or Dracula, who is supposedly Transylvanian, hails from continental Europe. As Pirie notes, the entire film is set in "a slightly caricatured Victorian England."[16]

Whereas in *Nosferatu* (1922) and Universal's *Dracula* (1931) the vampire is a foreign and perhaps Semitic threat to the bourgeois West, Hammer's Dracula is a vehicle for domestic fears about sex and class. Christopher Lee portrays him as a displaced English aristocrat, the embodiment of an amoral, parasitic and dying class, whom Van Helsing defeats in the name of English middle class respectability. Rather than contamination from the East, Hammer's Dracula is a symbol of rapacious class privilege, a nostalgic bogey-man defeated by Van Helsing's bourgeois virility and know-how. Appropriately therefore, Peter Cushing does not reproduce the comic foreign accent of the novel's Van Helsing, as Anthony Hopkins does in *Bram Stoker's Dracula* (1992). In *Legend* he is the consummate English gentleman abroad, kitted out in Edwardian explorer's gear complete with colonial pith helmet.

In *Legend* Dracula's foreignness is unavoidably accented because he has now become a symbol of the West. He does not function as a figure of "reverse colonisation", as Ken Gelder suggests he does in Stoker's novel–an Easterner revenging

The Legend of the 7 Golden Vampires

himself upon the colonial powers.[17] In *Legend* he is a freelance Western colonialist abroad in mainland China. But like the traditional conception of Dracula he remains an emphatically mobile figure, whose threat is global and cross-cultural. As Gelder remarks, the vampire is unassimilated into any culture. He is "a 'cosmopolitan' or internationalised character who is excessive to national identities, whose lack of restraint threatens the very *notion* of identity."[18] Dracula's role in *Legend* is therefore highly ambiguous. On the one hand, he is a symbol of the evils of colonialism and the depravity of the Western ruling class. (In James Forbes-Robertson's dreadful performance, Dracula is a lurid caricature of 'decadence'–a rouged and lipsticked old queen, which lends a homoerotic air to his union with Kah.) On the other hand, he symbolises the dangers of cultural hybridisation, of crossing over from the West to the East. He can therefore be read in alternative ways: as a Western colonialist who like Marco in *Emmanuelle* (1974) goes East to gratify sadistic sexual and feudal desires; or as that recurrent figure of Western nightmare, the man of power who goes native and like Kurtz in *Heart of Darkness* (1899) blends his identity with that of the Other. It is significant that, in the film's prologue, he should literally turn into an Oriental and merge his body with that of his disciple Kah–the film respects the Otherness of the East, but its chief symbol of evil is a man who wilfully transgresses racial boundaries.

Van Helsing represents a more acceptable face of Western influence. He is an anthropologist, sensitive to the value of cultural difference. While Dracula colonises by force and stealth, Van Helsing is the classic Orientalist who understands the East better than the Easterners themselves. Although the presence of a frail Peter Cushing ensured the continuity of the franchise, it is initially unclear why Van Helsing is required to defeat the vampires. Aside from providing moral support, he takes relatively little part in the action until he stakes Dracula in the perfunctory finale. He has little special knowledge to impart–he admits that he is unsure how to tackle Eastern vampires–and the seven vampires are defeated in bouts of martial arts to which he minimally contributes. But his presence underscores that the western threat of Dracula *needs* to be defeated by a Westerner: the Chinese cannot do it themselves. The trope is therefore a familiar one: the East is vulnerable and feminine–Dracula's victims are all young Chinese women–and its salvation will only come with western help.

Hammer horror often intelligently used the exotic to criticise Western attitudes. In *The Abominable Snowman* (1957), for instance, a clichéd Orientalist fantasy of Tibet is counterpointed with the grasping materialism of Western and especially American values. As Marcia Landy notes, the film "expresses discontent with the aggressive behaviour of Western males and uses traditional stereotypes of Eastern culture to undermine Western attitudes. The 'Orientalism', the portrayal of the Eastern way of life that is usually negative in the empire films of the 1930s is… inverted. The culture of the East is now seen as offering a corrective to that of the West."[19] Similarly the horror films *The Reptile* (1966) and *The Plague of the Zombies* (1966), both set in Britain, use otherwise racist tropes of foreign infection to depict colonialism as corrupting. *The Plague of the Zombies* constructs an explicit anti-colonial metaphor: workers in a Cornish tin mine are zombified using knowledge acquired in the West Indies–they suffer in effect the revenge of the colonial repressed. As Pirie remarks of these two films, "Both concern small Cornish communities threatened by a kind of alien and inexplicable plague which has been imported from the East via a corrupt aristocracy: both are, by implication at least, violently anti-colonial."[20]

In this context *Legend*'s representation of the East, like that of Dracula, is thoroughly ambivalent, both anti-colonial and patronisingly Orientalist. The East is sympathetically portrayed in the film and ultimate evil is identified with Western colonialism, yet the East is also shown as powerless and emasculated without Western knowledge and aid. But the picture is more complex still. The evil of the Chinese vampires is not a sign of the irredeemable evil of Otherness, as in the Fu Manchu novels and films, but the result of their corruption by a Western overlord. This echoes Hammer's earlier film, *The Stranglers of Bombay* (1960), in which the violence of Thuggee is depicted not as the brutality of a lower race but as a product of Western infection and interference. As Marcia Landy notes, "The Indians are portrayed as seeking to reappropriate what has been expropriated from them, and the violence of their methods, when read against the grain, is a distorted mirror of the methods of the expropriator."[21] Even so, as Landy goes on to remark, the film "dramatizes how the liberal Englishman must still regard the colonial Other from a position of rational superiority. The white man must save the Indians from themselves."[22] *Legend* gives Van Helsing precisely the same task in China.

It is important to stress the complexity of these representations and, as Landy suggests, to read them carefully and against the grain. Hammer's horror films were seldom merely racist in their treatment of Otherness, often criticising imperial practices and Western 'civilisation' at the same time as they reproduced residual colonialist ideologies and images. Of all Hammer's films *Legend* makes this ambiguity most explicit, with unusual self-reflexivity. Even as it titillates the audience with the spectacle of Eastern tortures, it emphasises that they are overseen by a Western aristocrat. The exotic sadism of the Other is shown to be orchestrated by and for the pleasure of the West.

An earlier version of this essay appeared in *Postcolonial Studies* Volume 3 Number 1 (April 2000).

Notes

1. Leon Hunt, 'Han's Island Revisited: *Enter the Dragon* as Transnational Cult Film', *Unruly Pleasures: The Cult Film and Its Critics*, ed. By Xavier Mendik and Graeme Harper (Guildford: FAB Press, 2000), pp.78–80.
2. David Pirie, *A Heritage of Horror: The English Gothic Cinema 1946 – 1972* (London: Gordon Fraser, 1973), p.51.
3. See Robin Wood, 'Burying the Undead: the Use and Obsolescence of Count Dracula', *Mosaic*, 16 (1979), pp.175–87.
4. David Thomson, A *Biographical Dictionary of Film*, rev. ed. (London: Andre Deutsch, 1995), pp.244.
5. Roy Ward Baker, *The House that Hammer Built* 10 (November 1998), p.108.
6. Tom Johnson and Deborah Del Vecchio, *Hammer Films: An Exhaustive Filmography* (Jefferson, NC and London: McFarland and Company, 1996), p.372.
7. Marcus Hearn and Alan Barnes, *The Hammer Story* (London: Titan Books, 1997), p.65.
8. Pete Tombs, *Mondo Macabro: Weird & Wonderful Cinema Around the World* (London: Titan Books, 1997), p.26.
9. Tombs, p.31.
10. Hunt, p.80.
11. Stephen Teo, 'Local and Global Identity: Whither Hong Kong Cinema?', paper delivered at the Second International Conference on Chinese Cinema, Hong Kong Baptist University April 19, 2000. http://www.sensesofcinema.com/contents/00/7/hongkong.html
12. Hunt, p.75.
13. Stephen Teo, *Hong Kong Cinema* (London: British Film Institute, 1997), p.219.
14. Ibid., p.223.
15. Ibid., pp.87-121.
16. Pirie, p.86.
17. Ken Gelder, *Reading the Vampire* (London and New York: Routledge, 1994), p.13.
18. Ibid., p.23.
19. Marcia Landy, *British Genres: Cinema and Society 1930–1960* (Princeton: Princeton University Press, 1991), p.418.
20. Pirie, p.124.
21. Landy, p. 420.
22. Ibid., p.421.

Part Three: Seventies Horrors
Xavier Mendik

In a period marred by real life social, political and military terror it comes as no surprise that horror proved one of the most popular genres of the seventies. It was not merely that the decade saw the explosion of new and disturbing types of celluloid savagery, it was also the fact that these images were largely produced from the independent and exploitation sectors, beyond the control of major studios. As with many of the other genres discussed in this volume, the social and political impact of the horror genre was particularly marked in American productions of the era. Here, wider national instabilities were reproduced in horror narratives where definitions of the monstrous and normality were frequently blurred and resolution (when it existed) no longer guaranteed the restoration of legality. In this concluding section of *Shocking Cinema of the Seventies* we examine key examples of horror cinema from the decade to consider their images in light of these wider issues of social change.

Our examination begins with Linnie Blake's article 'Another One For the Fire: George A. Romero's Apocalyptic Theology of the Seventies.' This paper indicates that the nihilistic view of America that Romero initiated in his 1968 classic *Night of the Living Dead* was also evident in his later work. Author Linnie Blake substantiates this view through a discussion of films such as *The Crazies, Martin* and *Dawn of the Dead*. These works remain disturbing not merely for their graphic images, but because they also reveal the degeneration of communal bonds between Americans. It is this sense of alienation which allows the American body to become either infected (*The Crazies*), ravaged by violence (*Martin*) and allowed to decay (*Dawn of the Dead*). In so doing, Romero's films can be seen as demonstrating a corruption of the 'civic body' forewarned by the religious leader John Winthrop as early as 1630. Winthrop's vision of a future America confirmed the need to build unifying bonds between its citizens in order to prevent the threat of violence from within. For Blake, Winthrop's fears are actualised in the seventies when American citizens found their rights and values continually eroded by a growing military presence. It is this threat that Romero explores in works such as *The Crazies*. Here, the inhabitants of a small American town are actually infected by a bacteriological agent bound for Vietnam. This provokes a literal corruption of the civic body as the citizens begin to engage in acts of mass slaughter, suicide and incest. However, as the narrative reveals, the signs of civic corruption are much more widespread, as indicated in the military's sanctioning of a nuclear bomb attack on the town. Blake usefully connects the (fatally) overblown military and masculine gestures of *The Crazies* to Romero's later works such as *Dawn of the Dead*.

Both films reveal an America struggling to see any common connections with its dead and infected (this being indicated in the latter film in a scene where SWAT teams fight with tenement dwellers over the corpses of former loved ones and religious leaders). Rather than seeing any division between the 'sick' and 'healthy' characters in Romero's films, Blake concludes these works to governed by the signs of a "nationally specific schizophrenia", a malaise which she further discusses in relation to the director's urban neo-vampire classic *Martin*.

It is the similar theme of nihilistic seventies American horror that dominates Jonathan L. Crane's article 'Come On-A My House: The Inescapable Legacy of Wes Craven's *The Last House on the Left*.' This discussion links Craven's gut-wrenching debut to a period of innovation occurring within horror during the decade. These changes undoubtedly reflected wider social upheavals, resulting in Crane's comment that seventies horror was dominated by a "feel bad factor." This resulted in horror being redefined as the evil of the everyday, rather than being a distant, foreign or supernatural phenomenon. Linked in with these changes was a disturbing focus on the pain and suffering of the victim's body (rather than that of the monster as had been the case in earlier horror traditions). Unlike previous decades of horror, the seventies productions also displayed their moral ambiguity through an absence of authority figures capable of either containing evil or restoring order. Crane maps these disturbing generic changes onto to Craven's brutal rape and revenge drama, noting a number of key features which distinguish it from its source material of Ingmar Bergman's *The Virgin Spring*. For the author, it is not merely budgetary and aesthetic qualities that separate these two productions, but rather the lack of any redemptive or authoritative figures in Craven's remake. Here, the forces of law and order are reduced to the level of bungling Southern caricatures, whose comic actions jar against the images of female torture and degradation that the film depicts. Crane goes on to identify other key features of the film's powerful effect in the latter part of his analysis. These include the use of musical score as a means of creating an incongruity between sound and image tracks, as well as a close-up focus on terror that refused any safe distance for either character or spectator.

Beyond Craven's film, Tobe Hooper's *The Texas Chain Saw Massacre* stands as another of the most notorious American horror films of the seventies. The film is the topic of Martin Jones' article 'Head Cheese: *The Texas Chain Saw Massacre* Beyond Leatherface.' This chapter dissects the disturbing basis of an otherwise bloodless tale of a group of hippie college kids slaughtered by a family of rural cannibals. Jones begins by commenting on the curious commodification of Leatherface, the film's key villain. Rather than dismissing the protagonist's cult following as a deviant trait specific to horror fans, he concludes that this character (and the film in general) embody a sustained condemnation of American culture that appeals to its audience.

In defence of his position, Jones draws on Robin Wood's famed analysis of *The Texas Chain Saw Massacre*, which argued the film to be drawing on the repressed social and sexual tensions. This traumatic 'return of the repressed' is evidenced in the film by a series of uneasy parallels between the monstrous cannibal family and the group of youngsters depicted as their intended prey. It is this set of uncanny connections that

Jones explores by comparing Leatherface with the wheelchair bound character of Franklin. Although Franklin represents "a pin-up to the meat industry" (as Jones terms it), his position of victimisation is complicated by his physical similarity to Leatherface, as well as his shared obsession with cattle slaughter. The film thus charts another example of the collapse between established definitions of evil and normality, a feature which Jones links to the period of the film's production. In particular, he notes that although the narrative employs many of the motifs of the hippie generation, these symbols of freedom are cruelly subverted by the actions of the cannibal family. For instance, he notes the crazed hitchhiker that the young group unwittingly pick up on the highway appears and behaves like a member of the by now infamous Manson family. (His fascination with photographing death and the macabre actually mimics some of the rumoured snuff movie practices of Manson's followers). If the film can be seen as a contemporary comment on the literal death of the flower power generation, it is also the 'ordinary' nature of the cannibals' depiction which provides much of the film's ability to shock.

While American horror of the seventies clearly concerned itself with the problematic distinctions between the monstrous and the normal, in Britain, the genre was more concerned with the boundaries between traditional and contemporary constructions of the urban space. This is the subject of Nick Freeman's article 'London Kills Me: The English Metropolis of the 1970s.' This chapter examines the extent to which British horror films of the seventies had to radically revise their depictions and directions as a consequence of the more extreme images of stateside savagery. Although companies such as Hammer attempted to tap into new youth markets by including more titillating fare in the later Dracula films, they remained limited by their eighteenth century depictions, which appeared far removed from contemporary concerns. One project which did shift the vampire myth into a modern urban space was *Dracula AD 72*, which Freeman discusses during his analysis. From the opening scene (where Dracula and Van-Helsing battle on board a Victorian stage-coach), to the film's following credit scene (revealing the sights and sounds of contemporary London), the narrative attempts to link these two time-scales together in an uneasy fashion. Thus, as Freeman notes, the film reveals a decidedly conservative and confused view in its depiction of London and its youth culture. For the author, a far more successful integration of the Victorian and contemporary London is contained in the later *Death Line*, which takes as its concern cannibalism contained in the London underground. Here, tube-bound, flesh-eaters are revealed as having distinctly Victorian roots (as descendants from abandoned nineteenth century labourers who built the tunnels), who later return to haunt the contemporary urban space. By drawing on Michel Foucault's concept of hetrotopia, Freeman agues that this film manages fuse apparently incompatible social and historical dimensions within a singular depicted location. A similar effect is found in the Vincent Price vehicle *Theatre of Blood*, which Freeman discusses at the close of his article. The film concerns a faded, melodramatic actor who takes a revenge on the theatrical critics who spurned him. Once again, the film manages to integrate the concept of hetrotopia shifting between the fashionable Knightsbridge hangouts of the potential victims and a far more Dickensian image of London inhabited by Price and his band of vagabonds.

While many of the articles in this section of this volume seek to analyse genre representations from one specific filmmaking culture, Andy Black offers a cross-cultural analysis of horror in the article 'False Gestures For a Demonic Public in *The Sentinel* and *The Anti-Christ.*' Here, the author discusses both American and Italian representations of the supernatural that followed on from the success of the 1973 film *The Exorcist*, as well as identifying some of the controversies surrounding these works.

While the wider social turmoil of the decade popularised narratives that depicted the struggle between good and evil, Black is here interested in pointing out how such factors affected the different depictions of demonic possession in these two films. As the author notes, in Alberto de Martino's film *The Antichrist*, evil occupation occurs as a distinctly physical and sexual affliction, which transforms a wheelchair bound heroine into an unholy vixen. Via these metods, the author sees the film as located in established exploitation traditions that seek to accentuate the sexual aspects of possession afflicting the female form for titillating effect. (This is further indicated in the film's over-reliance on spectacle and special effects as a way on enhancing the heroine's slide into the unholy). In comparison to de Martino's film, *The Sentinel* uses its supernatural underpinnings to explore wider contradictions in class and consumption in seventies America. By identifying these wider social concerns, as well as the controversies that movies such as *The Sentinel* raised, Black's article provides a fitting conclusion to a cinematic study of one of the most turbulent film periods of the twentieth century.

Another One For the Fire:
George A. Romero's American Theology of the Flesh
Linnie Blake

"It's not over with – it's going to come in through another door."[1]

The Enemy Within: Romero's Vision of the Seventies

In 1630 the religious radical John Winthrop, lately appointed Governor of New England, delivered a rousing sermon entitled "A Model of Christian Charity." [2] Here, he outlined the hopes and fears of the Pilgrims who had fled Europe in search of religious freedom in the New World. He also warned of the dangers that faced the settlers in their attempts to tame a wilderness: dangers from outside their walls but most importantly from within. Winthrop argued that the colonists who sought to redeem the sins of the old world by building a new society must "be knit together in this work as one man," looking upon each other as "members of the same body,"[3] a civic body of true believers engaged in the communal exercise of building a civilization on the edge of a hostile continent. Thus, entering into a "near... marriage"[4] with their God, the colonists could only hope to survive and prosper if they obeyed the injunctions of their creator. If they chose to place selfish desires over the common good and should "fall to embrace this present world and prosecute [their] carnal intentions, seeking great things for [themselves] and [their] posterity" then, as Winthrop warned, the Lord would "surely break out in wrath"[5] against them. They would, in short, be "consumed out of the good land."[6]

I resurrect the figure of John Winthrop for two reasons. Firstly, because back in the 1960s, when it still seemed possible to win both the war in Vietnam and the approval of the American people, a range of American presidents as diverse as Kennedy, Johnson and Nixon had actually sought to justify their nation's actions by re-mobilizing for themselves some of Winthrop's most potent images and ideas. Most commonly they had evoked his vision of America as a shining "city on a hill,"[7] a beacon of freedom, the light of which illuminated the oppression inherent in all non-American ethical, political or economic systems.

By the 1970s, though, the decade in which Vietnam was lost and the twin spectres of economic collapse and presidential corruption threatened to douse the shining city's illuminations for ever, Winthrop's imagery would take on a whole new significance. Now, American writers, artists and particularly film-makers became increasingly aware that they were in danger of being 'consumed' by their environment, not by any external threat but by the nation's own failure to live up to its original promise. Throughout the 1970s, against a backdrop of economic crisis, military defeat in Vietnam and the loss of faith in the moral leadership of the presidency engendered by Watergate, we can trace a resurgence of the decidedly apocalyptic consciousness that had informed Winthrop's early vision of the nation. This is a nation now trapped in the twilight nightmare of degenerating dreams that was the American 1970s. And nowhere is this more true than in the genre of cinematic horror.

Between 1973 and 1978, George A. Romero wrote and directed three uniquely pessimistic masterworks of horror cinema: *The Crazies* (1973), *Martin* (1976) and *Dawn of the Dead* (1978) that depicted in highly allegorical ways the historically-specific horrors of the decade whilst embodying a far older sense directly traceable to Winthrop. These texts indicated that America's civic body was under threat—not from any external enemy but from within. Besieged from without by governmental forces of authoritarian right-wing militarism and from within by the rapacious self-seeking individualism and consumption that the economic policies of successive administrations had so shamelessly promoted it is clear that Romero's 1970s America has failed to heed Winthrop's warnings. Here is a nation in which the social body is either infected, murderously divided or rapaciously decaying, an America in which the family exists in an ongoing state of disintegration, all cooperative endeavour appears condemned to fail and the individual seems destined to live, and to die, alone. This is an America of Winthrop's 'carnal intentions', an America of frenzied acquisitiveness, entrenched racism and class divisions, an America devoid of liberality, cooperation and the will to equality. It is an America in which the civic body is in such poor shape that the nation's claims to the moral leadership of the 'free' world are exposed as the hypocritical fantasies of a degenerate superpower in the final moments before its timely collapse.

Heaven Help Us: The Infected Bodies of Evans City

Released in 1973, the year in which the United States effectively lost the Vietnam War, *The Crazies* is very much a product of Nixon's first term of office. The film is set in Evans City, a small town in West Pennsylvania just north of Pittsburgh. Its narrative examines the legacy of an administration that had steadily rolled back the civil rights legislation of the 1960s, had cracked down hard on anti-war elements and other dissident groups and had engaged in the wholesale wiretapping of and file-keeping on hundreds of thousands of individuals and organizations across America. The film can be gauged against the might of the government-business matrix that had forestalled implementation of measures designed to protect the American environment from destruction or the American people from poverty whilst guaranteeing enormous expenditure on the military. In Romero's vision, the film has the citizens of Evans City accidentally exposed to a bacteriological weapon developed by their own government. (This bacteriological weapon presumably destined for Vietnam).

First encircled and then invaded by the faceless agents of the military-industrial complex (as once the New England Pilgrims had felt themselves encircled by

Dawn of the Dead

hostile Native Americans) the town's inhabitants either die immediately or go 'incurably mad', entering into an orgy of murderous destruction. Here, men bludgeon their wives to death and incinerate their children, fathers and daughters indulge in acts of consensual incest and gray haired grandmothers employ knitting needles as assuredly as Leatherface ever wielded a chain saw. As the American family is itself, consumed by murderous desires, a very Nixonesque President sanctions the 'accidental' dropping of an atom bomb on the town, an act designed to consume townspeople and virus alike in a conflagration of flame. Indeed, this flame, reminiscent of the US military's wholesale napalming of Vietnam and the earlier nuclear holocausts of Hiroshima and Nagasaki also connects with the purging fires of divine retribution that (according to Winthrop) would signal the death of the civic body and the failure of the American endeavour in the New World.

But the willingness of the President to slaughter the native-born Americans of Evans City should not, perhaps, surprise us. *The Crazies* was, after all, released in the year in which members of the Sioux nation gathered at the historic battle site of Wounded Knee, South Dakota to protest earlier administrations' crimes of genocide, broken treaties and civil rights violations. The 'real Americans' of the 1970s have, it seems, become so alienated from their elected representatives that they have more in common with the nation's original inhabitants. Dispossessed of their dreams of freedom by an administration that purposefully infects them with its poisonous lies (as once it infected the Native Americans with smallpox), ordinary Americans seem to have only two options: insanity or death. As the doomed scientist remarks: "The whole thing's insane, how can you tell who's infected and who isn't?" The entire civic body, it seems, has been over-run by a murderous will to mutually assured destruction.

It is notable, though, that the one community member ostensibly immune to the virus is David, the town's only green beret: a man who validates Winthrop's cooperative ideal of American social life through his work with the town's Volunteer Fire Department and who thus offers up a totemic challenge to the coercive strategies of the present administration. A veteran of the Vietnam war who uses the skills he acquired up country to attempt to breach the government-imposed perimeter with his best friend Clank, a regular army veteran, and his pregnant girlfriend Judy, neither of whom survive. David is the typically ambiguous Vietnam figure of Romero's '70s horror. (A killer by training if not disposition, David in many ways prefigures Peter of *Dawn of the Dead*, just as his friend Clank, with his gung-ho machismo, prefigures Roger). Unable to dissociate himself from the killing-machine his government has made him, unable to remake himself as a husband and father in a world of familial implosion and civil chaos David (like many of Romero's hero-protagonists) is effectively trapped between worlds: a condition echoed in the baffled speculation he repeats on several occasions-"Maybe we're in some kind of war. ... Maybe we are in a war."

Standing on the dividing line between foreign war and domestic peace, social cohesion and anarchic chaos, individual rights and totalitarian government, David may survive the virus but he is unable to escape its social ramifications. He cannot, Romero makes clear, survive alone. Without the support of his community, the assistance of his best friend and the love of a good woman Romero warns, as Winthrop warned before him, David is as doomed as his fellow countrymen. The radical individualism that Americans have so long prized, the individualism that imprinted the figure of the lone frontiersman, the gunslinger and later still the biker-outlaw upon the national consciousness is here found to be a sorry substitute for cooperative social endeavour.

Of all the townspeople herded into the gymnasium at the movie's close, David alone has his faculties. He may, then, offer a solution to the epidemic but, Romero makes clear, the authoritarian demagogues of the military are unable to recognise it so wrapped up in their macho power games as they are. In the figure of the veteran, then, destined by virtue of his past experiences to always stand alone and, in that solitude, to be destroyed, Romero encapsulates the baffled isolation of the American subject at the end of the Vietnam war. This atomized and solitary subjectivity (addressed in greater detail in *Martin*, and *Dawn of the Dead*) seems, for Romero, to be yet another symptom of the degeneration of the American civic body, another road to hell for the doomed American self.

Stockpiling Hardware After Vietnam

The Crazies is a film that beats to the rhythm of the military drums that furnish much of its soundtrack, playing taps for a community that has been infected, without their consent or will, by the zeitgeist of the Nixon era. The ongoing futility of the Vietnam war, lost but yet unfinished, is encapsulated in the inter-cutting of documentary footage of bombers in flight, as well as the auto-immolation of the priest who douses himself in petrol and sets himself ablaze with a zippo. Equally, in the military's incineration of the infected bodies with flame throwers and in the extensive damage caused to a technologically superior enemy by the townspeople of Evan City, the film focuses attention on America's ongoing love-affair with the gun. Certainly, the gun may be associated with the gas-masked white-suited soldiers who invade the peaceful environs of family homes in the manner of the Latin-American murder squads armed and financed by Nixon. But within these ostensibly peaceable familial spaces, Romero's *mise-en-scene* includes gun cabinets, mechanical machine guns for children to play with, toy soldiers and framed prints of fathers and sons in the military uniforms of their respective eras' wars.

In this context, it is noticeable that Judy is shot not by agents of the state but by gun-wielding teenagers guilelessly asserting their constitutional right to bear arms against a force that seeks to curtail their vision of freedom 'American-style.' It is no coincidence, in other words, that when the infected Clank is outnumbered by faceless gunmen (in winter woodland that is itself reminiscent of deforested jungle) his gaze falls on a snake making its way into the hollow of a fallen tree. The garden of the New World, the Eden of mankind's new beginning, is thus shown to harbour a viper in its bosom: namely that which has tempted Americans away from the straight and

Dawn of the Dead

narrow path of cooperative social justice 1960s-style into the despondent slough of the 1970s present. As Winthrop once warned, the nation has fallen into a state of corruption. As Judy dies with her unborn child still kicking inside her, her hopeless desire to name the baby after its father leaves us with the sense that both Evans City and the nation itself have no meaningful future. Both are thus doomed from the very start. For all the hopes of the original settlers, the New World has become a nation that can only bring forth death. The virus, we discover, has already made it to Louisville. The destruction of the Union is already underway and the only response the average American can make (in the words of Carole Baker Sager's mawkish protest pop that accompanies the film's closing credits) is to cry "Heaven Help Us." A most Winthroppian prayer.

The Vampire As Outsider: Nosferatu Hits Pittsburgh

This sense of a blighted future engendered by the sins of the past is most fully explored by Romero in *Martin*, a film released in 1976. (This was the same year in which Nixon's Watergate transgressions were unconditionally pardoned by Gerald Ford - one year after the fall of Saigon). This was a point in time in which the gulf between public opinion and official policy, the people's reality and that of their rulers had never seemed wider. As a result, this was a point in time in which the civic body had never appeared more divided or more corrupt. Filmed against the background of America's most severe economic crisis since the Depression, *Martin* is a strange tale of modern vampirism set in Braddock, a decaying suburban district east of Pittsburgh. Here is a city subject to galloping inflation, staggering levels of unemployment and imminent economic collapse, a city of urban decay and radio talk shows, car graveyards and bottle-hugging derelicts. Into such a world comes Martin, an individual who is either a psychotic teenage serial killer who drugs his victims prior to drinking their blood or as he and his cousin believe (and as the intercut monochrome homages to Universal horror classics show), an eighty-four year old vampire from the old country adrift in the modern American world.

Throughout the film, Martin's social contacts admirably evoke the fragmented social stratification of mid 1970s America. A single woman on a train heading for New York, a man engaged in extra-marital sex with the adulterous wife of a businessman away from home and a derelict who subsists in the abandoned warehouses and factories of the dying steel-town all provide Martin with a meal. More importantly, they also grant Romero a chance to play upon the huge disparities of wealth and power that characterised America during this period. Whilst biker gangs rampage across the neighbourhood, drug dealers meet in secret conference and young men harass and abuse shopping housewives, Romero again establishes a dividing line, a perimeter, a fortress wall between opposed and competing sectors of the American public. Outside stand the dispossessed, the disgruntled, the disposable byproducts of American consumer capitalism, their lives symbolically encapsulated in the strip show and porn shops of Braddock's less than salubrious side streets.

Within this perimeter are the tastefully furnished homes of the bourgeoisie –

homes like that of Mrs Santini, with its white walls and framed reproductions of Goya and the early Mondrian, homes like that of Martin's adulterous victim, with her glass walls and concealed doors, leather sofas, remote controlled garage and myriad electrical goods. Both outside and inside the fortress, it seems, sad, sordid and self-regarding lives are lived: Mrs Santini having compensatory sex with Martin as grocery boy, the adulterous victim doing the same with a self-serving and equally duplicitous lover and Martin's own family member Christine acting in much the same way with her boyfriend Arthur. In both worlds, most notably, children are altogether absent. Again palpable, as in *The Crazies*, is a sense of thwarted future and blighted present, a sense underlined by the highly ambiguous past of Martin our hero-protagonist who, as is usual with Romero, stands very much alone. As he himself declares "I shouldn't have friends, not even for the sexy stuff."

Working Through the Family Curse

It is possible to argue that *Martin* is somehow "about" the family's pernicious reinforcement of the conformist norms of a conservative society in a state of imminent collapse.[8] The teenage Martin, many critics have claimed, is a victim of a personality disorder brought on by his family's insistence that he is *Nosferatu*, a vampire whose soul must first be saved prior to his bodily destruction. For instance, throughout the film, Romero insistently highlights Martin's cousin Cuda's obsession with "the family curse, the family shame." This is also seen in the old man's penchant for the external symbols of religious superstition (the cross, the Madonna, the wreath of garlic) and his insistent belief that the decline of "the old ways" has led to the social collapse of the present. This is a static world of down-at-heel veterans exposed to public view in public washrooms, a debased chorus offering only banal platitudes to a world in which repeated shots of cars being crushed to blocks of metal in a wrecking yard mark the utter disposability of American culture, American dreams. In such a world as this, it may be argued, Martin becomes for his cousin Cuda, a convenient symbol for all that ails him, all the chaos, disorder and darkness that once lay outside the pilgrims' stockade and still lies out there in the Pittsburgh night, still lies deep within the breast of the American citizenry. According to such a reading, then, the interpolated Universal scenes (in which Martin's vampiric identity is re-cast in the cinematic language of the silver screen) may intimate the pervasive effects of family life, family drama and family trauma on the individual subject. Martin, one may argue, has constructed such fantasies in order to live up to the image of him projected by his family. He has internalised their belief system and found a way of making it relevant to himself.

However, the film is rather more ambiguous than this reading allows and contains rather more potent and disturbing ideas. Throughout the movie, Romero repeatedly invites us to countenance the possibility that Martin's vampirism is actually real. He encourages us to debate with ourselves, in the act of watching, whether Martin is, indeed, an eighty-four year old refugee from the old country. If this is the case, then he is not psychotic, but in fact drawing on very memories of the past that have been re-cast in the mass cultural vocabulary of his adopted homeland (specifically

in the cinematic lexicon of Universal horror movies). Shot in grainy black and white, these mass-culturalized images appear to offer Martin an heroic subjectivity absent from his dependent and infantilised present life. In them, he is positioned first as the romantic-hero-vampire offering his compliant and complicity victims a kind of sado-sexual release. This is a picture far different from the spirited resistance put up by the anonymous housewife or by the woman on the train who bites, kicks and wrestles with the "freak rapist asshole" and necrophiliac that Martin has become. Clearly, as the present-day sections of the narrative make clear, such fantasies (or re-constructed memories) have little to do with the America of the present. The Universal scenes of Catholic exorcism old-world-style may be echoed by Father Zulemas's present-day attempts to drive the evil out of Martin, but without the erratic low angle shots and extreme close-ups of tormenting Latinate priests and silent, complicity family members, this appears to be a hollow, outmoded and ultimately meaningless act. Rather, it is merely a game played by old men with too much time on their hands. As Cuda makes clear, the modern world has substituted science for religious faith.

In this environment, mass culturalised spectacles such as the horror movie or the radio freak show have come to replace any idea of authentic subjectivity. Martin is lost not to the dark forces of spiritual evil, but to the horrors of contemporary America, a man aware that he has lived "a long time full of crazy people" but powerless to effect his escape. Deploying the technology at his disposal in the form of sedative drugs, hypodermic syringes and remote control devices, Martin thus attempts to live out his vampiric destiny in the modern world. Rejecting the existence of magic and well aware that the cloak and fangs of mass cultural representations of the vampire are "only a costume", Martin thus synthesises ancient desires and new world technologies. He is a hybrid of forbidden lusts and contemporary consumer capitalism. The interpolated Universal scenes are then less a testament to the family's invidious affects on the individual than a representation of the ways the individual internalises their own commodification in the modern world. This is a world of banal radio phone-ins that position Martin as "The Count" and "a real live honest to goodness vampire" whose personal confusion is seen as little more than a means of increasing audience ratings and improving the returns for the show's sponsors.

Far from being a unique aberration, Romero seems to argue that Martin is an example of the pernicious effects that mass culture has on the subjectivity of the American individual; the individual who, like Martin himself, seems destined to suffer from a kind of nationally-specific schizophrenia. At this point in the nation's history, Romero seems to argue, every American contains within themselves a series of irreconcilable contradictions. Mrs Santini with her fine house and unhappy marriage, Christine with her yearnings for freedom and her regressive love of her family, Arthur with his strong work ethic and utter inability to find a job of work and Martin, with his thwarted will to social interaction and human warmth adrift in the harsh, abrasive and punitive world he inhabits; all of these bespeak a nation divided. On the one hand is the will to believe in a range of American dreams–dreams of equality, opportunity, freedom and democracy, on the other is the awareness that the America of the present is a land of social stratification, economic stagnation, civil liberties violations and corrupt government. By 1976, for Romero, the civic body has become inexorably divided. The idealistic visions of the past are pitted against the consumer durables of the present and both appear empty and devoid of promise. And it was with such ideas in mind that, two years later, Romero would release his 1978 masterwork *Dawn of the Dead*.

Cannibalism As Consumption: *Dawn of the Dead*

In *Dawn of the Dead* the controlled, contained or foreshadowed mayhem of *The Crazies* and *Martin* explodes into global apocalypse. America, it seems, has not only lost the right to the moral leadership of the world, but is incapable of handling the national disaster that faces it. For the past three weeks, the dead have returned to gorge themselves of the still-living flesh of their countrymen who, in turn, arise again to kill. Whilst, as in Vietnam, the disintegrating media continues to feed the populace on a diet of "moral bullshit" and false information, representatives of the state, such as the SWAT team sent to round up the dissident poor, either kill themselves, abscond or are driven murderously mad by what they see. This is a society at the point of meltdown where martial law has been declared and citizens, echoing the US policy of forced relocation in Vietnam have been forbidden from occupying private residences. Even at this early point in the narrative as Romero indicates in his own novelization of the film "the administration in power didn't have the faith and confidence of the people."[9] Here in the City of Brotherly Love, where once the Declaration of Independence was signed, the civil order has collapsed, with citizens actively disobeying the government's injunctions to turn over the bodies of their dead to specially equipped divisions of the National Guard. As Winthrop once warned, the people of America are being consumed out of the good land from within, the rest of the film delineating precisely which sins have brought them to pass.

That much of the remaining action occurs in a large shopping centre doubling as a Civil Defence bunker obviously enables Romero to embark on a protracted parody of the highly militarised consumer society that America of the late 1970s had become. As Roger, the macho SWAT member and Vietnam veteran (thematically descended from Clank of *The Crazies*) indicates, this self-sufficient and windowless place is "fat city," a veritable "gold mine" of consumer delights, fortress suburbia no less. Like the America that has been lost, the mall can be taken from the zombies who, in this context, are its original inhabitants and who, like the Native Americans that originally occupied the land mass, find it "an important place in their lives" whilst having no actual use for its many material resources. In this bizarre graveyard, Romero terrifies us with his grotesque superimposition of untouched consumer goods and ambulant corpses. The fact that the undead in depicted in workaday clothes (with plaid shirts aplenty, flared jeans and wide-lapelled suits, caftans, sportswear and ethnic-chic a-go-go) underscores our awareness that these people are, in fact, ordinary Americans of the late 1970s. Distinguished by their clothing (a nurse, a baseball player, a Hare Krishna devotee) yet homogenized by their deadness and their convulsive appetites that can never be truly sated, the zombies have become perfect and rather pitiful allegories of the American self under capitalism: children of the military-industrial complex whose

Dawn of the Dead

lives and deaths have been underwritten by the gun. Like media-generated images of the individual as consumer they are alike and interchangeable, lacking any interior consciousness, simply driven to consume.

Such a notion is emphasised, for example, when Roger and Peter turn on the power in the mall. Jauntily cutting (led by the swanee whistle that accompanies the comical Muzak in the mall) between the dials in the control room, the fountains, automated shop displays, turning mannequin heads and the zombies themselves, Romero conveys a distinct sense that we as consumers are ourselves manipulated by the environments we inhabit. We, like the zombies, metaphorically wander with arms outstretched through corridors of consumer delights, banging at the windows, attempting to lay our hands on the goodies inside then, tiring of those commodities and moving on to the next transient object of our passing desire. It is an impression further highlighted by the fact that throughout the mall scenes, the camera moves unmolested amongst the zombies as they stagger and stumble, bump and bounce upon their way. Coupled with the frequent point-of-view shots, when we see directly through the eyes of a zombie about to be dispatched, such techniques only encourage us the audience to denounce the government view that the zombies are not, strictly speaking, of our species. We know, as Peter does, that they are their audience and that the audience of the 1970s were as dead as their dreams of America.

Gun Crazy: Technology and Trauma in the Mall

In the light of the above discussion, it is notable how much our hero-protagonists have in common with the hostile forces that surround them. Both humans and zombies are, after all, attempting to survive; both are capable of reproducing themselves; both must destroy the enemy in order to do so. All that distinguishes the groups, it seems, is their choice of weaponry: the hands and teeth of the very many zombies versus the military hardware of our small band of heroes once again echoing the ill-fated technological superiority of American forces in Vietnam (and, earlier still, against the Native Americans). The gun, in fact, is an important means of social bonding in this movie. For instance, Steven increasingly participates in the macho camaraderie of the two Vietnam veterans as his shooting skills improve. Similarly, Fran's dependent femininity transmutes into a highly autonomous parody of the female outlaw as she becomes increasingly attached to the guns that are both an erotic accessory and a means of survival for her and her unborn child. However, as in *The Crazies*, Romero is keen to emphasise that the gun, no less than the zombie hoard, is a potent agent of infection unless one actively guards against its insidious effects. It is, after all, Roger's gun-wielding machismo that brings about his end and Steven's taking pot shots at the invading bikers that gets him killed and returns the mall to zombie hands. Only Peter, it seems, is immune from the effects of such weaponry. It is he who chastises Steven for his dangerous shooting at the airstrip and Roger for his reckless antics in the truck. It is Peter who urges Roger to relinquish his weapon to a zombie, trading arms for survival. At the movie's close he too passes on his gun to the same zombie, who holds it aloft like a cross, an icon, a totem of all that America has become.

Clearly this is not to argue that the four key protagonists function like avenging angels immune from the sins of the nation, redeeming America through their high-minded creation of a New World from out the ashes of the old. Timely reminders of the sins of the forefathers are thus embodied in the dangerously macho Roger and the superficial and greedy Steven. The former whoops like a cowboy in victory and groans "we whipped 'em, we whipped 'em good" (in the manner of a dying Indian killer) in defeat (the intermittent western-style crescendos that accompany each of our heroes victories on Romero's soundtrack echoing the frontier motif). Stephen, of course, points to the dissolution of such intrinsically destructive American dreams at the hands of consumer capitalism. Here is a man who builds himself a penthouse apartment in the bunker, furnished with state-of-the-art electrical goods, tasteful furniture and top-of-the-range tableware whilst proclaiming "it's ours, we took it" before plunging himself into the world of the dead and his companions into ruin.

Thus, both Roger and Stephen function more as echoes of the outlaw biker gang that brings about an end to their empty idyll than as ideological or moral repudiations of it. Both groups, like the zombies themselves, are quintessentially American, and each encapsulates disparate fragments of American history and its attendant myths. Clad in a range of western regalia and sending forth US cavalry bugle calls, the gang that has survived so long on the open road clearly embodies many of the skills and values of the men that tamed a wilderness. Here is murderous strength and the utter absence of any moral scruples that accompanies playful sadism and a childish greed. The group's behaviour echoes that of US soldiers in Vietnam or US soldiers on the prairies of the West, soldiers who sledge hammered Native American culture as assuredly as their descendants sledgehammer the mall's teepee display or the people of Vietnam.

In the bikers' astonishing theft of rings and jewellery from an African American zombie who screams and slashes in outrage, we can also see the historic institution of American slavery reenacted as a crime that must, somehow, be punished. In the gang's ultimately destructive will to plunder, we can see the fate of the American people writ large. Pillaging an eclectic selection of non-essential items from the stores, goods that echo the watches and rings, fur and leather coats, luxury foodstuffs and branded liquor previously coveted by our heroes, the bikers illustrate the progressive degeneration of the pioneer ideal. Hypnotized by the spectacle of so many goods so readily attainable the group thus comes to share the desires of the undead and, in so doing, to invite their own destruction. Only Peter and Fran, it seems, can see beyond the spectacle that mesmerises the others, can acknowledge that, like all Romero's 1970s Americans "we're the thieves and the bad guys" and that for all its ostensible delights, the mall, the nation, is "a prison too."

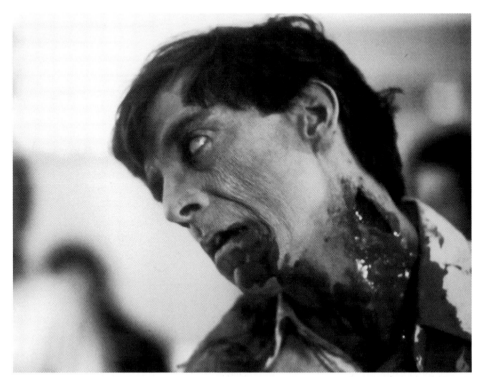

Dawn of the Dead

The final re-taking of the mall by the zombie hoard marks the end of the American endeavour as Winthrop originally conceived of it. The entrenched social divisions that lie at the heart of American society, that pit Puerto Rican immigrant and dispossessed African American against the government, biker gang against urban-professional-thirty-something can only be healed by death. Indeed, it is this death that transforms each into a tottering parody of 1970s US citizens. Each competing group, alongside the Johnstown rednecks who, as Stephen observes "are probably enjoying the whole thing," have internalized the pervasive violence of the American project to the extent that they have become inseparable from it. "I'm a man" plays Romero's soundtrack over the zombie hunting scenes, replete with group photos of the military and men in hunting shirts picking off the undead whilst popping open another can of beer. And with the exception of Peter, whose own future is highly uncertain, this model of beer-drinking, woman-abusing, easy-killing manhood appears to be not only culturally pervasive, but obligatory. Here, the cooperative and communal ideal that Winthrop espoused for the New World is shown to have been eviscerated by an overweening if entirely illusory individualism. This is symbolized at the movie's opening and closure by the spectacle of starving zombies fighting over dead meat. The Puerto Rican priest may warn Americans to "stop the killing or ... lose the war" but at this movie's very inception that war has been lost, not to any outside enemy, but to the enemies within. And like Winthrop before him, Romero seems to argue, the loss of that war has been America's longtime fate.

The 1970s horror movies of George A Romero remain some of the most visually arresting and politically challenging works of the decade. Each, in its own inimitable manner, conjures up the spectre of that darkest and most dishonest of decades in all its duplicity and despair. Each provides the viewer with a haunting series of images to remind us of how frequently Americans have come close to being consumed out of the good land and how, very probably, that fate has been deserved. Like the church bells that ring out their ode to joy at *Martin's* end, each of these movies is an elegy to the dreams of the nation's founders, the hopes of each generation of American selves. Each is a death-knell marking the total dissolution of the American civic body–now an infected, divided and corrupted corpse fit only for the fire of perdition.

Notes

1. Tony Williams, 'Wes Craven: An Interview', *Journal of Popular Film and Television*, Volume 8, Number 3 (1980), 10-14 (p.10).
2. John Winthrop, 'A Model of Christian Charity', in *The Norton Anthology of American Literature*, ed. by S. Gottesman, S. Murphy et al (1630; New York: WW Norton, 1979) , pp.11-25.
3. Ibid., p.23.
4. Ibid., p.22.
5. Ibid., p.23.
6. Ibid., p.24.
7. Ibid., p.24.
8. See, for example, Tony Williams, *Hearths of Darkness: The Family in the American Horror Film* (London: Associated UP, 1996).

9. George A. Romero and Susanna Sparrow, *Dawn of the Dead* (London: Sphere, 1979), p.15.

Come On-A My House: The Inescapable Legacy of Wes Craven's *The Last House on the Left*

Jonathan L. Crane

Horror: The 'Feel Bad' Genre of the Seventies

Horror, of all hardy film formulas, is the most periodic of genres. Since the thirties, horror has followed a regular sine wave of innovation, exploitation, parody and decline. Within these regular cycles, central, defining works in the genre have typically explored the horrific with stock characters, common themes and shared special effects that are either abandoned wholesale or radically reworked in the next cycle.

The seventies, a period of radical innovation for the horror film, marked the beginning of a new turn for the genre. Signal efforts: *The Last House on the Left* (1972), *The Texas Chain Saw Massacre* (1974), *Halloween* (1978), *Shivers* (1976), *Snuff* (1974) and *I Spit on Your Grave* (1978) all ran pioneering changes on the genre. The new directions explored in these normative films severed them from work belonging to previous cycles while reformulating the conventions that would come to rule the genre for the next twenty-five years.

While these works do evidence some singular characteristics (they are not, even as defining genre efforts, exactly the same film), they also strongly manifest some indelible resemblances that have had an unavoidable influence on subsequent depictions of the horrific. Firstly, these films are extraordinarily negative viewing experiences. Much of the video nasty debate can be traced to this simple, uncontestable observation. If 'feel good' is the favoured adjective for the popular mainstream film that promises to pleasure the spectator for two hours, then these films are 'feel bad.' With little or no humour, (levity generally belongs to the parody phase of the cycle), these films are relentlessly and antagonistically grim. The hallmark of the seventies horror film is sustained, unavoidable anguish with no promise of catharsis. There is, for many, something radically suspect about films designed to assault the senses. For viewers unaccustomed to films that refuse victims and audience succour these are puzzling and distasteful entertainments.

Pain in the dominant seventies horror film is heightened by a rejection of the occult, foreign or otherworldly that might help to safely distance the audience from the dark, dogged spectacle cast before them. When evil arises in the fourth dimension, via the arcane stratagems of the necromancer, or atop a remote Balkan aerie, it is relatively easy to dismiss the action on screen as fantastic twaddle. In these films horrific spectacle is enacted on familiar ground. When forced to suffer, the audience is not allowed to do so in realms far removed from ordinary life; instead, horror is visited upon the audience in familiar harbours. In the seventies, horror comes home.

One of the primary reasons horror occupies intimately familiar ground is budgetary constraint. Independent filmmakers shot the most innovative horror films of the seventies on very low budgets. Without even modest studio support these films were shot on location, oftentimes as guerrilla shoots, with relatively undressed sets. Unloosed from the standard set pieces of the Studio film (the heavily armoured castle keep, the fully stocked laboratory alive with burbling retorts and smoking alembics), the horror film immediately feels more real, becomes more threatening, as violence explodes in a room of our own. Along these lines, the recent success of *The Blair Witch Project* (1999) belongs in great measure to the use of cheap technology to document the eruption of horror in familiar surroundings. Devoid of any noteworthy landscape, the generic woods of *Blair Witch*, as with all the locales of seventies horror films, are common ground. In addition, like the low budget 16mm cameras employed in many independent seventies productions, the video cameras used to track the Blair Witch are the same cameras used by much of the audience to document their own lives. Sadly, the singularly hapless video shooting in *The Blair Witch Project*, with too rapid pans, fumbled cameras, and errant focus exactly matches the style that most home videographers employ as everyday life is put on tape.

The Last House on the Left

The Last House on the Left

Alongside an implacable devotion to suffering enacted in generic locations, the seventies film inscribed the weight of horror directly on the flesh of ordinary men and, (most often) women. Whereas previous eras had typically registered horror in the ruined flesh of the monster, (consider the horrible visages of Chaney and Karloff), or in the destruction of property, (Tokyo crumbling under Godzilla's scaly heel), this unbridled era made weeping scrimshaw out of the plastic bodies of screaming victims. Under the impress of degenerate tattoos, the shredded body became the best measure of the monstrous. Unmitigated suffering was, in and of itself, a questionable genre practice, but suffering predicated on endlessly inventive vivisection was, and continues to be, too far beyond the pale for many.

While there are other trademark codes and practices common to the seventies horror film, (narrative incoherence, infinitely deferred denouements, random victimisation), the code which is most closely tied to the elaborate destruction of victims is the absence of authority figures. It is these characters who once served to dispatch the monstrous and offer affirmative wisdom that effectively counterbalanced the lunatic appetites of venomous madmen. In most films from this era no empowered authority figure or potent institution shields the victim from the blade of the omnipotent butcher.

In nihilist narratives celebrating release from hope, the vulnerable body stands outside the purview of anything but the bedrock authority of death. Here, in the seventies horror film, impotence and legitimate authority are synonymous. Once Van Helsing, the able scientist, could have driven a stake through the ravening heart of evil. Once the cagey psychiatrist could have unravelled the madness that lies within and eventually, in making sense of insanity, prevailed against menace. Even the good cop had a place in the horror film. No longer. In this turn, the genre strips recognized authority of all efficacious power and leaves victims to their own pitiful devices.

Against this generic backdrop, shared by nearly all the normative horror films of the seventies, we can begin to examine how Wes Craven's *The Last House on the Left* worked to instantiate these codes. The narrative functioned in concert with other genre efforts, effectively defining what can be done in the genre for years to come. In addition, aside from what the film does in sync with other horror movies, we can also determine what singular contributions separate *The Last House on the Left* from other genre efforts.[1]

Rural Rape and Revenge: From Bergman to Craven

Unlike any other notable horror film from the seventies *The Last House on the Left* has a distinguished pedigree. Most epochal horror films from this era draw from some combination of urban legend, *Snuff (1974)*, fuzzy history, *The Texas Chain Saw Massacre (1974)*, and genre conventions that build on and depart from passe codes

The Last House on the Left

The Last House on the Left

cribbed from once salutary chillers. *Last House*, despite introductory titles that boldly claim what we are about to see is based on true events, remakes Ingmar Bergman's Oscar winning *Jungfrukallen* (*The Virgin Spring*, 1959) which in turn is based on a 14th century Scandinavian legend. While remaining ostensibly true to *The Virgin Spring*, which documents the violent punishment meted to a band of itinerant shepherds for the rape and murder of a favourite daughter, *Last House* reconfigures Bergman's troubling meditation on the profound difficulty of following God's will into a bleak, horrorshow void.

The Virgin Spring, the first film shot with Bergman by celebrated cinematographer Sven Nykvist, meshes model compositions of foreboding smoky chiaroscuro, mainly interiors, and striking, dichotomous whites and blacks. These powerful images serve to foreground both the difficulty and the necessity of divining the presence and direction of God. Masterfully shot, this is a film where, even if beyond one's own reach, the hand of God remains palpable. In dismal contrast, the inept shakycam and cheap colour stock of *The Last House on the Left* bleeds the on-screen world of tangible gravity. Given that the film was most often screened in drive-ins, where ambient light and long projection distances wash out the image even further, this is a film where the world is worn to a flimsy, washed out scrim. In this place, a vitiated stage bleached of mystery and substance, could anything matter? Perversely, as the violent havoc claims our attention, like the mangled wreckage of a smash-up drawing rubber neckers, and we succumb to narrative drive, any interest in the ends of the contestants is undermined by the shoddy arena in which they struggle to survive.

The Virgin Spring also demands attention by virtue of the cast's prowess. Lead by a young, sternly robust Max Von Sydow, these players give a sobering phenomenological depth to their parts that is almost entirely absent in the characters embodied by The Last House on the Left company. Aside from the performance of David Hess, as the repellent Mansonesque ringleader Krug in Last House, these are paper-thin creations. Whether unable, unwilling or undirected, the Last House actors fail to do much more than scream and writhe with conviction. Even those with the greatest experience and the strongest motivation, soap opera actors Gaylord St. James and Cynthia Carr playing parents of murdered and raped Mari Collingwood enter the fray bemused or benumbed. Collectively, nearly all of the cast are negligible actors and evanescent on-screen presences. Barely acting, they don't eat the scenery-they simply disappear into it.

In most other productions a barely discernable world blighted with stilted performances would merit little attention. Yet, The Last House on the Left, soon to be reissued in high resolution DVD, managed to draw large audiences for years wherever it was not banned.[2] And even in those countries where it can not be legally screened, the United Kingdom, Australia, and New Zealand, it must have some mimetic power to convince concerned authorities that it carries a significant threat.

The Last House on the Left

The Last House on the Left

Low budget horror, especially meat movies like the groundbreaking *Last House* and other landmark horror films of the seventies reaps an unexpected benefit when quality doesn't get in the way. Absent captivating performances and mesmerizing cinematography the audience is free to concentrate on the nature, meaning and manner of spectacular violence. What makes *Last House* so unforgettable is the cruel violence employed by the gang as they prey on the innocent *and* the feral savagery of crazed parents hungry for their pound of flesh. Even while it tells the same basic tale, *The Virgin Spring* is so well crafted, so freighted with portentous significance, that terrible violence pales before the question of what men and women should do when confronted with insufferable transgressions in a world where God's grace is not readily discerned. *The Virgin Spring* is diffident theodicy. *Last House on the Left* is an unmitigated assault.

Unlike *The Virgin Spring*, where the authority figure is (presumably) a caring God, *The Last House on the Left* embodies authority in human form. Bergman would have you search your soul, in league with the characters struggling on screen, to test for the presence of Authority. *The Last House on the Left* and its ilk demand less from the audience by giving authority a human face in the concrete form of cops, psychics and psychiatrists, mothers, dads and other traditional figures of strength, guidance and comfort. Unfortunately, even as horror films of this era accommodate the demand for corporeal authority, with protagonists who embody the Law, the Good,

The Last House on the Left

and Reason-the entire phallic spectrum, authority cannot prevail in normative seventies horror.

This standard code helps us make sense of perhaps the most maddening feature of *Last House in the Left*. In a sub-plot with no parallel companion story in *The Virgin Spring*, a rube sheriff and even dimmer deputy, who fritters away his empty shift reading a Classics Illustrated comic, have their puerile misadventures intercut with the ultra-violent rapine and mayhem. The officers spend the duration of the film overlooking the obvious and never catching sight of the murderous gang. Hoofing it to the crime scene, after running out of gas and failing to hitch a ride on a chicken truck, the Law arrives in time to do absolutely nothing. A long-time, staple figure in drive-in movies, the redneck oaf of a sheriff provides welcome comic relief in many low genres.(This figure reached an apotheosis in the roughly contemporaneous *Smokey and the Bandit* (1977, 80, 83) features). In Craven's film, these moronic interludes regularly interspersed with the prolonged torture and execution of both the innocent and the vicious work to provide a remarkably maddening film experience. The continually abrasive shift from dopey law to savage lawlessness, from fourth-rate Benny Hill buffoonery to death from a thousand cuts, with close-ups of handy knife-play and brain splatter, works to create near impossible tension.

Cutting back and forth between the posse and the imperiled has long been a convention common to a variety of genres. As the menace looms larger, as the train bears down on Pauline and Dracula moves in for a last kiss, tension is pleasurably heightened as the film cuts to the rescue team in pursuit. And while it seems as if help will never arrive, and pressure mounts, with the audience wound tight with bated breath, we are all engaging in a fanciful suspension of disbelief. We know, however long the camera lingers on help's rough passage, that all will be as it should— except in dominant seventies horror. In *Last House* we have to learn that help, the long, comforting arm of the Law, will rarely ever reach those in need. In this tutorial, cutting between vapid authority and barbarous abuse makes a lash of the edit. Every switch in scene, from hicks afoot to abattoir, is a nasty swipe at the audience.

A Record to Nowhere: The Use of Soundtrack in *The Last House on the Left*

This is not that only aberrant and abrasive shift to which the audience is subject. In a manner which closely resembles Arthur Penn's *Bonnie and Clyde* (1967), another violent ground-breaker, *The Last House on the Left* employs a jaunty, celebratory score accompanying the gang as they scramble from one killing floor to the next.[3] Featuring the instrumental genius of Flatt and Scruggs playing breakneck breakdowns as Bonnie and the boys blow through the Midwest, *Bonnie and Clyde* employs music that works to both sanctify giddy violence (a fast picked banjo rarely produces sounds that lead to melancholy introspection), and to estrange the audience from the pleasure they might initially take in gutshooting bankers, deputies and G-men. Grafted onto exhilarating gunplay and dynamic edits between multiple camera positions, these reels first lead to toe tapping, but eventually, even though the shootouts and instrumentals share a wild rhythmic core, knee-slapping tunes don't perfectly mesh with the discharge of lethal weapons. Still, the music does, for at least a time, manage to contain contraries. As unstoppable folk music the score harmonises with Bonnie and Clyde's status as Depression era heroes. As woefully inappropriate accompaniment, gangsta pickin', the music satirises the notion that Bonnie and Clyde can claim to be anything more than greedy sociopaths.

The Last House on the Left aims to employ similar music to similar effect, attempting to construct ancillary music that manages to make both heroes and anti-heroes of Krug and his gang. Employing the banjo, a la Flatt and Scruggs, but also the kazoo, the ersatz Aquarian folk music of *Last House*, which in one number describes the "quartet in harmony" as "barbershop bad" the soundtrack jars because it is completely out of kilter with the perverse, Sadean suffering the gang inflicts on their prey.[6] Again, as with the painful cutting between errant lawmen and the grotesque appetites of the gang, the inappropriateness of the music makes the film all that much more difficult to bear. For the entire course of *The Last House on the Left* irreconcilable sounds and vision buffet and chaff anyone hoping for consonance and a complementary sensory experience.[4] Once more, grating inconsistencies and dashed expectations make for a more horrific film. A related blasphemous mismatch between sound and vision is engineered by Stanley Kubrick in *A Clockwork Orange* (1971). Here, however, Kubrick exactly choreographs the blows issued by malevolent thugs with the score in order to both aestheticize mayhem, violence as a modern dance, and to critique the notion that a beaten, broken body can ever become an *objet d'art*

Family Violence in *The Last House on the Left*

There are two final deeply frustrating oppositions that work to make *Last House* an exceptionally disturbing work of horror. Early on in the film a radio announcer details the daring daylight escape of the gang. In his description of the felons we, along with the doomed kids gaily cruising with the radio on, are told that the gang comprises murderers, drug pushers and rapists. Furthermore, the ringleader has hooked his own son on heroin in order to foster filial obedience. As if fathers fixing sons were not enough, the announcer continues to elaborate the gang's egregious sins by noting that they killed prison guards and kicked a German shepherd to death on their break to freedom. Finally, the gang is known to rape nuns. Described in gravid stentorian overkill, by the time the laundry list of criminal offenses includes inexcusable canine abuse and nun rape it would be natural to assume the film has spun off into hyperbolic parody. This is the dysfunctional Manson family fit for a John Water's fantasia.

In concert with a supporting score that rivals needledrop pornographic soundtracks for vapid affect, the radio primes us to expect a preposterous menace of ludicrously overblown proportions. As with nearly all sensible expectations predicated on familiarity with previous genre exercises, this reasonable demand goes callously unmet. Instead, the gang metes out a sadistic regime of torments that is unequalled by nearly any previous or contemporary horror film. With brutal rapacious glee the gang beats, cuts, rapes, torments, humiliates and executes their charges. Even worse, a hand held camera films these rites at a very intimate distance. At close range the participatory camera merges with the circling antagonists. Any measure of comfort that is provided by a more detached, voyeuristic camera is simply unavailable from this noxious, confederate point of view. It is a relief when Mari finally staggers, under her own power, into a scum-covered and algae choked pond to die apart from her attackers. As the shore-bound camera marks Mari's descent into the pond and she puts some space between herself and her assailants, the only moment of secured dignity in the film, her last act of agency generously allows the audience to put some welcome distance between themselves and the unwarranted, unforeseen slaughter that has been too closely monitored.

At this moment, in league with a scant handful of other incendiary scenes, the genre is gutted, unmade and, for better or worse, remade. (The final, never-ending twenty minutes of *Texas Chain Saw Massacre* is another such primal scene). There can be no innocent return to earlier modes of spooky torment post *Last House*. Certainly, films can and have been made which reject this model, but filmmakers and audiences alike must now manufacture belief under a new regime. Whenever discrete violence is preferred, whenever the camera shyly looks away, whenever the body is not torn, a conscious choice is made between turning back or savouring the once unimaginable. Now, even when ultra violence is eschewed, we know what could have been. Prior to *Last House*, the audience was not at liberty to envision the impossible.

The ultimate indignity of *Last House* comes at last, not with the end of the innocent, but rather with the grand destruction of Krug and his companions by Mari's parents. Given that so much of popular film, in and out of the horror genre, depends on the revenge story, with the protagonists manfully claiming their due, while villains get what's coming to them, it's no shock for *The Last House on the Left* to climax with all wrongs righted. But, as with so much of this film, the chasm between what is duly expected and what is given to the audience cannot be bridged. Even though audience expectations are nothing more than candied delusions, given the ferocity with which *Last House* attacks the unwary and the genre, the last battle still manages to come as an unwelcome surprise. Despite time and again demonstrating how much further there is to go, the last third of *Last House* manages to shock. Done with Mari and her friend the gang dons spare clothing, shedding their blood spattered duds, and seeks shelter in a nearby dwelling. Unknowingly, unbelievably, they have ended up at Mari's home. The same thing happens in *The Virgin Spring* except that in Bergman's version a ridiculous coincidence reads as Providence with the Lord delivering up one's enemies. No matter, absurd plot contrivances, like all other narrative niceties figure little in the withering light of savage retribution. Mari's parents, good souls that they are, welcome in the strangers despite being burdened by concern for their missing daughter. When they eventually discover the killer's misdeeds the parents become, in an instant, homicidal monsters themselves. With teeth, chainsaw, shotgun, shaving cream and other handy implements the killers are, collectively, sawn, shot, electrocuted, drowned, castrated and finished. Again, the camera works in close and there is no remove from the violence at hand. Whether merited or not, all violence is shot in the same brutally intimate fashion. In this regard the earlier sequences, with the gang in control, cannot be used against *Last House* as evidence of an especial disregard for women. No matter who is dealing the blows or receiving them, the camera will not let go. Horrific affect is radically magnified, when, under the new rules of the game, menace cannot be defeated. The resultant affect is perversely cinematic: whatsoever menace elects to do must be directly, closely, and endlessly detailed. The notable horror of the seventies lets horror have it way while never, ever granting the audience shelter or respite.

Yet, didn't Mari's parents carry the day as the film expires the moment the last gang member dies? Can we legitimately claim for the formative horror of the seventies that menace most always trumps the specious good? Yes, because the pyrrhic victory of the Collingwood's necessitates that they become even more grotesquely vicious than their antagonists. Unlike the typical action film death, wherein villains are dispatched with a quip and smile by collected heroes, this version of the horror film only allows monsters to succeed. Potential victors must be willing to become their worst enemies. In this regard, the violence that men, women and monsters do is infectious. The carrier may be dead but the contagion lives on.

Seen by some as the most potent genre film of the era, while dismissed by others as a hack job, *The Last House on the Left* continues to plague the genre after twenty-five years the horror film has still not recovered from mutations in the code wrought by a cheap remake. Bergman, for all his orotund skill is a filmmaker without heirs, while Wes Craven's *The Last House on the Left* has, for over three decades of genre filmmaking, continued to maintain a considerable and unmistakable influence.

There is, as *Last House* makes perfectly clear, no justice.

Notes

1. The most exhaustive treatment of *Last House* is David Szulkin, *Wes Craven's The Last House on the Left: The Making of a Cult Classic*, rev. 2nd edition (Surrey: FAB Press, 2000).

2. Aside from fanzines and a host of home pages and web sites dedicated to canonizing the best in film horror, the Internet Movie Database (http://us.imdb.com/ and http://uk.imdb.com/), provides a useful and extensive compendium, from pan to rave, of fan reaction to *The Last House on the Left*.

3. The soundtrack to *The Last House on the Left* is available from the David Hess website at http://www.davidhess.com.

4. For a detailed explanation of how avid film fans find enjoyable work in making sense of films cleft by radical incongruity see Xavier Mendik and Graeme Harper's 'The Chaotic Text and the Sadean Audience: Narrative Transgressions of a Contemporary Cult Film', in *Unruly Pleasures: The Cult Film and Its Critics*, ed. by Xavier Mendik and Graeme Harper (Surrey: FAB Press, 2000), pp.235-249.

Head Cheese: *The Texas Chain Saw Massacre* Beyond Leatherface

Martin Jones

> Where you come from is gone, where you thought you were going to never was there, and where you are is no good unless you can get away from it.
> - *Wise Blood*, Flannery O'Connor. [1]

Behind the Mask

Masks. Posters. Chain-saws. Bootleg videos. Screaming. Model figures. Icons. It's as difficult to separate the character of Leatherface from *The Texas Chain Saw Massacre* (1974) as it is to bisect Siamese twins with a rusty nail...but, for now, just try. Try and forget that Leatherface has become an inspiration for countless heavy metal bands and gorehounds and merchandisers. Forget that, as with other contemporary horror icons, he wears a mask. Just like Jason and Michael and Ghost Face, numerous actors hide beneath the constructed features. Mask equals cool. These hooded fictions are (anti) heroes because they exist entirely on a surface level, and so are easy to reproduce into figurines and masks. Put one on and <u>you</u> become the character. Check out your local comic store and see how many Norman Bates figures are left on the shelves. The masks of his celluloid successors offer expressions of terror and death. If they were to be taken off, underneath you'd find... nothing.

Leatherface is the main attraction on the turbulent surface of *The Texas Chain Saw Massacre*. A one-track anti-hero who delights audiences and alienates film critics. In his essay, 'The American Nightmare: Horror in the 70s', Robin Wood notes:

> Watching it recently with a large, half-stoned youth audience who cheered and applauded everyone of Leatherface's outrages against their representatives on screen was a terrifying experience...it expresses, with unique force and intensity, at least one important aspect of what the horror film has come to signify–the sense of civilization condemning itself, through its popular culture, to ultimate disintegration, and ambivalently...celebrating the fact. [2]

Christians to the lions. Half the films' cast are sacrificed to the fetishistic chain-saw, with Leatherface as warrior number one. In a character line-up, he is the easily identifiable poster child. If, as Kim Newman has stated, "*The Texas Chainsaw* [sic] *Massacre* is only defensible as a nightmare"[3], then the nightmare lies beneath Leatherface's gleeful slaughter. He pulls the punters in; but, like a bloody, intrusive eclipse, his bloated frame blocks out more subtle aspects of this particular horror story.

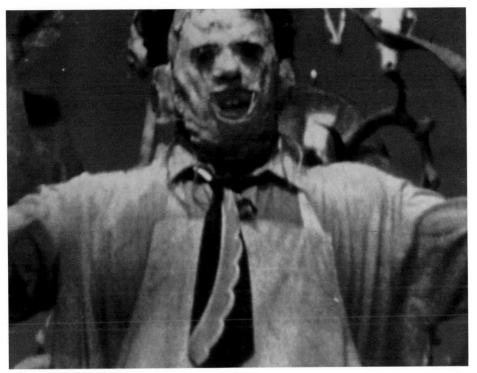

The Texas Chain Saw Massacre

All that has to be done is to glance past that stained apron, that chain-saw, that mask...

Come With the Gentle People

In Russ Meyer's dazzling *Beyond the Valley of the Dolls* (1970), a foxy three-piece girl pop group (plus manager) drive out to California in search of fame and fortune. They find it, fuck it, and overdose on it, until death and a moralistic narrator intervene. In Tobe Hooper's *The Texas Chain Saw Massacre* (1974), five young people drive into America's rural South in search of reassurance and family history. Death and events beyond the realms of reasonable control intervene. Far from the streets they are used to, both sets of kids face unnecessary danger. However, in Hooper's film, the danger signs are all around. The curiosities of urban folk are discouraged in the dry landscape of *The Texas Chain Saw Massacre*: look too close, and you might get hurt. Just as its title suggests, the film is saturated with piercing noise, lethal machinery and desperate screams reverberating across burning Texas dirt tracks. Within eighty-or-so minutes, all three: title, chain-saw, and screams-compete to be the loudest...

Jerry and Sally (Allen Danziger and Marilyn Burns), Kirk and Pam (William Vail and Teri McMinn), plus Sally's wheelchair-bound brother, Franklin (Paul A. Partain), are on a road trip towards family history. They are driving back into the past, a place far,

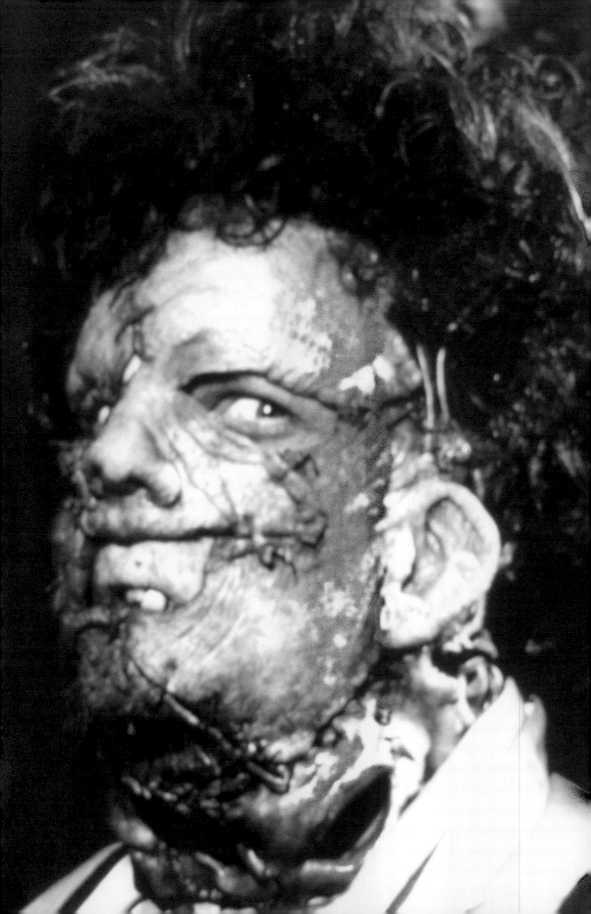

far away from their regular lives. In this past men found it necessary to take on jobs that bloodied their hands and clouded their minds. The countryside around them is occupied by graveyards and dust, water-starved fields and dilapidated, half-remembered houses that reek of faded childhoods. The kids are driving into it to find out if the grave of Sally and Franklin's grandpa has become victim to a recent spate of disinterments. The day out will also encompass a visit to the old family farmhouse. "A fun trip." But, as the all-knowing opening narration states, "For them an idyllic summer afternoon drive became a nightmare." Of the group, Jerry and Kirk are flawed adverts for their country, perhaps in need of a haircut and sideburn shave. Jerry wears a flowery shirt and sports glasses and a curly hairdo. Kirk is less extravagant, and was probably once a quarterback for the team back home, the template of a thousand parental dreams. The girls are complementary. Fragile brunette Pam is akin to a Hollywood laboratory experiment that terminated somewhere between Goldie Hawn and Sally Field; in her backless bikini top and red denim cut-offs, she should be wandering through Frankie Avalon's last beach party, not these dangerous backwoods. Sally has *Brady Bunch* blonde hair and wears a purple and white vest and thigh-hugging white flares; she looks like a survivor, not as breakable as Pam. Only Franklin is the aberration in this collection of gentle people, a by-product of the American Dream, a *doppelganger*–as noted by Robin Wood-of its nightmare:

> The young people are, on the whole, uncharacterized and undifferentiated...,
> but in their midst is Franklyn [sic], who is as grotesque, and almost as
> psychotic, as his nemesis Leatherface.[4]

But never as dangerous. Not only is Franklin fat, whiny and sweaty as his monstrous mirror image , but he's also in a wheelchair. This means that the others are responsible for him at all times. Towards the climax of *The Texas Chain Saw Massacre*, it also becomes apparent that the family are responsible for Leatherface's welfare. Resentment spans across both parties. America never wanted to be the land of the infirm or retarded. To the kids, Franklin is a four-wheeled cramp on their style: the dweeb left alone at the end of the party. Their behaviour confirms that the "monstrous cruelties of the slaughterhouse family have their more pallid reflection within normality."[5]

The ripples of this cruelty expand far. Franklin is not a beautiful person. He is a liability to fun. A target. The narration paints him as such, and warns those outside the picture of what will happen: "The film you are about to see is an account of the tragedy which befell a group of five youths, in particular Sally Hardesty and her invalid brother, Franklin." Sally, Franklin, and the others are passing through dead lands, unaware of the horror that surrounds them. As Kirk wheels an ungrateful Franklin out of the van in order to urinate, news reports seep from the radio: murder, accidental death, natural disaster. Horror surrounds them. Death is all around. A dead armadillo lies belly up on the roadside, its solidity hazed by heat lines (excised scenes from the released film included a dead dog at the bottom of an embankment).

Heat isn't good for flesh, unless it's being barbecued: too many flies, too

The Texas Chain Saw Massacre 2

much smell. The wide open graveyard where Sally and Franklin's granddaddy is buried is a natural heat conductor. Why don't all the corpses raise a stink from beneath the ground? As the kids get closer to their destination, it becomes clearer that their trip is laced with morbid fascination: they are driving towards dead people and dead places. And those who are not dead live on the borderland between the two. An idyllic summer afternoon drive?

The Mad and the Macabre...

Degenerate Texan musicians *Ministry* have numerous side-projects: one of them is *Revolting Cocks*. In 1993 the Cocks released a sleaze-injected version of Rod Stewart's 'Da Ya Think I'm Sexy?' In the song's promotional video, Southern brother Edwin Neal reprises his role as the Hitchhiker from *The Texas Chain Saw Massacre*. Almost twenty years down the line, Neal is again windmilling his limbs and blowing raspberries at the camera, as if obeying a sign on the Texas border that cheerfully reads: "YOU'LL NEVER LEAVE!" Perhaps he never will leave. The role, that is. Its claim on him is as unremovable as the lurid birthmark on the Hitchhiker's face. But who would want to be remembered for anything else? The Hitchhiker is the wild card in Hooper's film; wilder than lumbering Leatherface (Gunnar Hansen), who obediently waits at the family homestead, butchering tools at the ready.

Before the film's apocalyptic opening titles, a camera flashbulb illuminates a body for split seconds at a time. After these glimpses of decay, the picture widens to show two dug up corpses tied together, horrific news reports the accompanying soundtrack. This is the Hitchhiker's work, or rather, his hobby. Whilst the rest of the family slave over cooked and uncooked meat, this spindly delinquent roams the parched graveyards, photographing his lovingly-constructed tableaux. Just as the Zapruder film captured the brain of a president, the Hitchhiker captures death in photographic records. Although there is no coincidence in where his lens is directed. With his manic face (birthmark, grin), greasy hair and ragged clothes, the Hitchhiker could almost be the last lost member of Charles Manson's Family, wandering through the South four years after the Tate-LaBianca murders. Like those mythical tales of soldiers fighting wars long-finished, the Hitchhiker has gone beyond any plans outlined by Manson, with his Robert Heinlein novels and hallucinogenics. He is the illegitimate child (the legitimate child was Marilyn Burns, taking a part as a Family member in the 1976 film *Helter Skelter*), who would rather get on with cutting someone up than listen to another Beach Boys record.

Rumours of snuff movies floated around the fringes of Manson's world, magnified by Ed Sanders' freaky-deaky true-crime study, *The Family.*[6] The word 'rumours' doesn't exist in the Hitchhiker's limited dictionary. His motto could well be: "less talk, more action." Even from the relative distance and safety of their van, Pam remarks, "oh, he's weird looking!" But this is just an indication of what the kids think

The Texas Chain Saw Massacre

is weird. After the passenger has made himself comfortable, Franklin says, "I think we just picked up Dracula." Yes, the Hitchhiker is weird looking. He's too weird looking to be a hippie, a love-child, a peacenik. He is beyond any of those (middle class) labels. In the Southern Gothic world of *The Texas Chain Saw Massacre's* family, the Hitchhiker is the deformed brat they keep in the barn and try not to talk about.

An irksome bunch of Satan-worshipping hippies feed an old-timer LSD–for kicks–in *I Drink Your Blood* (1971). In return, the trippin' granddaddy's son offers them rabies-infected meat pies. Result: the freaks turn even more bloodthirsty and over-the-top. All this caused by reactions to chemicals and disease. There's nothing but red, red blood pumping through the Hitchhiker's veins. "My family's always been in meat," he tells the open-mouthed kids. The Hitchhiker has expanded his perimeters beyond the slaughterhouse of his childhood, the hammer-and-pull gang his formative experiences. Unlike the crazed hippies of *I Drink Your Blood*, no additives made him like this, it's just the way he is. The lines of difference have already been drawn. Previously dismissive of Franklin's tales of slaughterhouse lore, the kids are now face to face with the meat industry. A little too close: a bit like ordering your burger and then having to watch as–behind the sizzling skillet–the teenage staff struggle to kill an uncooperative cow. They don't think about how it gets into their hands because it's not part of their everyday lives. Fingers in the ears time. When Franklin crosses an anecdotal line, Sally whines, "I like meat, please change the subject." So far, the kids have driven through these dead lands with the van protecting them from unappetising sights. Now, the Hitchhiker is the living embodiment of what they don't want to see, sitting just feet away...

With an undemanding song playing on the radio, the kids stare at the Hitchhiker as they would a mutant cow in a freak show. His birthmark marks him out as an abnormity, a complicated birth. In Hooper's *The Funhouse* (1981), a travelling fair houses such a bovine, cleft palate and all. But whoever decided to let Hitchhike Senior live, now he runs free. Pulling a Polaroid camera from his kitbag, the Hitchhiker photographs Franklin, who acts suitably violated. (The military connotations of the kit bag are further underscored when a similar character is painted as a deranged Vietnam veteran in the 1982 sequel *The Texas Chain Saw Massacre 2*). But why not photograph him? He is–after all–the fattest, juiciest, slowest, and so the easiest to slaughter. Good riddance, the audience (and his friends) say. Those wheels will prove to be a hindrance later. Franklin has become a pin-up for the meat industry. The Hitchhiker's slaughterhouse mind has already marked him out as the first to go.

There are weird, ritualistic talismans attached to the Hitchhiker. Within their van, the kids also wander in the arena of the speculative, thanks to Pam's astrological readings, which warn that malefic Saturn is in retrograde, apparently bad news for anyone (Sally) whose sign (Capricorn) is passing by that way. Pam's interest has become the hidden code of the film. Robin Wood writes:

> We infer near the opening of *Massacre* that the age of Aquarius whose advent was so recently celebrated in *Hair* [contemporary nude hippie musical]

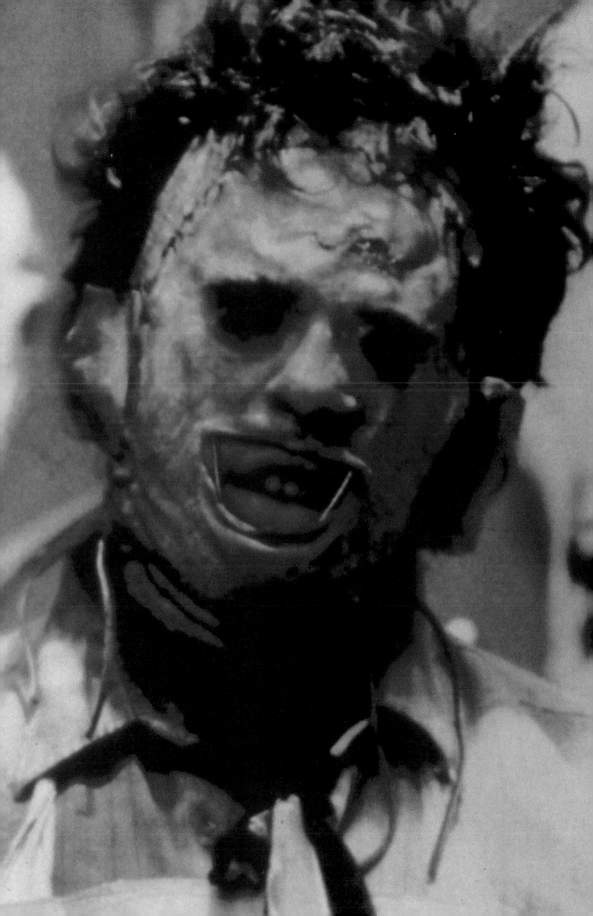

has already passed, giving way to the Age of Saturn and universal malevolence. Uncontrol is emphasized throughout the film: not only have the five young victims no control over their destiny, but their slaughterers (variously psychotic and degenerate) keep losing control of themselves and each other.[7]

The author JG Ballard once wrote: "Deep assignments run through all our lives; there are no coincidences."[8] The kids may have no control over the 'assignments' of their lives, but someone, somewhere is always pulling the strings. Growing up, Sally and company have had more than enough time to realise this. For every Kennedy assassination and Hollywood murder and Vietnam, there is a Mafia, an ex-convict, a government, in total control or not. The kids are victims of North America's meat industry, mere grains of sand, as Kim Newman has pointed out:

> The only cerebral reading of the film sees it as a rabid vegetarian tract: the people in the movie suffer exactly the same atrocities daily inflicted on beef cattle in the name of Ronald McDonald.[9]

If trust has been put in something so ethereal as star-signs, there's no real reason why the kids should be freaked out by the Hitchhiker's ways. After Franklin refuses to buy the Polaroid ("You can pay me now. Two dollars. It's a good picture!"), he pulls a lump of tin foil out of the fur pouch around his neck, unfolds it, places the photo in its centre, adds some inflammable powder, and lights the whole thing up. Rituals of death: the Hitchhiker is literally taking Franklin out of the picture, setting fire to him with Texas heat. The foil covers up the evidence of this burning easily, but, just to add a further touch to his ritual, he quickly cuts Franklin's forearm with a straight razor. Cast out of the van amid panic, the Hitchhiker smears his own blood-the result of a self-inflicted wound made in front of the kids-on its side panels. Later, only Franklin will stop to consider this mark, but even he cannot realise its full meaning: the Hitchhiker has painted a cabalistic symbol on the kids van, a sign to his kin that they have been targeted as fresh meat.

After shedding their malevolent passenger, the kids pull into a garage forecourt. Thanks to the Hitchhiker's bloody smear-symbol, Sally, Jerry, Kirk, Pam and Franklin are already on the conveyor belt, and the hammer is hovering above their heads. This is a gas station without gas. There is a coke machine out front, and barbecue cooking inside, but nothing to propel the kids vehicle beyond their visit to the old homestead. Business has dried up because civilisation has been redirected; but, just like the Bates Motel in *Psycho* (1960), the proprietor carries on regardless. The kids are too polite, too nice, to be around places like these. As the Old Man (Jim Siedow) who runs the garage tells them: "you boys don't wanna go messing around in an old house. Those things is dangerous. You're liable to get hurt." If the incident with the Hitchhiker didn't warn them of impending doom, then this dying place should.

A forecourt crony (Robert Courtin) stares up at a golden coin of a sun. His large, angular forehead points to signs of acromegaly, or perhaps gigantism, which makes you wonder what's in the water, or the meat. With a bucket and cloth he wipes the dirt and flies from off the van windscreen, an automatic gesture activated whenever the Old Man approaches. As far as *The Texas Chain Saw Massacre* goes, the Old Man is the most regular character encountered. Hell, he even has a job. Only buck teeth offer clues to abnormality. He sells the kids some barbecued meat and cordially warns them of the dangers of exploring unstable buildings (even when he learns that Franklin and Sally have a hereditary right to). He wants them to stick around, where he can watch out that they don't get up to mischief. Noticing Sally and Pam gathering drinks from the vending machine, he tries to appeal to the men's sense of gallantry: "Them girls, now, they don't wanna go messing around no old house. Do they?" No, they don't. Sally's white flares would get dirty. Pam might graze one of her bare knees.

Beetles and Vans: Symbols of Freedom

Comparisons have been made between *The Texas Chain Saw Massacre* and rational ghost-hunting cartoon *Scooby Doo*, but it's too easy a reference. In their groovy van, a good-looking bunch of kids investigate spooky happenings in an old, dilapidated house. Can you really imagine Fred with a meat-hook up his rectum, or Thelma's bloody limbs flying through the air? Staying in the same area, *The Texas Chain Saw Massacre* might be better suited to a reinvented *Wacky Races*. The family in some kind of souped-up dragster, pursuing the kids' van down a lonely highway: buzzing chain-saws, scraping hooks, engines and screams. *Mad Max 2 (1987)* for flower people. It's a scene that damn near happens at the beginning of Hooper's belated sequel, *The Texas Chainsaw Massacre 2 (1986)*, where Leatherface (same mask, different actor) and company rule the road in a four-by-four truck, decidedly more high-tech now. A better class of murderer.

The sequel is nothing more than its predecessor pumped full of movie hormones. Everything is cranked up ready to fly way over-the-top. A great deal of the film takes place in an inexplicable subterranean stage set, like the producers discovered it left over from something else, and didn't want it to go to waste. The dirt and viscera of the 1974 production is replaced with new Hollywood-funded slop. The most memorable aspect of *The Texas Chainsaw Massacre 2* is the short blast of The Cramps' sublime 'Goo Goo Muck', a song which had the right idea all along. When the sun goes down and the moon comes up, it's best not to be within the boundaries of strange territory. Behind the ancestral home, Kirk and Pam go in search of an old watering hole, only to find a dried-up creek instead. That isn't all they find. Past the creek stands another—seemingly occupied—house. One that has played no part in Sally and Franklin's childhood memories. People equals gas.

On their way to the place, Kirk and Pam wander through a field of bright, healthy sunflowers; this pleasant juxtaposition in homicidal backwoods cinema being a consistent trait in seventies 'backwoods horror.' For instance, in *3 on a Meathook* (1973), nice young Billy takes his potential girlfriend on a slow-guitar stroll through summer cornfields. But, in *The Texas Chain Saw Massacre*, flowers are as far as the peace gets. Stray from the path, and there is the split-second glimpse of a ripped, abandoned tent; rusty mugs and utensils hanging from a tree above it. Are these the remains of a rock festival that never happened? Or did the campers set up their tent in darkness, unable to scan the landscape around them? Did they ever see daylight again? Kirk thinks that whoever lives in the house will accept his guitar as security for some gas, but the undiscovered canvas graveyard indicates otherwise. How many other easygoing types have passed by this way? Beneath camouflage netting that belongs in Manson's desert hideaway, Kirk and Pam find a collection of stationary cars and pick-ups. Have they stumbled onto a free-living commune? Or is this just a trophy cabinet of vehicles? Amongst the regular wheels are some prime Volkswagen movers: a dirty white Beetle, a pale green Beetle, a two-tone camper van. Beetles and vans: symbols of freedom, of independence. The 'let's do it now' mentality. Let's drive out into the countryside and explore. How many of these vehicles' occupants encountered the Hitchhiker? How many stopped for gas at the Old Man's garage? Freedom-hogging young kids on a road to somewhere, their journeys suddenly cut short.

In Wes Craven's edgy *The Hills Have Eyes* (1977), the mutant hillbilly patriarch tells his civilised counterpart, "Don't you come out here and stick your life in my face." The Hitchhiker and Leatherface and the Old Man probably feel the same way about the urbanites who disturb their shimmering landscape. In the van, the Hitchhiker gets agitated when Franklin talks about new methods of killing cattle ("The old way...with a sledge!") He and his kin are clinging onto the only lives they know, unconcerned as to how such ways might look to outsiders. The new has no place here. Even a filling in a lone tooth counts as an invasion from the modern world. Kirk finds the tooth on the porch of the house, and uses it to gross out Pam. But its presence there is ominous. A filling says 'recent.' A filling says: whoever dwells within has no respect for the modern world. Being the first to find the place, Kirk and Pam are–naturally–the first to die. This backwoods homestead hides a slaughterhouse conveyor belt, where live meat travels unwittingly to its doom. Inside, Kirk moves down a shadowy hall, enticed by what sound like pig noises. But something is amiss through the frames of the next doorway: the wall is red, and covered with animal skulls, hung like trophies. Before Kirk can even begin to take in these anomalies, he trips and comes face to face with Leatherface, who sledgehammers him across the head and then slams a steel door shut on the scene, as if to say: "it's not for you to see what happens next."

Pam may be lined up next on the conveyor belt, but at least she gets to see some of the horror contained within the house before she dies. Quite a lot of it, in fact. This place is a mausoleum of body parts, as Pam discovers when she stumbles into a room–hidden, vaudeville-style, behind a curtain–whilst looking for Kirk. Feathers choke the floor, limbs make up sections of furniture (an 'arm' chair; a lamp-holder), too-big chickens live in too-small cages, eyeless skulls stare at nothing. The room is an exaggeration of fact: in 1957 farmer, mummy's boy and necrophile Edward Gein was arrested for the murders of two women. Further investigation unearthed a collection of female body parts in his house, and numerous items of clothing made from human skin. Gein lived in the Northern state of Wisconsin, but his lifestyle is at home in any rural backwater, and grotesque enough for any filmmaker ready for the challenge: from Hitchcock's chubby hand, through to the biographic *Deranged* (1974) and *3 on a*

Meathook. Gein's pleasure has now become Pam's pain, and a set decorator's nightmare.

Kirk and Pam have had their freedom curtailed. At least Kirk didn't know what hit him. Pam has gone through the whole horror mangle, and it doesn't end there, as she is now the unlucky party in a universal fear. Confronted by Leatherface, she makes it to the front door of the house, even gets onto the porch, but is pulled back into the shadows by the lumbering slaughterer. The beautiful day-blue skies, blazing sun-was just seconds from her grasp, and now it is gone. Pam's alternative is a slow, painful death: Leatherface deposits her on a meat-hook whilst he goes to work on Kirk, giving the eponymous chain-saw its debut. Within hours of setting out to go swimming, Pam is futilely struggling with a hook stuck deep in her back whilst a taciturn, masked figure cuts up her boyfriend with a power tool. A more horrible reversal of fortune on such a pleasant day could not be imagined.

The Pickup Drives off With the Screaming Girl

The antagonists of *The Texas Chain Saw Massacre* are a pond-life bunch of misfits. Brought together, all they do is squabble and shout: cartoon villains with no manners. The family hierarchy is unveiled when the last survivor of the kids day-trip is captured and dragged into the home. As the sun fades over this alien territory, only Sally and Franklin remain. Jerry went to look for Kirk and Pam, but stepped on the conveyor belt and got hammered by Leatherface for his troubles. In darkness, Sally struggles to push Franklin's wheelchair over uneven ground, trying to follow Jerry's steps through hindering brambles. There is no escape for Franklin when Leatherface emerges from the darkness and shoves a whirring chain-saw into his gut. This four-wheeled death signifies the beginning of Sally's descent. As the opening narration has pinpointed, the tragedy befalls Sally and Franklin, in particular. But whose end is the more tragic: Franklin's, or his sister's?

Sally's terrified flight from Leatherface glues *The Texas Chain Saw Massacre* together like a freakish jigsaw puzzle. Beneath a wave of screaming and chain-saw, she crashes into the garage encountered earlier, straight into the arms of the Old Man. Now it all begins to make sense. Whilst the Old Man goes to get his truck, Sally's eyes fall on the barbecuing meat (after all the film has revealed, it now looks strangely human). In the background, endless radio reports of grave robbing continue, a sound-loop of sudden realisation. That Sally has come so far, and avoided so much physical damage, is the perverse final piece in the jigsaw. It is even stranger that she is finally subdued with an ordinary household item: chased by a chain-saw, beaten unconscious with a broomstick. The Old Man knocks her senseless with it as he tries to reason with her. Although he's the sanest member of the family, his repression soon fades when faced with fresh meat. But-as pointed out later-he's just the cook, a person feared by Leatherface and ridiculed by the Hitchhiker: "I heard you, but it don't mean much!"

With his catch half-unconscious, restrained by sack and rope, the Old Man can indulge in his guilty pleasures, something to bring a goofy smile to his face. Driving back home, Sally helpless on the floor of his pick-up truck, he tentatively pokes her with the broomstick. Each scream of response brings on another attack, and another. The Old Man enjoys his sadism whilst no one else is looking, keeping his respectable side for the garage customers, if there ever are any. The Hitchhiker, however, is uncontrollable. He is still travelling the dusty roads when the Old Man gets to the family home; but no amount of berating ("C'mere you nap-haired idiot!") can harm him, and he taunts the Old Man mercilessly, blowing raspberries and slamming truck doors, avoiding his elder like a manic, devilish child.

A cinema poster for *The Texas Chain Saw Massacre* asks: "Who will survive and what will be left of them?" Blonde Sally survives, and she's still intact. Bruised and cut, but still intact. Her hair is matted and dirty now, her tight vest is torn, her hip-hugging jeans no so white, but she's still alive. Whether this is a good thing, she does not yet know. For now, tied up, face to face with maniacs she thought she'd never see again (Hitchhiker: "I thought you was in a hurry?!"), it is all too much. Her eyes go wide before she blacks out. And then she wakes, from one nightmare into another.

"I just can't take no pleasure in killin'," the Old Man moans to no one in particular when the family are seated at the dinner table. But he still enjoys the end results. Like the encounter with the Hitchhiker back in the kids van, he betrays a sympathy with them, remaining reluctant to have knowledge of the methods and workings of animal slaughter. Sally's waking eyes fix on a meal from hell: skulls and bones and slabs of unappetising, pale meat. She starts screaming again, and doesn't stop for a long, long time. He don't take no pleasure in killin', but the Old Man loves joining in with the family taunts. As Sally takes hysterical stock of her situation, he jumps around by the doorway, laughing, as if reluctant to commit himself wholly to this madness. There is much to covert on Sally: a fair amount of succulent flesh to go round, and a head of golden hair, a sought-after possession by Leatherface, one more accessory for his masks...

There is an end to this nightmare. Sally manages to escape, to smash through a window into daylight, and make her way onto the highway. The Hitchhiker gets pureed under the wheels of a truck; Leatherface is left standing alone with his crazy chain-saw; the Old Man survives to turn up in *The Texas Chainsaw Massacre 2* as a parody of himself; and Sally...Sally scrambles into the back of a passing pick-up: alive, bloody, but a giggling, shaking mess. Perhaps the vehicle is taking her to act out more of the same in Hooper's next film, *Death Trap* (1976), another prime cut of Southern Gothic?

Sally Hardesty has survived the family's conveyor belt. But it is only a kind of survival. It is all the more tragic in that she was young. She and Franklin and Jerry and Pam and Kirk came into contact with things they knew nothing of: a lifestyle they could not comprehend; values alien to them; seemingly barbaric methods of existence. Before her escape—when she was tied up—great emphasis was made on close-ups of Sally's green eyes: wide, terrified, more white than green. When the Hitchhiker cuts her finger to feed blood to their fossilised grandfather (who should really be dead in the ground, just like Sally's), her eyeballs look like planets of terror; and on the scleral surface of these violent planets: veins, grit, oceans of tears. Perhaps one is Saturn. Pam warned that Sally's sign would pass by it: "There are moments when we cannot believe that what is happening is really true. Pinch yourself, and you may find out that it is." But who was going to take any serious notice of her hippie ethos, words from a cheap astrology magazine? Cultures collide like planets in *The Texas Chain Saw Massacre*, and peace and love is no protection against the business end of a meathook.

Notes

1. Flannery O'Connor *Wise Blood* (London: Faber and Faber: 1989), p.159.
2. Robin Wood, *Hollywood: From Vietnam to Reagan* (New York; Guildford: Columbia University Press, 1986), pp.93-94.
3. Kim Newman, *Nightmare Movies* (London: Bloomsbury, 1988), p.53.
4. Wood, p.92.
5. Ibid, p.92.
6. Ed Sanders, *The Family: The Story of Charles Manson's Dune Buggy Attack Battalion* (London: Panther Books, 1973) , see chapter 13 'Getting the Fear.' A comprehensive overview of this subject can be found in David Kerekes and David Slater *Killing For Culture: An Illustrated History of Death Film from Mondo to Snuff* (London: Creation Books, 1998).
7. Wood, p.90.
8. JG Ballard, *The Atrocity Exhibition* (London: Flamingo, 1993), p.4.
9. Newman, p.53.

London Kills Me: The English Metropolis in British Horror Films of the 1970s
Nick Freeman

Monsterising the Metropolis

In the early 1970s, the British horror film was in crisis. A series of high profile rows over censorship, notably concerning Ken Russell's *The Devils* and Sam Peckinpah's *Straw Dogs* in 1971, had led to a general reconsideration of film content. This process given added impetus by the underground success of George Romero's *Night of the Living Dead* (1968), with its cinema vérité style and cynical narrative morality, and the enormous box office and critical acclaim of William Friedkin's *The Exorcist* (1973), nominated for multiple Oscars. As Kim Newman points out, these problems combined with the wider plight of the British film industry to render the "small-scale Gothic horror film" obsolete.[1] Audiences expected more gore, and expensive special effects, and were no longer satisfied by Hammer's increasingly desperate attempts to graft their (late 1950s-1960s) formula onto contemporary genres such as soft core pornography (*The Vampire Lovers* (1970), *Lust for a Vampire* (1970), *Twins of Evil* (1971)) or the violent 'meat' movie (*Scars of Dracula* (1970)).

Gothic cinema in the States was equally threatened, and indeed would die out in the mid 1970s, finished off by the explicit brutalities of *The Texas Chain Saw Massacre* (1974), but it at least managed to ring a few changes on older ideas with films such as *Count Yorga, Vampire* (1970) and its sequel, *The Werewolf of Washington* (1973), the *Kolchak* and *Dark Shadows* TV series and so on. What distinguished American horror of this period was its willingness to exploit the contemporary cityscape: to site events in recognisable everyday surroundings rather than the favoured settings for British horror films. These were, in the main: ersatz 18th century European villages, peopled by a stock company of emblematic authority figures, aristocratic wastrels and damsels in distress. Both the characters and the locations which surrounded them (i.e. dark foreboding forests) lent themselves to Freudian interpretation. Meanwhile the company depicted Victorian London as a garishly lit theme park of rhubarbing Cockneys, pub sing-alongs and doomed tarts. Audiences were so familiar with the conventions of these settings that the films which used them became intensely predictable, yet those which offered imaginative variations on the Gothic paradigm such as *Vampire Circus* (1972) and *Captain Kronos, Vampire Hunter* (1972) or on the Victorian one, *Dr. Jekyll and Sister Hyde* (1971) for example, often disappointed precisely because they refused to obey the rules. The only option for British film-makers was to drag the horror film into the world its viewers knew only too well-the modern conurbation. Confronted with this change of emphasis, horror audiences would, it was hoped, be able to savour new thrills, and be drawn back to the British product.

Unfortunately, exploiting the resources of the metropolis was no easy task.

American horror writers, especially Robert Bloch and Fritz Leiber in the 1940s, had succeeded in using the contemporary city as a setting for horror narratives. Such authors recognised that the alteration of the quotidian is, if done even passably, far more frightening and immediate than the alteration of the fantastic, historically distant or unknown. British and American film makers, however, had been reluctant to use the city in the same way, despite the possibilities shown by such works as *London after Midnight* (1927), *Dark Eyes of London* (1939) and *Cat People* (1943). The city had passed into the hands of genres such as gangster movies, *noir*, thriller, the 'problem picture' and musicals. From *Scarface* in the 1930s to *Singin' in the Rain* in the 1950s, the city had been exploited as a venue for intricate social relationships, manic high-spirited spectacle, social crusades and clashes between cops and robbers. However, few directors had used it as a venue for out and out horror films. It was one thing to show a city under threat from a single marauding creature as in *King Kong* (1933), *Godzilla* (1954), *The Beast from 20,000 Fathoms* (1953), or *Gorgo* (1960); quite another to see its institutions and values being challenged from within by subversive intelligences or the supernatural. In the monster movies of the 1950s, citizens and their leaders invariably unite against a common foe, but this is far more difficult when they are not sure whom or what that foe may be. Don Siegel's allegory of McCarthyism, *Invasion of the Body Snatchers* (1955) used the corruption of a small town as a microcosmic symbol of the wider threats to American life-when the film was remade in 1978, the

Dracula A.D. 1972

setting was changed to San Francisco with far less success although in some ways more unsettling overtones.

Yet the city suggests itself as a richly imaginative horror setting, offering as it does so many contrasts and juxtapositions between for example, interiors and exteriors, danger and safety, technology and barbarism. The city shows man at his most sophisticated and masterful, but at the same time more insignificant and vulnerable than ever before. Its many faces can conceal Satanic corruption behind a facade of quintessential good-neighbourliness as in Roman Polanski's *Rosemary's Baby* (1968), or lead one to question what is taking place behind locked doors, as the same director did in his extraordinary *Repulsion* (1965).

Georg Simmel and later sociologists have noted how the city is often organised by its inhabitants on the lines of individual relationships and needs-it has no necessary centre, as each of us approaches it as an individual. The gulf between the personal metropolis fascinatingly explored by Jonathan Raban in *Soft City* (1974) and the wider, impersonal conurbation is one which crime films have often utilised. The detective, be he Sherlock Holmes, Father Brown, or Lieutenant Columbo, has traditionally been able to decipher the city's intricate codes and introduce an element of justice as an organisational principle. However, although horror often uses many of the same devices, it does not need to solve narrative or moral puzzles in the same way.

Dracula A.D. 1972

Dracula A.D. 1972

London Kills Me!

1972 and 1973 saw a clutch of British films which attempted to challenge these ideas, and exploit London as a setting for a modern horror movie. Each approached the task in a different way, and the results were consistently entertaining, if critically mixed. During the 1960s, London had served as an effective backdrop for the range of genres identified above-crime films, spy thrillers, caper comedies, explorations of social problems and so on, but its potential as a setting for horror films remained largely untapped. There were some notable exceptions: Michael Reeves's inconsistent but imaginative *The Sorcerers* (1968) found Ian Ogilvie stalking a city of clubs and discotheques in search of thrills for the old couple who control his life by means of an hypnotic process, while Gordon Kessler's *Scream and Scream Again* (1969) which owed as much to science fiction and conspiracy thrillers as it did to horror. However, such films only served to emphasise that British horror was still adjusting to the urban environment. *Dracula A.D. 1972*, *Death Line* and *Theatre of Blood* all tried to redress the balance, and reveal London's potential as a city of nightmare.

Hammer's *Dracula A.D.1972* is a strange concoction, and one that divided studio personnel. Anthony Hinds and Christopher Lee deplored suggestions of a *Dracula* film with a contemporary setting, but Sir James Carreras was far more impressed with the idea and encouraged development of Don Houghton's original screenplay, tentatively entitled *Dracula Chelsea*. The title shifted to *Dracula/Chelsea 1972* and then to *Dracula Today* before shooting began at the end of September 1971. Such confusion undermined the film from the very beginning, and to make matters worse, its "perspective on youth culture . . . seemed a good decade behind the times."[2]

   Dracula A.D. 1972 begins with an excitingly shot Victorian sequence depicting the vampire and Lawrence Van Helsing (Christopher Lee and Peter Cushing) fighting to the (un)death on board a stage coach careering through Hyde Park in September 1872. This sequence finishes with an abrupt cut from Van Helsing's funeral to the same churchyard a century later-a jet airliner screams overhead and the electric guitars and brass of the title theme roar into life. However, the switch from past to present was less easily accomplished. James Barnard's famous motto theme sounds before the opening distributor credit, jarring with the more 'contemporary' score of Mike Vickers on the credits themselves. The familiar medieval letters of *Dracula* visible at the start of the titles are then replaced by Times Roman capitals, while the memorable stage-coach fight overshadows the montage of modern London-a building site, flyovers, traffic jams, a steak house(!) and red buses. While a film such as *Taste the Blood of Dracula* (1969) had used a Victorian setting to articulate late twentieth century anxieties about familial collapse, *Dracula A.D. 1972* created a division between the Victorian and the modern that seemed far greater than a hundred years. This in itself could have had interesting imaginative and narrative consequences, but Houghton's

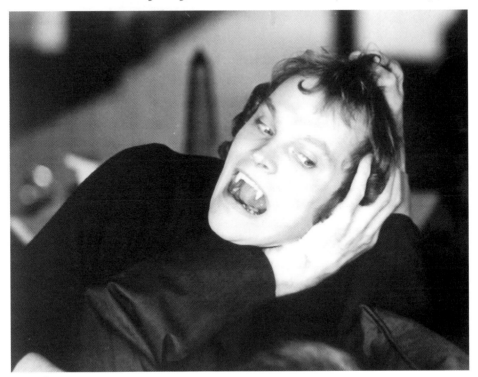

Dracula A.D. 1972

Dracula A.D. 1972

script had little idea of how to exploit their potential.

The film's aggressive emphasis on youth further weakens its impact. Christopher Neame plays Johnny Alucard(!), Dracula's Triumph Stag-driving disciple, as an all-purpose hustler, scene-maker and Mister Fixit. The character inhabits an elegant Mews house and exerts an unhealthy influence over a group of fashionable Chelsea teenagers. He encourages them to experiment with 'black magic' in the ruins of St. Bartolph's church, where Dracula's remains had been concealed in 1872. Their rites resurrect Dracula, who is soon back to his old ways, vampirising attractive young women such as Caroline Munro and Marsha Hunt and coming into conflict with both the Metropolitan Police and Van Helsing's descendants.

The film reunites Hammer's most famous pairing, Christopher Lee in the role of the Count, and Peter Cushing as his long-standing nemesis, Van Helsing. The film was directed by Alan Gibson, a Canadian who had previously directed *Crescendo* for Hammer in 1970. As the above synopsis suggests, *Dracula A.D. 1972* is an attempt to update the Gothic formula rather than break new ground, and the compromise is a fatal one. Reviewing the film for the *Monthly Film Bulletin*, Clyde Jeavons called it "abortive and totally unimaginative"[3] , a fair summation of critical responses to the work, and one that is unlikely to be challenged. The film now offers a parade of kitsch pleasures, with its 'The Time... The Place... The Killer' poster, post-psychedelia fashions and dated teen slang, but it remains flawed in a number of crucial respects.

Dracula A.D. 1972

As usual, Lee and Cushing are excellent, but their skills only throw into relief the dramatic poverty of most of the cast, although Neame might have made a passable understudy for Malcolm McDowell in *A Clockwork Orange* (1971). Lee in fact hated the new Dracula; the purist in him was appalled by the script's apparent conflation of the Count with Satan. More worrying than the variable acting, however, is the central problem of Dracula's acclimatisation to the late twentieth century. George Hamilton's coming to terms with present day America in *Love at First Bite* (1979) provides some slick comic moments, but Don Houghton's script for *Dracula A.D.1972* flounders, failing to suggest the Count's timelessness, his Victorian inheritance or the potentially fruitful encounter between high Gothic and neon-lit modernity. Lee's stately presence and unchanging iconography clash interestingly with rock music and mini-skirts, but the film does not pursue these contrasts, settling instead for a predictable battle between the new generation of Van Helpings and the vampire. Recalling the London of 1971 in *Stardust Memories* (1983), Ray Connolly remarks:

> Somehow the idea of sitting in the back of a Rolls, cruising back to town looking at the pretty, leggy girls in Knightsbridge has always seemed to me to be one of the most lasting images of London when it was just about to stop swinging.[4]

Hammer's film inhabits this transitional city, poised between the fag-end of

Death Line

psychedelia (one character drives an elaborately painted Citron, while Alucard has a groovily painted mirror) and the emergent styling of glam rock. Indeed, one of its U.S. titles was *Dracula Chases the Mini Girls*! In a scene towards the beginning of the film, San Francisco also-rans The Stoneground play at a Chelsea party to an audience of hippies, evening jacketed straights and a girl in silver lurex hot-pants and crop-top. Neck-chokers, Afro hairstyles and skull-caps suggest a confusion of fashion and sub-cultural allegiances unlikely in a world in which Gaynor (Marsha Hunt) can pronounce mini-skirts a thing of the past. The film's Chelsea set congregates in the neon-lit Cavern coffee bar on the King's Road to drink coffee at twenty pence a cup and dream of tickets to the Albert Hall Jazz Spectacular. Their dialogue would not have seemed anachronistic in *Beat Girl* twelve years before, but elsewhere, Hammer did make a more determined effort to seem better informed, with passing allusions to the Manson murders and a general attempt to engage with the early seventies' popular enthusiasm for 'black magic.' Even here though, dialogue such as "Dig the music, kids!" and "I demand an audience with his satanic majesty" did the film no favours. "The trendies vampirised by the resuscitated count... are patently phoney... and the attempt to reconcile Transylvania with SW3 merely sends the script haywire", reported the MFB.[5]

Alan Gibson never comes to terms with how he wishes to use London, even though the city enacts the very encounter between ancient and modern that the film seeks to dramatise. By concentrating on a group of teenagers, he offers a contrast between youth and age, but even this is flawed by the fact that most of the cast is manifestly older than the characters they play. A case could be made for the creation of a temporally or chronologically uncertain city, but Gibson uses only convenient establishing shots, and never succeeds in using St. Bartolph's church, where much of the action takes place, as anything other than a venue for vampirism and occult experimentation: an impressive set, it is largely wasted. Ultimately, the film presents a dated version of Swinging London, complete with shots of *Chelsea Male* and other boutiques which middle aged film executives patronisingly assumed would attract the youth market and suggest something of London's position as the world's trendsetting capital city. One could hardly blame Lee's Dracula for wishing to destroy the world in *The Satanic Rites of Dracula* the following year. The credit sequence of that film also hints at an intriguing mixture of ancient and modern. To the strains of an up-tempo action film soundtrack, with brass and wah-wah to the fore in the style of *Enter the Dragon*, a menacing silhouette of the vampire looms over famous London landmarks. Once again however, the film promises more than it delivers.

Terror Under the City: *Death Line*

Dracula A.D.1972 failed to meet the challenge of reconciling Transylvania with fashionable London, and only succeeded in hastening Hammer's demise. Hearn and

Death Line

Death Line

Barnes are more charitable, suggesting that it "gets more entertaining with the passage of time" and is "perhaps best enjoyed as an endearing, if naïve, picture of an era that never was."[6] *Death Line* however emerges as a triumphant success. Directed by Gary Sherman, a young American who had previously specialised in advertising commercials, the film is a terrifying yet moving piece which solves the clash of ancient and modern far more effectively than Hammer's trite fusion of Dracula and dolly birds. The London Underground is the venue for a series of mysterious disappearances, culminating in that of a high ranking official from the Ministry of Defence. It transpires that he has been abducted and killed by a cannibal, the last survivor of the descendants of a gang of labourers engaged in building a tube station in 1892 who were trapped by a cave-in and left to their fate by unscrupulous railway companies. Two students, Patricia and Alex (David Ladd and Sharon Gurney) who were the last to see the official alive, are drawn into the investigation, as is lugubrious police inspector Colquhoun (Donald Pleasance) and his assistant Detective Sergeant Rogers (Norman Rossington). Patricia is snatched by the cannibal, who, lonely and grief-stricken following the death of his pregnant mate, seeks a replacement for her and takes the girl to his body-strewn charnel house somewhere beneath the British Museum. Her subsequent escape occurs only after a touching and macabre scene in which she is wooed by the monster, whose only remaining snippet of language is a half-articulate cry of "Mind the Doors!"

Death Line tackles London in a number of ways. Rather than fall back on the clichéd location footage of what Alan Parker has denounced as 'red bus films' (red buses can be seen on several occasions in *Dracula A.D. 1972*), Sherman uses defiantly ordinary locations. Pleasance and Rossington get drunk in one of the few vaguely realistic pubs in English cinema; the two students live in a messy flat that might actually be inhabited by the people they are supposed to be. The director's real triumph however is his use of the London Underground, a genuine meeting of Victorian and modern technology, which he shows as dirty, antiquated and consistently menacing. Anyone who has travelled alone on a subway train will appreciate the masterful control of sound and lighting in the tube scenes. Rather than making use of exaggeratedly menacing tracking shots, Sherman employs a deliberately flat style which makes shocks all the more unexpected, especially in the sequence when the cannibal attacks three night workers and there is a desperate fight on the station platform. Alex Thomson's photography further enhances an atmosphere of claustrophobic dread, as does the film's minimalist electronic score.

The cannibal, or 'The Man' (Hugh Armstrong) as he appears on the film's credits, is a bridge between past and present. Inbred, bereft of companionship and driven by needs he can neither understand nor control, he inhabits a bleak subterranean world analogous to the class position of his forebears, whose rescue from the collapsed tunnel shaft was considered "economically unviable." Sherman

Death Line

DEATH LINE

creates a dialogue between the surface city, typified by the official's expensive flat and Christopher Lee's suave intelligence man, and the railway tunnels beneath it, in which Patricia acts as an unwilling intermediary. The film can also be read as a political allegory in similar terms, with the privileged few living above those they have oppressed and rendered inhuman. In this reading, the fact that the two students are studying at the London School of Economics assumes a certain significance, as does the ironic siting of the cannibal's lair beneath one of the nation's leading cultural depositories. Sherman does not drum the message home, preferring to leave the viewer with the final shots of Colquhoun uncovering the hide-out and requesting an ambulance. "Get these kids out of here" he says, a comment that might be applied to the cinema audience as well as the film's youthful protagonists.

Death Line succeeds because of the way it manages to combine English and American readings of the city. It draws upon elements of European, especially Italian, horror cinema in its use of cannibalism, (its alternative title was Raw Meat) and sometimes suggests the subterranean Paris of The Phantom of the Opera. Alex is from New York, and brings to the underground an intensely urban sensibility based upon caution, distrust and callousness. Typically, when the couple find the man from the ministry unconscious at the start of the film, Alex believes him to be a drunk, Patricia to be a diabetic in a coma. "In New York, you walk over these guys" Alex remarks, only to be met with her principled, "We're not in New York." Alex's apparent harshness is the protective shell of the city dweller, that identified by Simmel in 'The Metropolis and

Mental Life' (1903) but one that Patricia has yet to acquire.[7]

Simmel posited that the figure he designated as "the metropolitan type"[8] adapted to its environment in particular ways, creating "a protective organ for itself against the profound disruption with which the fluctuations and the discontinuities of the external milieu threaten it."[9] "Instead of reacting emotionally, the metropolitan type reacts primarily in a rational manner",[10] he argued, "thus creating a mental predominance through the intensification of consciousness, which is in turn caused by it."[11] Simmel believed that the 'intensification of consciousness' was in fact a safety device, allowing the 'metropolitan type' to cope with the flood of diverse imaginative stimuli to which it was subjected. The experienced urbanite, far from celebrating unique epiphanies, shunted them into a cerebral siding where they could not derail the more urgent mental processes of everyday survival. "The reaction of the metropolitan person to those events is moved to a sphere of mental activity which is least sensitive and which is furthest removed from the depths of the personality"[12] he concluded, anticipating the blasé attitudes of many late 20th century city-dwellers. Alex's treatment of the stricken official suggests that he is the 'metropolitan type' personified.

As an American, Sherman looks at the underground itself in a different way - few English cities, even now, have subterranean railway networks, but Sherman is obviously blasé, and his cool compositions reveal the squalid heart of the London transport system. The slow passage of the camera through the lair shows the juxtaposition of modern bodies with Victorian memorabilia, and offers a glimpse of the world Michael Foucault has called "the epoch of simultaneity.. the epoch of juxtaposition, the epoch of the near and far, of the side-by-side."[13] This environment Foucault terms the *heterotopia*, "capable of juxtaposing in a single real place several spaces, several sites that are themselves incompatible."[14] It is, he posits, "the space in which we live, which draws us out of ourselves, in which the erosion of our lives, our time and our history occurs."[15] The erosion of the gap between past and present would seem very much part of the imaginative engagement with the heterotopia, and here *Death Line* excels. Foucault suggests that heterotopic spaces exist outside of conventional chronology and association, being "something like counter-sites, a kind of effectively enacted utopia in which the real sites, all the other real sites that can be found within the culture, are simultaneously represented, contested, and inverted."[16] The metropolitan interpreter grapples with the complex interplay of personal and extra-personal spaces within an apparently unified (if not unitary) realm. In *Death Line*, Sherman posits that London is what Henry James termed "a collection of many wholes"[17], a number of cities at the same time, with the cannibal's lair serving as a focus for Alex and Patricia's disturbingly disordered encounter with London's histories. By contrast, *Dracula A.D.1972* could only offer a cluster of largely unimaginative locations devoid of wider meaning and suggesting merely tangential connections with the London of the film's audiences.

The City and the Stage: *Theatre of Blood*

Douglas Hickox's *Theatre of Blood*, released in 1973, was undoubtedly one of the most enjoyable horror films of the decade, mixing *grand guignol* with deft humour. Vincent Price is Edward Lionheart, a melodramatic Shakespearian actor determined to be honoured with the Critics' Award following a triumphant theatrical season. When the Critics' Circle rewards the endeavour of a young actor Price considers "a twitching, mumbling boy", he throws himself into the Thames and is presumed dead. The following year, however, he returns, aided by his beautiful daughter Edwina (Diana Rigg) and a gang of psychotic tramps, in order to kill off the critics who spurned his talents. This he does by restaging and, on occasion, rewriting the death scenes of his final Shakespeare season, with the critics filling the roles of the victims, hence its American title, (*Much Ado About Murder*). Although it is nowhere near as profound a film as *Death Line*, *Theatre of Blood* makes stylish use of its London locations. Once again, the film employs the device of the past being at war with the present as Price takes the Shakespearean canon back to the world of Victorian melodrama, and then into a bloody confrontation with modernity.

The film's emphasis on theatricality creates a variety of interesting effects. Price's multifarious disguises correspond to the urbanite's protean constructions and varieties of self, mixing individual personality with the demands of circumstance. His daughter's employment as a make-up artist is another witty hint that, in the modern city, all is not as it seems. The critics too suggest something of the difference between looking and seeing that distinguishes the urban semiotician or detective from the more passive city-dweller.

Hickox employs London as a theatrical backdrop to Lionheart's crimes, and manages to show the city as a series of contrasts, again in the manner of the Foucauldian heterotopia. (Although the abandoned theatre where Lionheart rehearses his infamies does not offer quite the same imaginative juxtapositions as the cannibal's lair). The film opens with George Maxwell (Michael Hordern) being stabbed to death by Price's tramps in a derelict warehouse, and from there takes in a wine merchant's, a fencing school, a fashionable Knightsbridge boutique, a restaurant, luxurious riverside housing, the critics' penthouse overlooking the Thames, and the poorer quarters where Price and the tramps hide between murders. In one memorable sequence, Price reveals how he survived his apparent suicide, being washed up on a muddy riverbank where he greets the drunken tramps inhabiting it with lines from *The Tempest*, "O brave new world, That hath such people in't." The film's structure plays on the twin poles of the penthouse and the theatre, returning to each or either after every outrage. And yet, while Sherman could give a strong sense of place from just a few tube signs, Hickox's London exists as a series of free-floating set pieces rather than a coherent vision of the metropolis. London is of course all the settings that Hickox employs, but is also the sum of them and more. The episodic construction of the film never manages to create this element of montage.

It does however encourage the viewer to see the modern city as a theatre-

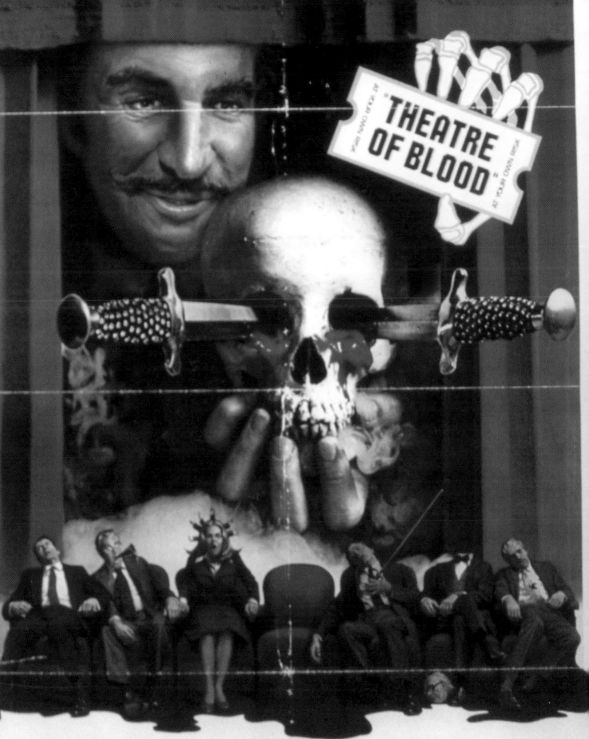

not in the way Hammer's Victorian London was obviously set-bound and often imaginatively feeble in terms of a convincing metropolitan locale, but as a performative space in which anything is possible. The laws of the city apply neither to Price and his gang, nor to the places that they inhabit. Anthony Greville-Bell's script and the sets of Michael Seymour and Ann Mollo combine to transform mundane settings such as a hairstylist's studio into venues for Price's transgressive activities. Despite a considerable police presence, nobody is safe from Lionheart. The depiction of a city under this type of siege is a cliché, invariably signified by the favoured device of the news-stand and its hoarding, or, in more recent films, the overheard radio or television broadcast. However, because of the very precise targets of Price's vengeance, Hickox never needs to show London being menaced in its entirety; as in his earlier incarnation as Dr. Phibes, Price has specific subjects for vengeance and the wider population is not at risk from his activities. Instead, Hickox conveys the destruction of the Critics' Circle by constantly returning to the penthouse where it met, the camera revealing the steadily increasing number of vacant chairs.

The film's finale promises much, but is eventually rather conventional. Peregrine Devlin (Ian Hendry), the last remaining critic, is kidnapped by Edwina and taken to Price's theatre where he is cast as Gloucester in an impromptu production of *King Lear*. He is told that unless he reconsiders the decision of the Circle, and presents Lionheart with the award, he will be blinded "to improve [his] vision." Devlin refuses to give in to Lionheart's threats, whereupon the meths-drinking tramps run amok, the theatre catches fire, and the police arrive just in time to free Devlin and see Price plummet from the roof into the flames. Although this is a dramatic spectacle, it suffers in comparison with the kidnapping sequence itself, in which Hendry is struck down by a rag-and-bone man on a desolate stretch of road.

In scenes such as this, Hickox blurs the final years of a vanishing Victorian city with the contemporary-Edwina drives off with the unconscious Devlin in her fashionable sports car. The rag-and-bone cart, like that of *Steptoe and Son* on British television, and the revelry on the mud-flat which accompanies Price's 'resurrection', belong not to the London of 1973 but to a sinister Victorian past coexisting uncomfortably with it. Lionheart belongs to the world of 19th century melodrama, a point reinforced by the film's antique style credits and score, and his assistants are equally rooted in the past, particularly resembling the river scavengers of Henry Mayhew or Charles Dickens's *Our Mutual Friend* (1865). Once again, the present triumphs over the past but at terrible cost-despite Devlin's cheap exit line, the abiding memory is of the dying Edwina's exchanges with her father, and Lionheart himself, cape swirling, standing on the roof of the blazing theatre before vanishing into the flames. As Leon Hunt has remarked, "how can one side with modernity when the 'past' is embodied in such persuasively flamboyant and wittily elegant form?"[18]

The naïve updating of *Dracula A.D. 1972* represented Hammer in terminal decline, entertaining though the film is today. *Theatre of Blood* offered an intriguing perspective on the city as theatre, but one which was perhaps undercut by its elaborately formulaic narrative structure. Of the three films discussed here, only *Death*

Line managed a genuinely exciting development of the representation of London within the horror genre. However, as a low budget independent film with two largely unknown leads and a villain who is both repellent and pitiful, it did not inspire imitation. It might also be suggested that *Death Line* gains many of its effects by comparing and contrasting surface and subterranean Londons, in some ways taking a stage further the ideas of Nigel Kneale in *Quatermass and the Pit* (1967). The film was therefore less interested in London's everyday surfaces than in their relationship to the world beneath them. Perhaps this is because of the film's limited budget did not encompass lengthy location shooting, perhaps because for the protagonists of *Death Line*, life has become uncannily similar to a tube journey: they trace daily paths between fixed points, university to bookshop to flat, or from police station to crime scene to home, just as commuters traverse identical routes on the underground each day. For Alan and Patricia, not to mention Inspector Colquhoun, the city has contracted to a series of individual associations and personal paths. As Jonathan Raban observed, in the London of the early 1970s:

> we map the city by private benchmarks which are meaningful only to us. . .The constrictedness of this private city-within-a-city has the character of a self-fulfilling prophecy. . .one builds a grid of reference points, each enshrining a personal attribution of meaning.[19]

In that sense, the film's characters are just as trapped and confined as The Man, another method by which Sherman suggests not the alterity of horror, but our kinship with it.

The death of the British horror film in the mid-1970s, and the wider collapse of the British film industry meant that the innovations of *Death Line* went largely unnoticed. Such a film was unlikely to inspire a cinematic re-envisioning of the English capital, but it showed nonetheless what could be done with the modern metropolis. Unfortunately, almost thirty years later London seems firmly in the hands of television crime dramas and the occasional Hollywood thriller, its potential as a setting for horror cinema still largely unrealised.

Notes

1. Kim Newman, *Nightmare Movies* (London: Proteus Books, 1985), p.23.
2. Marcus Hearn & Alan Barnes, *The Hammer Story* (London: Titan, 1997), p.156.
3. *Monthly Film Bulletin*, Vol. 39 No. 466 (November 1972), pp.230-231.
4. *Stardust Memories: Talking about my Generation* (London: Pavilion, 1983), p.132.
5. *Monthly Film Bulletin* (ibid.) p.231.
6. Hearn & Barnes, p.157.
7. 'The Metropolis and Mental Life' (1903) in Philip Kasinitz, ed., *Metropolis: Centre and Symbol of Our Times* (London: Macmillan, 1995) pp.30-45, p.31.
8. Ibid., p.31.
9. Ibid., p.31.
10. Ibid., pp.31-32.
11. Ibid., p.32.

12. Ibid., p.32.

13. Michael Foucault, 'Of Other Spaces' [lecture, 'Des Espaces Autres', 1967], tr. Jay Miskowiec, *Diacritics* 16, 1 (Spring 1986), 22-7 (p.22).

14. Ibid., p.22.

15. Ibid., p.22.

16. Ibid., p.22.

17. Henry James, 'London' in *English Hours* (London: Heinemann, 1905), p.30.

18. Leon Hunt, *British Low Culture: From Safari Suits to Sexploitation* (London: Routledge, 1998), p.144.

19. Jonathan Raban, *Soft City* (London: Hamish Hamilton, 1974), pp.166-167.

False Gestures for a Demonic Public in The Sentinel and The Antichrist
Andy Black

"We were banished because of our beliefs and the methods we have used to rid the earth of the disciples of the devil. Ex communication has been a small price to pay for the fulfilment of our destiny." - minister from the Brotherhood of the Protectors in *The Sentinel*.

"I find New Yorkers have no sense for anything but sex and money." - Miss Logan (Ava Gardner) to Alison (Christina Raines) in *The Sentinel*.

"If god performs a miracle for you he's good, he exists, he's your protector. If not, it's supposed to mean he's abandoned you but it's not quite like that, it's not so simple." - The bishop (Arthur Kennedy) in *The Antichrist*.

"Sects of devil worshippers are springing up everywhere...it's a symptom of the spiritual crisis of our time." - The bishop (Arthur Kennedy) in *The Antichrist*.

The Supernatural Seventies

Given the spectacular success of *The Exorcist* in 1973, regaling a captivated cinema-going public with the spiritual battle between good and evil, god and the devil as physically manifested upon the pre-pubescent body of a helpless teenager Regan (Linda Blair) via such flagrant means as levitation, stigmata and projectile vomiting, the success of *The Exorcist* appears almost inexorably linked to the traumas of seventies Amercia.

For instance, in his book *Hollywood From Vietnam to Reagan*, Robin Wood has linked the film's conflict between good and evil as an apocalyptic comment on the structure of Amercian ideals during the era. He notes that this nihilistic vision produced not only in the profound questioning of the amercian family as a structure of normality and stability, but also recast childhood innocence via the figure of the "Terrible Child."[1] The monstrous nature of the possessed child is clearly signalled by the hideous transformation of Reagan in the film, and her more excessive physical and sexual displays motivated much of the visceral excess of the imitations and sequels that followed Friedkin's film. Indeed, it is fascinating to see how this age-old struggle for spiritual utopia is handled in contrasting styles by British director Michael Winner's *The Sentinel* (1976) and Italian director Alberto de Martino's *The Antichrist/The Tempter* (1974).

For while the demonology in *The Sentinel* is avowedly implicit and material-delineating a Brownstone building which happens to be built over the gateway to hell, the demonology in *The Antichrist* is assuredly explicit and emotional with Carla Gravina as Ippolita, a crippled young woman who becomes possessed by the devil.

As a result of her afflictions, the normally virginal heroine becomes increasingly aggressive and sexually devious, much to the disgust of her close companions. While the protagonist's exaggerated gestures are clearly modelled on *The Exorcist*'s most shocking scenes, their impact goes beyond their use in Italian exploitation productions. Rather, the figure of Ippolita like Reagan before her, indicates the currency that the female body and the female sex organ has within the possession film of the 1970s. As Carol J. Clover has noted, in these narratives supernatural domination is evidenced through aggressive sexual displays, pointing to long held cultural myths that connect the vagina as an entry point to demonic possession. Through these beliefs, the female openings of the possession film:

> ...stand in a long line of female portals, from the equally gullible Eve through the professional portals-sibyls and prophesses-of classical and medieval times to the majority of psychic and New Age channelers of our own day. Certainly the portals of occult horror are almost invariably women.[2]

The Antichrist

The Sentinel

The Antichrist continues the theme of the "colonised body"[3] that Clover finds in many of the narratives of this type, situating a theme of female possession alongside that of dysfunctional patriarchal attempts to restore the order that excessive female sexuality threatens.

Whilst Winner chooses to explore the tangential effects of spiritualism via the extra-dimensional portal which leads beyond the physical world, de Martino firmly roots his battleground for spiritualism inside the human body-that of Ippolita to be precise.

By jettisoning the graphic displays of possession which inform *The Exorcist* and *The Antichrist* and a legion of other similar films, Winner creates a more cerebral canvas upon which he adds splashes of mental anguish. Alongside issues of sexual repression, the director situates the pivotal religious/secular conflict through a powerful condemnation of the political and social injustice of the seventies American society.

Winner's choice of his central character Alison (Christina Raines) in *The Sentinel*, a fashion model, serves to emphasise the superficial nature of modern society with its accent on materialism and artificiality as opposed to spirituality and strength of character/depth of purpose. The most glaring example of this occurs during one of Alison's photoshoots for a wine commercial where repeated 'takes' prove necessary

The Antichrist

due to her failure to leave the wine bottle and its brand label facing the camera.

Blind Faith?

Contrast this obsession with the importance of all things visual, all things seen with the figure of Halloran (John Caradine)-a blind priest who inhabits the top floor of Alison's house, blankly staring out of the window.

"Blind, well then what does he look at?" Alison enquires of her unusual neighbour. Casting aside any flippant comments regarding 'blind faith', the question is not so much *what* can he see, but can he see *more* than a sighted person. Perhaps he can see more than the immediate horizon which Alison sees all to easily, perhaps he can see beyond and deeper into the very soul?

No such existential debate or soul-searching in de Martino's avowedly more visceral *The Antichrist* as the tormented Ippolita ponders far more prosaic concerns- enviously eyeing her father Marino's (Mel Ferrer) blonde girlfriend Gretel (Anita Strindberg) from the confines of her wheelchair-"She's pretty and young and intelligent. She should be loved, she's a woman" Ippolita opines.

Having then discarded a tarot card into an open fire, whereupon wind and demonic voices howl around the spacious family home, Ippolita explains to her uncle, a bishop (Arthur Kennedy)-"The blasphemous image of christ was an image of the devil, uncle."

She then utters her plaintive philosophy; "Then why doesn't god make himself understood. The devil does and clearly too. He has been very clear to me. Has god forgotten you ? Has your father forsaken you ? Are you alone, unhappy, desperate ? Here I am. All you have to do is call me and I will be with you. I'll give you everything you have been denied" concludes her rhetorical question to the devil.

"God is testing you" her uncle replies, continuing to her that; "You're too possessive with your affection for your father. You must learn to know yourself honestly. Your jealousy is absurd."

Whilst Ippolita's 'possession' is subsequently revealed to be the external manifestation of her own inner demons and ancestral bloodline, Alison's battle with the forces of evil is not so much the result of any emotional baggage she carries with her but rather the unfortunate consequence of fate as she discovers that she is predestined to become one of the guardians (or sentinels) to the entrance to Hell, over which her house is built.

"To thee, thy course, thy lot, is given, change in strict watch to this happy

The Antichrist

place, no evil thing approach or enter it" from Milton's *Paradise Lost* proves to be the prophetic words which guide Alison's destiny.

When her boyfriend Michael (Chris Sarandon) does some investigating of his own amongst the secret records of the mysterious Brotherhood of the Protectors sect, he discovers the apocalyptic truth that "If these files are right, father Francis Matthew Halloran dies, the same day that Alison Parker disappears and becomes Sentinel Theresa... tomorrow."

During the film's conclusion when estate agent Miss Logan (Ava Gardner) is seen showing some prospective tenants around the now familiar Brooklyn house, she is asked if "the neighbours are quiet", to which she replies that one woman is a recluse. "She's a nun", whereby the camera pans away to reveal a now blank-eyed Alison silently staring out over the river as the Brotherhood's earlier prediction is proved to be true.

It is not prophecy but regression which provides the self-revelatory undercurrent in de Martino's film as we see a "practising psychologist" Dr. Sinibaldi (Umberto Orsini) persuade Ippolita to undergo regressive hypnosis in order to contextualise her inner demons in the hope of providing her with some form of emotional (if not physical) catharsis.

The Sentinel

The Sentinel

During the hypnosis Ippolita is transported back in time to the personal trauma of her mother's death in a car crash-Ippolita escaping the flaming wreckage only to discover that her legs are now paralysed-"My legs are dead" she screams. The surreal image of her now writhing on the psychiatrists couch, engulfed by flames like a witch being burnt at the stake becomes highly symbolic as Orsini tells her to meet her past-"Who are you?" he asks. In a dream/flashback sequence we see Ippolita transformed, now sporting long blonde hair and held captive in a circular cage as white-robed monks encircle her. It transpires that she is on trial as a heretic and is later sentenced to death at the stake before the therapy session abruptly ends.

Her father and uncle subsequently inform her that one of her ancestors was a nun forced into the path of religion and who later revolted by escaping to join a devil-worshipping sect. "So much family history, it can be a burden" she is told.

It is then the sight of Massimo and Gretel making love which acts as the catalyst in awakening Ippolita's angst, frustration and jealousy as she is shown writhing on her bed, apparently floating skywards. Transformed again into the blonde devil figure, we are transported into the ethereal setting of a fairytale wood-incantations, tribal drums, a masked figure-"You are about to become a daughter of Satan" the announcement as fog swirls around. An eerie azure filter colours the scene as we see a toad's head torn off and fed to Ippolita, whereupon she lasciviously licks

The Sentinel

the blood up from the floor, before then being penetrated by the masked figure - all cross-cut with Ippolita on her bed as the mattress ripples, curtains billow and the sky casts a shimmering aura.

As her regression therapy sessions advance, they culminate with the now shaven-headed Ippolita on trial, still imprisoned in her cage before Orsini asks her to try and walk-to his astonishment, she does !

"I feel so marvellous, as if I've been reborn" she gushes. We then see her ravenously tear into her meat at dinner and consume copious amounts of wine before then writhing and speaking in a latin tongue-"Look at my arse you whore, how many men have you had?" she spits forth at Greta. Continuing unabated, in suitably demonic tones, with foaming white mouth, lights flickering, doors banging and wind raging outside, she utters; "I have been waiting 400 years for today but I piss on that time."

During the graphic conflagration between Ippolita and the exorcising priest father Mittner (George Coulouris), all manner of demonic trickery is unleashed from levitation, to crockery smashing, to glass breaking, to projectile vomiting, explained by Orsini as being the product of "sexual frustration that brings on hysterical phenomena" -go figure eh, ever the psychiatrist.

Even the family's reaction is totally unreal-their response to Ippolita's behaviour being an intellectual debate on the mores of demonic possession rather than a shocked rebuttal of her behaviour.

She later confronts her sickened uncle-"Here is the devil" she shouts at him as she opens her legs up before him, later claiming that "You with your doubts priest and you're fragile faith-stop reading that idiocy" she demands as she makes the bible he is grasping burst into flames.

"You will not prevail" the bishop repeats as he brandishes his cross and places it upon Ippolita. As father Mittner begins reading his incantations her powers begin to ebb away as the triumphant priest claims "Behold the cross of God, Satan be gone... I exorcise you."

This battle of moral and gender wills reiterates Carol J. Clover's view that for the woman, the possession film is a "body story with a vengeance"[4], which forces women to reveal the inner most sexuality to male inquisitors. As Clover states:

> Film after film interrogates... the "physical presence" of a woman: forces it to externalise its most inner workings, to speak its secrets, to give a material account of itself-in short, to give literal and visible evidence. It is remarkable how many of these films in fact put the female body to some sort of formal trial.[5]

As the raging storm and demonic voices begin to calm down, we can hear church bells toll all around us as a new day begins to dawn-so good *has* prevailed over evil.

Freaks and the Normal

Unlike the overtly fantastical special effects and over the top exploitative approach of de Martino's film to its demonic possession subject matter, Winner's more prosaic, earthy approach lends an entirely more realistic tone to its supernatural subject matter. This was all the more problematic given his use of genuinely deformed and handicapped people, who help make up the 'legions of hell'-the ghastly apparitions who populate Alison's house and simultaneously haunt and terrorise her.

For some critics, this was all simply *too* distasteful-"A thoroughly execrable enterprise" according to *The Aurum Book of Horror* and lacking the sympathy and dignity afforded to the similarly real-life disabled who appeared in Todd Browning's controversial *Freaks* (1932).

Robin Wood went much further in his condemnation of the film. Commenting in the volume *Hollywood From Vietnam to Reagan*, Wood concluded that while it is normality which has the power to define the marginal nature of the freakish and 'abnormal', Michael Winner's use of real freaks in *The Sentinel* made this "the worst-most offensive and repressive-horror film of the seventies.[6]

Interestingly though, Winner gives a different insight into such prejudices when I interviewed him on the subject-"These people we found all came with their carers, were so happy. I got reviews and letters saying "I didn't know there was anyone else in the world like me, I thought I was the only one." They all enjoyed themselves. But do you know what happened? I suddenly sensed that something was happening on the set. I called over the first assistant director and said "Are they union representatives that have arrived and he replied "Yes." So I said what the hell do they want. Anyway, it turned out that the crew did did not want to sit at the same lunch table as the disabled actors. The union representative told me that the crew wanted a screen put up, they didn't want to see these people having lunch. So they put this screen up and I went furious and told them that if they didn't take it down I would come out and sit and eat with these so-called freaks. And the union fella replied "We don't care what you do Mr Winner, you won't even eat with the crew!" Perhaps just as faith can be blind, so too can prejudice, ironic given the subtext within *The Sentinel*.

In conclusion, whether you prefer the explicit, graphic approach of de Martino, or the implicit, mind-games of Winner, *The Antichrist* and *The Sentinel* remain thematically similar films, both drinking from the same trough and yet offering a diverse, hybrid approach to the same subject, an approach particularly styled and inflected by the unique decade both films were born (nay, spawned) into.

Notes

1. Robin Wood, *Hollywood From Vietnam to Reagan*. (New York: Columbia University Press, 1986) P.83.
2. Carol J. Clover, *Men, Women and Chainsaws: Gender in the Modern Horror Film*. (London, BFI Publishing, 1992) p.70-71.
3. Ibid., p.82.
4. Ibid., p.82.
5. Ibid., p.82-83.
6. Robin Wood, *Hollywood From Vietnam to Reagan*. (New York: Columbia University Press, 1986) p.153.

Notes on Contributors

Andy Black is editor of and contributor to the *Necronomicon* book series for Noir Publishing as well as writing freelance for a number of diverse magazines including *Terrorizer, Shivers, Marquis, Men Only & Club International*. He is also the author of *Oliver Reed-Ten Top Films* and *Leonardo Di Caprio-Ten Top Films* (both for Glitter Books, London).

Linnie Blake is a Senior Lecturer in the Department of English at the Manchester Metropolitan University where she teaches film and American studies. A founder of the journal *Angelaki*, she has published on subjects as diverse as minoritarian literatures, Anarchism in America, cult movies and the serial killer as last American hero. She is currently writing textbooks in her research areas, whilst undertaking a longer project on necrophilia in the movies.

Garrett Chaffin-Quiray received his BA and MA from the University of Southern California School of Cinema-Television. He has sponsored film festivals, taught TV and cinema history, and published various movie and video reviews. His research interests include analyses of pornography and its transition through video into the Internet age, post-War American cinema, the cinematic response to Vietnam, the cult of mass media-aided fame and the pleasures of graphic violence. He now lives in New York City developing scripts, writing criticism and working on his third novel.

Paul Cobley teaches Communications at London Guildhall University. His publications include *Introducing Semiotics* (1997); *The American Thriller: Generic Innovation and Social Change in the 1970s* (2000) and *Narrative* (2001). He has edited the *Communication Theory Reader* (1996); *The Media: An Introduction* (co-editor 1988); and *The Routledge Critical Dictionary of Semiotics and Linguistics* (2001).

Jonathan L. Crane is Assistant Professor in the Department of Communication at the University of North Carolina at Charlotte He has published widely on such topics as Top 40 radio, horror film specatorship, and music censorship. His book, *Terror and Everyday Life: Singular Moments in the History of the Horror Film*, was published by Sage in 1992.

Benjamin Halligan lectures in film in the Department of Theatre, Film and Television Studies in the University of Wales, Aberystwyth. He has recently written a study of

Bertolucci's *La Luna* for Cinetek/Flicks Books and is currently preparing *Graven Images: The Life and Films of Michael Reeves*.

Leon Hunt is a Lecturer in Film and Television Studies at Brunel University. His research interests include Hong Kong Cinema, Martial Arts Films, Horror, British Cinema and Cult TV. He is the author of *British Low Culture: From Safari Suits to Sexploitation* (Routledge 1998), a study of 1970s British popular culture. He has written for *Framework* (on Martial Arts Films), *Velvet Light Trap* (on Italian Horror), and contributed chapters to *Me Tarzan: Masculinity, Movies and Men*, *British Crime Cinema*, *Unruly Pleasures: The Cult Film and its Critics*, *The Horror Reader* and *Action TV*.

I.Q. Hunter is Senior Lecturer in Film Studies at De Montfort University, Leicester, and editor of *British Science Fiction Cinema* (Routledge, 1999). He is currently writing a book on Hammer's fantasy and science fiction films.

Nick Freeman is a Lecturer in English at the University of the West of England. His research interests include 19th century literature and art, contemporary fiction, British cinema and post-war popular culture. He has written on a range of topics, from Victorian serial killers to Mervyn Peake and *Jason King*. He is currently working on a book about late Victorian London.

Martin Jones is the author of *Psychedelic Decadence: Sex Drugs Low-Art in 60's & 70s Britain* (Critical Vision). He has also contributed to *Headpress*, *Bedlam*, *Necronomicon*, *Penthouse*, *Chaotic Order*, *Samhain* and the *Amygdala* web-site. His interests include the music of The Cramps, the books of Edward Gorey, and the films of Christina Ricci.

Stephen Keane is a Lecturer in the School of Cultural Studies, Bretton Hall College, University of Leeds. He has published articles on contemporary literature, media and culture, and is the author of *Disaster Movies: The Cinema of Catastrophe* (Wallflower Press, 2000). He is currently writing a book on Cyberculture for Polity Press.

Xavier Mendik is Director of the Cult Film Archive at University College Northampton as well as a Lecturer in Media and Popular Culture. He has published, broadcast and toured cinema events around the themes of psychoanalysis and its application to cult and horror cinema. His publications in this area include (as Co-Editor) *Unruly Pleasures: The Cult Film and its Critics* (Fab Press, 2000) and *Dario Argento's Tenebrae* (Flicks Books, 2000). Xavier is currently undertaking researching for his new book entitled *Fear at Four Hundred Degrees: Structure and Sexuality in the Films of Dario Argento* (Flicks Books, forthcoming). Beyond his academic research in this area, Xavier Mendik has also conducted interviews with many of the leading figures of cult cinema as well as sitting as a jury member on several leading European film festivals. Details of his interviews and jury accounts can be found on the website www.kamera.co.uk.

Christopher Norton received his BA in English and Film Studies from Oakland University, Rochester, Michigan and an MA from the Department of Cinema Studies, Tisch School of the Arts at New York University. A former editor at the web-based journal *Images: A Journal of Film and Popular Culture*, Chris has written extensively on blaxploitation, Black independent cinema of the 1970s, the star image of Paul Robeson and other areas of critical race theory. An avid hockey player and scuba diver, he now specialises in start-up and implementation of New Media companies and the development of products. Chris currently resides in Norwalk, Connecticut.

Mark Sample is a doctoral candidate at the University of Pennsylvania. His research interests include the relationship between mass media, fugitives and manhunts, both historical and fictional. Other published works include the edited *Works and Days* volume "Intentional Media: The Crossroads Conversations on Learning and Technology in the American Culture and Classroom," ed. Randy Bass, Teresa Derrickson, Bret Eynon and Mark Sample, Spring/Fall 1998, 16:1-2.

Steven Jay Schneider is a PhD candidate in Philosophy at Harvard University, and in Cinema Studies at New York University's Tisch School of the Arts. He has published widely on the horror film and related genres in journals such as *CineAction*, *Post Script*, *Film & Philosophy*, *Hitchcock Annual*, *Kinema*, *Journal of Popular Film & Television*, *Paradoxa*, *Scope*, *Kinoeye*, and the *Central Europe Review*. He is currently co-editing two volumes, *Dark Thoughts: Philosophic Reflections on Cinematic Horror* (Scarecrow Press) and *Understanding Film Genres* (McGraw-Hill).

Index of Films
Page Number in bold indicates an illustration

Noir Publishing
Mail Order Sales:

PO Box 28
HEREFORD
HR1 1AY
UK
email: noir@macunlimited.net

Noir books should be available from all good bookstores: please ask your local retailer to order from:

UK & EUROPE:
Turnaround Publisher Services
Unit 3
Olympia Trading Estate
Coburg Road
Wood Green
LONDON
N22 6TZ
Tel: 0208 829 3000 Fax: 0208 881 5088

USA:
Last Gasp
777 Florida Street
San Francisco
CA 94110-0682
Tel: 001 415 824 6636 Fax: 001 415 8241836

Canada:
Marginal Distribution
Unit 102
277 George Street
N. Peterborough
Ontario
K9J 3G9
Tel/Fax: 001 705 745 2326

Please note:-
Necronomicon Books One & Two are still available from the publishers:-
Creation Books, 4th Floor, City House, 72-80 Leather Lane, London. EC1R 7TR
Tel: 0207 430 9878 Fax: 0207242 5527

Other titles available from Noir Publishing:-
Necronomicon Book Three   Necronomicon Book Four   The Dead Walk
Once Upon A Fiend